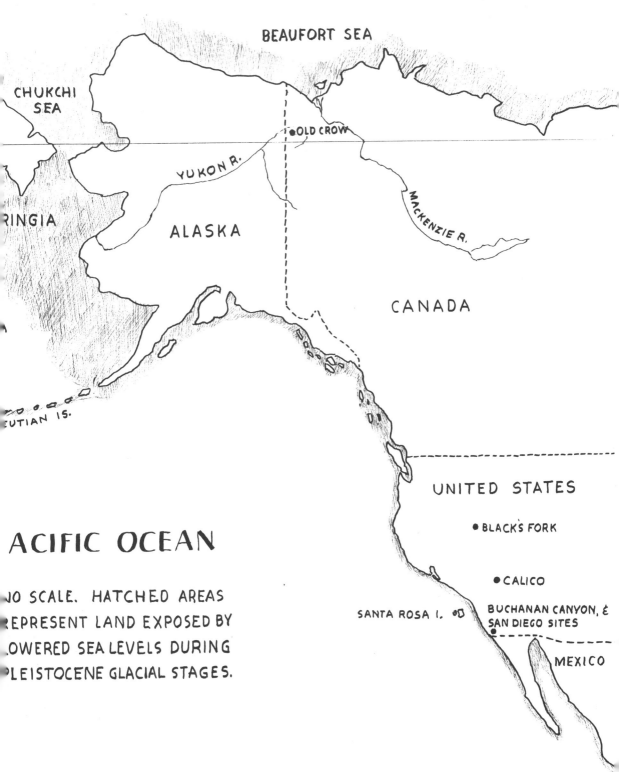

BEAUFORT SEA

CHUKCHI SEA

●OLD CROW

YUKON R.

MACKENZIE R.

...RINGIA

ALASKA

CANADA

...UTIAN IS.

...ACIFIC OCEAN

...O SCALE. HATCHED AREAS
...EPRESENT LAND EXPOSED BY
...OWERED SEA LEVELS DURING
...LEISTOCENE GLACIAL STAGES.

UNITED STATES

●BLACK'S FORK

●CALICO

SANTA ROSA I. ●▫

BUCHANAN CANYON, &
SAN DIEGO SITES

MEXICO

BUCHANAN CANYON

Ancient Human Presence
in the Americas

Other Books by Herbert L. Minshall

Glimpse of the Sea
(Poetry)
1970

Yonder the Sea
(An anthology of poetry and prose exerpts about the sea)
1973

The Broken Stones:
The Case for Early Man in California
1976

Window on the Sea:
A Nostalgic View of the Changing Environments of the Two Californias
1980

BUCHANAN CANYON

Ancient Human Presence in the Americas

Herbert L. Minshall

Slawson Communications
San Marcos, CA 92069

ISBN 0-932238-47-5

Library of Congress Card Catalog Number: In process

Avant® Books
165 Vallecitos de Oro
San Marcos, CA 92069

Cover design by Herbert L. Minshall
Illustrations by Herbert L. Minshall
Interior design by Dave Morgan, Slawson Communications, Inc.

Printed in the United States
10 9 8 7 6 5 4 3 2 1

Contents

Preface

Early in 1988, Henry de Lumley of France and eight colleagues; French, Brazilian, Japanese and American, reported in a publication of the French Academy of Sciences an amazing discovery. At the lowest level of a stratified floor in the Toca da Esperanca, a large cave in northeastern Brazil, flaked quartz and quartzite tools in close association with extinct horse bones showing evidence of human alteration were found. The nearest natural source of the quartzite was at least 10km from the cave. Several of the bones were dated in three different laboratories: in France, Los Angeles and Menlo Park, California, by uranium series. Ages obtained were between 204,000 and 295,000 years before the present.

Anthropologists and archaeologists, both in North America and abroad, have been almost unanimous in their insistence on recency for human occupation of the Western Hemisphere, many refusing to accept dates of over 12,000 BP for man in America. But few sciences have been changing more rapidly in recent years than the studies of paleoanthropology and archaeology; specifically the study of very early man around the Pacific Rim. Those who write about such material inevitably find their views and beliefs becoming altered almost immediately after their earlier perceptions have become frozen and immutable in print.

This book is, in a sense, a follow-up of an earlier work written over twelve years ago, *The Broken Stones*, published by Copley Books at La Jolla, California, in 1976. That book described in considerable detail the discoveries of evidence of very early man in the San Diego coastal zone, and other related investigations and conclusions regarding the first humans in the New World.

Today far more is either known or deduced on the subject as the result of ongoing fieldwork, the discoveries of new sites and localities yielding important records of very early human presence both in the Western Hemisphere and in East and Northeast Asia, the development of new dating methods and laboratory procedures, and new insights into the adaptability of very primitive humans to the sometimes rigorous environments they occupied.

While much of the material presented here is the result of personal investigation in the field, it is primarily a synthesis of the work of others. Interpretations of evidence and conclusions drawn from it are in many cases controversial, sometimes with some merit on both sides but often caused by firmly-held convictions and preconceptions which the evidence would tend to invalidate if accepted.

The view that the advancement of knowledge can only be attained through irrefutable empirical demonstration; that is, in the case of the presence or absence of very early man, with the discovery of pre-sapiens skeletal remains in an indisputably very early geological context, is emphatically rejected. We should examine impartially all of the evidence available to us and reach conclusions based on reason and common sense, but be flexible enough to change our opinions when new and more persuasive evidence is offered, even when it conflicts with previous beliefs.

In the present work, in order to present adequately the current state of early man studies and investigation, a certain amount of review of background events and previously described sites has been found necessary. It is hoped that readers of *The Broken Stones* will forgive the inclusion of such repetitive material, and appreciate the need for it.

This book is not intended to be a detailed scientific report of the sites, artifact assemblages and geological contexts presented, nor is it directed primarily at the scientific community. It does seek to argue conclusively its major premise: that human populations must have occupied the Americas far earlier than has generally been supposed. The principal purpose here has been to offer an overview of significant developments in the ongoing study of early man in the circum-Pacific region and particularly in the Americas, in a manner that both academic readers and interested non-professionals might find rewarding.

In the following pages, factual presentation of the rapidly changing developments in the search for very early man in both hemispheres around the Pacific rim will be interspersed with fictional episodes called "Cameos" in order to illuminate the human elements of the story. These segments are entirely imaginary. They are intended to emphasize my belief that human emotions — fear, courage and tenderness — are surely rooted far back in our distant past.

Herbert L. Minshall

INTRODUCTION

The Storm and the Canyon

The rain beat down in almost solid torrents. It drummed on rooftops and windowpanes like spent birdshot, went roaring down the storm drains and down the floor of Buchanan Canyon in a brown, churning flood; down Mission Valley to the sea. The streets above ran curb to curb with water that in prehistoric times would have soaked into carpets of grass and spongy turf and thick chaparral, but now the mesa top was covered with the urban works of man. Now the black clouds dropped their burden on wood, plaster, concrete and asphalt. The concentrated fury swept away the accumulated soils and gravels of thousands of decades from the canyon bottom, laying bare ancient sediments that might not have been exposed since before the onset of the last Ice Age, some 70,000 years ago.

Figure 1. The gully floor and wall in Buchanan Canyon after the cloudburst and flood down the canyon in 1970.

That cloudburst in the winter of 1970 was soon over, but in less than two hours it had dropped five inches of rain on the district called University Heights in San Diego, California. Most of it fell on the 500-acre watershed of Buchanan Canyon. I had enjoyed the spectacle of the storm from my home on a ridge above the canyon, and a few days later, when the trail had dried somewhat, I descended to the canyon floor.

This was a beautiful, wild enclave near the center of the surrounding city. Sirens could sometimes be faintly heard from a distant freeway and airliners occasionally droned high above, but the impression down in the canyon was one of a different world — an earlier world almost untouched by civilization. Coyotes sang their mournful choruses, raccoons, foxes and cottontails lived in the tall chaparral, and the liquid music of canyon wrens and thrashers rippled over the slopes. An air of timeless serenity, as perceptible as the odors of drying buckwheat and sage, seemed to pervade the canyon.

As I made my way to the bottom after the storm, I was surprised to find that what had formerly been a grassy, brush-studded floor had been transformed into a wide gully or ravine ten feet deep in places, with scattered pools of water sparkling in the sun. The bottom was paved with water-worn gravels from pebbles to boulders in size, giving the impression that an ancient streambed had suddenly been resurrected. Its many-colored stones, their hues intensified by the crystal-clear water, glowed like a rich mosaic along the floor of the wash. (figure 1.)

The walls of the gully were cleanly cut and displayed a number of different strata or layers. The topmost level, a dark brown loam, was a recent topsoil apparently formed from organic materials like those on the heavily-grown south wall of the canyon. Well below that and just above the floor of the wash was an ancient-appearing, heavy yellow clay similar to other soils in the region that I knew were pre-last-glacial in age and required scores of millennia for their formation.

As I picked my way over the stones of the wash, my eye was caught by a mahogany-colored piece of quartzite that was wedged among the cobbles on the bottom. About six inches long and shaped like a giant pumpkinseed, it had long and regular flutings along its sides, going to a rather blunt and battered point at one end. Its symmetrical shape and regular flake removals seemed impossible of achievement by any natural force known to me, and I felt certain that this was the work of man. The battered end and the long, concave flake scars running parallel to the axis of the core could only have resulted from a flintknapping technique known as bipolar flaking, in which a cobble is held vertically on a stone anvil and struck powerful blows by a skilled craftsman in order to utilize the knife-like blades thus removed.

As I held the worn and polished stone in my hands I felt a strange sensation. A feeling of awe and almost reverence swept over me, as though I had been permitted a glimpse far back into the distant past. I knew with certainty that the fluted stone had been washed out of that ancient clay; that it had been entombed there over vast periods of time, covered by the dust of a far younger canyon. I saw vividly in imagination the swarthy, black-browed maker of the core, naked and somewhat stooped but with enormous, powerful arms and shoulders and yellow, cracked and broken nails, standing there before me in my peaceful canyon. I resolved to penetrate if I could the mysteries surrounding this human predecessor, to know his origins and culture, to trace in time and space the long journey of his kind from somewhere in the Old World to this place and my own time.

In the intervening years much has been learned by personal investigation and by piecing together the reports of other workers in the field. Some has been deduced through logical conclusions, but a great deal remains shrouded in the shadows of ages past. It has been a long and difficult effort, plagued by huge gaps in the chain of evidence caused mainly by post-glacial elevations of sea levels, and hampered continually by the unshakable convictions of recency for man in this hemisphere still held by colleagues and influential critics.

Nevertheless, a new and completely different view of human first arrivals in North America is beginning to emerge, based on evidence that, although still meager and incomplete, can no longer be dismissed or denied. Like the fluted core in Buchanan Canyon, it can only be explained by the presence of man far earlier than most anthropologists have been prepared to contemplate.

CHAPTER 1

Challenge and Enigma
at San Diego

In its lower reaches, the valley of the San Diego River is called Mission Valley, named for the early establishment of Mission San Diego de Alcalá a short distance up the river from its juncture with the sea. It lies well down the eastern margin of the North Pacific Ocean in the coastal zone of Southern California. The valley with its tributary canyons is the setting for what appears to be a series of localities of very early human habitation; among the earliest yet discovered in the Western Hemisphere.

The river rises some 50 miles behind the coast in the vicinity of the Laguna Mountains of the Southern California Peninsular Range. It has cut down over millions of years across the slowly rising foothills and the coastal plain; down through the 40,000,000-year-old clays and massed cobbles of mightier Eocene rivers; down through the bleached white limestones of ancient Pliocene sea floors; down to the beaches of the present interglacial high sea stand. Subdued now by a semiarid climate and intermittent periods of drought, the river flows in its lower reaches only after substantial winter storms, and in the dry summer season in Mission Valley it sinks below the sand.

Today the valley floor and its margins are covered with shopping centers, hotels, high-rise office buildings and automobile agencies, while an eight-lane interstate highway fringed with crossing overpasses carries an endless stream of traffic. Despite the teeming activity in the valley, some of its side canyons are still wild, tranquil and almost untouched by modern civilization; disturbed only by the music of coyotes and the harsh bark of foxes.

In the first half of the present century Mission Valley was almost completely undeveloped, a wide flood plain with a few dairy and truck farms. The broad, sandy riverbed meandered down its center, set with sycamores, cottonwoods and shady, tule-fringed ponds. A series of uplifted terraces flanked the edges of the valley, truncated flood plains abandoned by the river far back in the Pleistocene Epoch. At the mouths of the side canyons cobble-rich alluvial fans emerged and spread onto the elevated valley floor remnants. The fanglomerates were interbedded with silts from the main stream at flood stage, as were soils washed down from the valley walls.

During the early 1940's a sand and gravel company established a large borrow pit at one of the most prominent terraces, excavating it in order to obtain rock for commercial gravel. When the operation was terminated, steep and almost vertical walls displayed in cross-section the layers of silts and cobbles which composed the terrace, a visible record of the geologic past going back several hundred thousand years. The faces or cuts, each fifteen to twenty feet high, were stabilized by horizontal pediments or benches and were clearly observable from the narrow country road that ran up the valley. The borrow pit was about a quarter of a mile from Texas Street, which mounted to the top of the mesa.

In 1947 George F. Carter, then a professor of geography at Johns Hopkins University in Baltimore but a native San Diegan, was studying local marine and stream terraces during a summer sabbatical. He had taken a Bachelor of Science degree with a major in Anthropology at the University of California, worked at the San Diego Museum of Man for several years, then went back to the university for a doctorate in Geography, which he felt would be useful in understanding the movements and environment of very early humans. He later moved to Texas A and M University and taught there until his recent retirement. Although a professor of Geography, his principal field of interest was and is still the search for early man in America, but he has made important contributions in other fields, particularly in plant geography and the pre-Columbian movements of colonists between the Old World and the New.

Driving up Mission Valley in 1947, Carter stopped to examine the engineered faces of the Texas Street borrow pit, and was struck by some localized areas of broken and heat-reddened rock deep in the terrace clays. Close investigation of the cliff faces and benches revealed a number of stone objects which were puzzling. Their means of formation were difficult to explain by any natural agency and suggested human alteration. Also displayed in cross-section were what appeared to be basin-shaped hearths with charcoal, discolored, soot-stained earth and broken rocks. Since the geological features of the formation clearly indicated to Carter an age of well over 70,000 years for the stone specimens and basin features, their positive identification as man-made would have more than quadrupled the time most scholars believe man has been in the Western Hemisphere.

Carter suspected that the elongate, polyhedral stone objects were cobble cores that had been held upright on a stone anvil and struck with a heavy stone hammer to produce long, slender blades, a technique called "bipolar flaking." This practice was then little known and rarely recognized by American archaeologists, although it had been commonly practiced from the most ancient times in China. (Figure 2.)

Figure 2. Bipolar cores. The two center specimens are from the Texas Street site; the outer ones are from Imperial Valley in southeast California.

The cores were from two to five inches long, with many flake scars running the length of the pieces so that little or none of the cobble cortices or rinds remained. Many of the scars were concave or fluted, a decisive aspect, since critics have later theorized that such cores can be produced naturally by heat spalling, and it is perfectly true that some rocks, especially granites and quartzites, do shed thin layers of outer surfaces under certain conditions. But such spalls always follow the contour of the stone, leaving a "skinned" look, whereas concussively struck blades are frequently triangular in cross-section while natural spalls never are.

Carter experimented by heating cobbles to high temperatures and dropping them into cold water to see if the same effect could be produced by heat spalling, but was consistently unable to replicate the flake scars on the Texas Street specimens by this method (Carter 1957:315) although curved spalls were easily removed. Such spalls bore a distinctive reddening or heat staining easily recognized, and Carter was convinced that the Texas Street specimens represented human alteration. By placing cobbles vertically on a stone anvil and striking them sharply with a steel hammer, he was able to split off long, slender flakes or blades, leaving flake scars like those on the collected cores.

Charcoal removed from one of the basin features that Carter identified as hearths was submitted to a radiocarbon laboratory for dating, but was found to be beyond the range of measure, or older by an unknown factor than 35,000 years. Finally convinced that the quartzite cores could only have been the result of human activity, and that the isolated and soot-stained basins could only have been the remains of fires built by humans no more recently than during the last interglacial period over 70,000 years ago, Carter reported his findings in a scientific journal (Carter 1950).

Although a few of Carter's colleagues concurred in his findings, the reaction of the vast majority of archaeologists was one of skepticism and disbelief. The bipolar cores were rejected and even ridiculed as evidence of early man and attributed to some unknown natural process, and the purported hearths were dismissed as residue from brush fires, perhaps burnt tree stumps to account for the basin-shaped depressions. The elevation of the terrace above the modern flood plain was laid to recent seismic action and not to slow regional uplift or an interglacial high sea stand, as Carter claimed.

Few of Carter's critics visited the site at Texas Street. Some of those who did listened politely to his arguments and nodded affably as though in agreement, but he was later surprised to read published comments by those same affable visitors expressing complete disagreement with his views. None of the negative reviews offered convincing evidence refuting Carter's conclusions. Even after his book, *Pleistocene Man at San Diego* (Carter 1957), was published presenting his evidence in considerable detail, the site was generally rejected or ignored. The bipolar cores, labeled "Carterfacts" by a skeptical critic, continued to go unrecognized as products of human activity.

Carter finally decided that only the discovery of irrefutable evidence of human antiquity would prove him right, and he turned his attention to other matters. The failure of the scientific community to appreciate the importance of the Texas Street discovery is perfectly understandable, for the bases for his claims were indeed uncompelling, and contradicted the prevailing and solidly-established doctrine of recency for humans in North America.

Early Man research might have ended in the San Diego coastal zone had it not been for the fortuitous cloudburst in the winter of 1970 described above. Previously unimpressed with the Texas Street evidence of 20 years earlier, I became convinced of its validity after my own discovery in Buchanan Canyon, less than a mile from Texas Street as the crow flies. I began a period of intermittent field and literary research which has lasted for over 18 years.

In the months that followed the first discovery, I found many more stone tools and cores either in the gravels of the wash or weathering out of the ancient clays at the base of the gully walls. They were completely unlike the artifacts of the known prehistoric cultures of Southern California, none of which was considered to be older than about 10,000 years, and with which I was very familiar. Most of the pieces were very large, even massive, and crudely flaked of quartzite, a type of rock which does not lend itself to delicate, fine workmanship but which produces very sharp and durable edges and was widely used by very early humans in other parts of the world. (figure 3.)

The tools appeared to have been quartzite, and occasionally andesite, river cobbles which were split by being placed on a stone surface, probably a boulder, and struck on the end with a very heavy stone hammer or maul, several of which were found in the canyon. The resulting halves were then shaped by hand-held percussion to suit the intended function, usually by sharp blows to one or both faces, which produced fairly regular flake scars and those typical marks of percussion by which human alteration is usually recognized.

Tool types could be roughly classified into choppers and chopping tools; heavy scrapers including a few with concave edges which appeared to be the right size for dressing down spear shafts; some large pointed tools with triangular cross-sections and heavily abraded ends, probably used for digging; and backed, lunate tools with the curved edges sharpened, which I took to be skinning and butchering implements. I later learned that such tools are called *skreblos* in Russian, and have been called "one of the diagnostic traits of the Siberian Paleolithic" (Powers 1973:4), and are common in China. Many of the specimens, although clearly formed by humans, could not be readily classified as to function or appeared to have been used for different purposes, such as both chopping and hammering or slicing and scraping. Small flake tools were rare, and secondary flaking or retouch along flaked edges was not employed and apparently not needed, the quartzite material being as sharp as broken glass when roughly flaked.

In 1970 the vast majority of American anthropologists believed, and most still believe, that humans have been in the Western Hemisphere less than 20,000 years. The most conservative scholars insist that there is no convincing evidence of human presence earlier than 12,000 years ago. It is also almost universally believed that stream battering, mudflows and earth pressures can and do produce stone specimens that look like genuine Paleolithic tools, although this fallacy has never been demonstrated. Thousands of professors have repeated the myth to their students, having had the warning impressed upon them by their own professors until it has become standard and unquestioned doctrine. So when I invited a professor of archaeology and former colleague over to examine the gully exposure and the specimens, he carefully explained to me that they had obviously been broken and chipped by stream action, since they lay directly in a streambed. Furthermore, he said, he often sent his students down a gravel-strewn wash near the college to collect psuedo-artifacts or Nature-facts, and that if one searched carefully in streambeds he could usually accumulate a nice collection of what appeared to be ancient tools.

Figure 3. Quartzite tools from Buchanan Canyon. In the top row are skinning and butchering tools called skreblos in Siberia. In the second row from the top are heavy ovoid choppers. Below them are specimens presumed to be scrapers, and the two on the bottom are picks, probably for digging in the ground.

Unconvinced, I took a sample box of specimens to the San Diego Museum of Man and showed them to Dr. Emma Lou Davis, then Curator of Archaeology and a scholar who has since become convinced of their human origin and antiquity. But then she also warned me about the danger of being fooled by stream-broken stones, and that if you hunt long enough in a high energy streambed you can find almost any kind of flaked object.

Still dissatisfied with these opinions, I sent some photos to George Carter in Texas. His reply was noncommittal; he couldn't tell from the photographs what the specimens represented, and he suggested that I show them to Professor James R. Moriarty III of the University of San Diego, whom Carter considered to be the best informed person in the area on the prehistory of the San Diego region. Moriarty examined the specimens with great interest and agreed with me that they were clearly of human origin and did not represent any culture then known in the area, but was unwilling to speculate on their age. He did consider that they represented a "pre-desert culture" which presumably meant that they must have been deposited in the terminal Pleistocene, or more than 10,000 years ago.

Although I felt that the tools must be far older than Moriarty was prepared to accept, I had finally found a colleague who shared in some degree my excitement and recognized the specimens from the canyon as human artifacts that were at least older than the known cultures of the coastal region. Moriarty and I jointly published a brief article (Moriarty and Minshall 1972) announcing the find and providing drawings of the most typical tools. It was greeted with dead silence, but this was quite expectable.

Since the artifacts had been dismissed by several so-called experts as merely stream-broken rocks, I had no hesitation in collecting a representative assemblage. Specimens found weathering out of the clay walls were carefully removed and photographed, then returned to their casts when possible. Over 200 artifacts were collected ranging from massive quartzite choppers over six inches long and weighing more than five pounds, to small, thin bipolar blades less than two inches long. Most tools were far larger than those of better-known and more recent industries.

I soon realized that if I had any hope of understanding this apparently unknown industry and its origins, I would need to rely to a large extent on my own investigation and research. This was unexplored territory — virgin ground, I believed, that no one else had trod. But I discovered that this was only partially correct. Others had found crude and apparently ancient artifacts in various parts of North America: Matthew Lively in Alabama, Thomas E. Lee at Sheguiandah on Lake Huron, E. B. Renaud along Black's Fork in southwestern Wyoming, W. Morlin Childers in the deserts of southeastern California, and Louis Leakey and Ruth D. Simpson at the Calico Mountains near Barstow, California. Renaud, Lively, Leakey, Lee and Childers have since died, and only Simpson is still actively engaged in the search, as are many other scholars today.

One of my first concerns was to satisfy myself that the stone objects exposed by the flood in Buchanan Canyon were indeed man-made, and not simply split and flaked by a high energy stream, by earth pressures, by brush fires or by tumbling down hillsides. Heating, freezing and earth pressures could easily be eliminated, since many of the tools showed typical marks of percussion well-known to all archaeologists: bulbs, eraillure scars, ripple lines of force, beta angles of less than 90 degrees, etc. Rolling and bouncing down steep hillsides and striking other rocks on the journey could certainly break and chip rocks, but could hardly produce symmetrical flaking all along an edge, much less a carefully shaped point. Heavy stream action seemed to be the only possibility; it was most often cited by critics and certainly seemed the most likely mechanism for broken stones recovered from a wash or streambed.

So on one of the rare days of heavy rain in San Diego, I went floundering down the trail into the canyon wearing rubber hip boots. Runoff in copious amounts was rushing and even cascading down the cobble-strewn floor of the ravine. The din of rocks clacking together was almost deafening, a frightening uproar in view of the experiment I had in mind. Nevertheless, I clenched my teeth and waded into the rushing water. I discovered with surprise that, although cobbles and even boulders were coming downstream, they were almost floating! They bumped against my legs without nearly enough force to bruise me, let alone shatter or flake tough, hard quartzite rocks in their path and fixed in the bottom. A few nearly-buried boulders showed scars like skinned areas on their tops.

Careful observation in flume experiments has shown that hydraulic energy applied to solid objects is dissipated in a vertical rather than horizontal direction. Stones on a streambed are raised and lowered and tend to bob along downstream far more often than they are rolled. In heavy storm surf on rocky beaches, stones are often hurled with great force onto the shingle, causing flakes or chips to be removed, but as in the case of hillside tumbling, this cannot result in symmetrically flaked edges on which the scars are all of the same generation.

Almost without exception the principal action of streams and surf is abrasion rather than breakage. Irregularly shaped rocks such as are formed in talus slopes, when subjected to stream battering, are pecked down to rounded cobble forms eventually. If a brick is put into a high energy stream, it will soon become rounded but rarely broken despite its relatively fragile composition. Most of the world's sand has been produced this way, by rocks striking together and removing small particles from the contact surfaces.

In regard to stream breakage, I was delighted to find this judgment expressed by the Abbé Henri Breuil, a French prehistorian of exceptional prestige in Europe: "In normal times a stream or river does not break anything resting on its bed. Should a flood occur, however, all the stones on the bed are carried farther along, and are knocked together fairly gently. . . . No current is able to fracture stones in any way comparable to human chipping, or to split slabs of flint, still less of quartzite." (Breuil and Lantier 1965).

In numerous places in the San Diego area extensive exposures of ancient riverine heavy gravels and clay are now available for examination, deposited by enormous Eocene rivers over 40,000,000 years ago. Almost without exception the cobbles and pebbles composing the formations are unbroken. Surely if rivers break rocks, one would expect to find masses of fragments here. But one searches in vain for a single specimen with a sharp edge or flaking of any kind, and even broken rocks are rare.

Satisfied that the flaked rocks from the canyon could only have been shaped by humans, I carefully inspected the Texas Street exposure where Carter had worked twenty years earlier. I found that more bipolar cores had weathered out of the man-made cliffs, and a few very crude stone tools lay on the benches. More importantly, it was as obvious to me as it had been to

Carter that the sediments were extremely old; clearly pre-last-glacial and probably far older. If the tools from the canyon represented the same cultural horizon as those of Texas Street, they could be placed into that pre-glacial time period with confidence. I boxed up the Buchanan Canyon assemblage and headed for Texas.

In Carter's office at Texas A & M University we laid out the two collections side by side. For the first time it was obvious that both represented the same industry. The tools from Buchanan were unequivocably the work of man, and were similar enough to the Texas Street pieces to demonstrate a common source; in a sense they validated the human origin of the latter. The geological formation at Texas Street is clearly pre-last-glacial, a fact that is almost universally accepted, so that it could be safely assumed that the Buchanan Canyon assemblage had equal antiquity, whatever that might prove to be.

As might be expected, Carter was greatly pleased by these new developments, and we decided to mount excavations at both sites in the hope of finding more conclusive evidence. In the early summer of 1973 we were ready to start excavations on the floor of Buchanan Canyon and on one of the stabilizing benches about fifteen feet below the original surface at Texas Street. The project was sponsored by the University of San Diego, with assistance from Texas A & M University. Moriarty, Carter and I would direct the operations, with the crews composed of archaeology students and interested volunteers.

I worked at Texas Street, where a grid of two-meter squares was laid out on one of the fifteen-foot-wide benches. It would be difficult to convey, to those who have never experienced it, the surging excitement we felt as we dipped in our trowels. What revealing and conclusive discoveries might lie just below the surface waiting to be exposed? Human fossil remains? An ancient living floor complete with tools, implements, a hearth with preserved food remains like bone or shell? It is this compelling and permanent thrill of anticipation, perhaps like that of horse players and lottery ticket buyers, that keeps those eager toilers on archaeological digs eternally hopeful.

The soil at the level at which we were digging was composed of a very indurated yellow clay. At about six inches below the surface I began to encounter black, soot-stained earth and charcoal. We had found another of the fire basins that Carter had reported earlier. It had the same red, fire-broken rock and was about three feet in diameter. A few days later a quartzite scraper was uncovered at the same level and a few feet from the basin.

During the course of the investigation several other artifacts were recovered, some of them displaying what appeared to be use wear on their flaked edges. No bone was exposed nor was shell found at the site, but it seems likely that these might have long since disintegrated in the very acid soils if they had ever been deposited there. We felt that the area at the mouth of the canyon had probably been an occasional camping place rather than a permanent living site, and that the presence of an estuary nearby in the valley during a period of marine transgression may have been the attraction at that particular location. Little blobs of lime in the soil suggested that shells had decomposed into unrecognizable forms there.

Work at Buchanan Canyon, supervised by Moriarty, was quite different from that at Texas Street. The question of where to dig was far more perplexing. Artifacts had been gathered from locations all up and down the gully, a distance of nearly half a mile. Most had been surface finds obviously recently deposited among the cobbles of the wash, and had been collected. A few had been seen weathering out of the gully banks, but also in gravel strata that could easily have been reshuffled countless times since their original deposition.

Late in March of 1973 a quartzite chopping tool considered to be indisputably the work of man was seen weathering out of the ancient clay stratum up near the head of the canyon. By chance this find was beside a level and fairly wide area of the canyon floor which lent itself ideally to fencing and digging operations and which in addition, unless the topography of the canyon had very radically changed, would have been a logical campsite for early man. It even seemed to me that I could see, on the canyon wall, a place where an overhanging mass of clay and conglomerate might have collapsed.

Permission to excavate was obtained from the city, which owned the land, and the project was begun early in the summer. Operations at this site consisted at first of heavy pick and shovel work, since the upper four feet clearly had been recently disturbed for sewer installation and our purpose was to expose the clay stratum seen at the base of the nearby gully wall. Nevertheless, meticulous control was exercised by Moriarty, and dozens of modern fragments of brick, glass, plastic and metal were faithfully collected and recorded as the work proceeded. These upper levels consisted of slope-washed soils and loose sand and gravel in which the sewer-laying operations had been conducted, and it was difficult to conjure up the vision of a shaggy-headed and black-browed hunter in such surroundings.

At a depth of about four feet the clay stratum was finally penetrated. It proved to be rock-hard, and its similarity to the soil in the pits at Texas Street was very marked, suggesting for it a similar antiquity. Two specimens were found solidly in place in this clay matrix, both about twelve inches below its upper boundary or disconformity. One was a roughly conical object of andesite believed to have been the snapped-off end of a bipolar core, or possibly an intentionally-shaped scraper plane. The obviously methodical removal of flakes all around this tip decisively established its human alteration. The other piece was found at the same level in the clay, about three feet horizontally from the core. It was a quartzite flake that had been symmetrically flaked along two edges.

Unfortunately the project had to be terminated before more than a few cubic feet of the indurated clay could be examined. Under our agreement with the city, the excavations had to be backfilled and the land returned to its previous condition. Nevertheless, the exposure of two manmade objects in a context apparently immune from stream action strongly suggested the presence of humans at the time when the clay soils represented the surface of the canyon floor, as surely as if fifty tools had been found. But this was far from the indisputable and convincing evidence we sought, as were the results at Texas Street, being at both sites undatable.

Since the excavation at Buchanan Canyon, the exposed wash and gully walls have been carefully monitored, particularly after heavy rains. Artifacts have been examined but not collected. Only one small fragment of fossil bone has been recovered from the clay stratum in the gully wall. When I found it I felt a leaping surge of excitement — perhaps this was from an ancient human inhabitant of the canyon — but it turned out to be the toe bone of an extinct bovid, a musk ox or bison species.

A site of primary deposit for the stone artifacts has never been found, but several possibilities can be visualized. The people may have lived on the edge of the mesa above the canyon, and their artifacts may have been washed and tumbled down the steep canyon slopes as the canyon widened itself over the scores of millennia since the tools were discarded. They might have been buried in the floor rubble of rock shelters or caves on the canyonsides, long since eroded away with the debris swept down to the foot of the slopes. The walls of the canyon are formed of soft Tertiary limestone that is easily carved with stone tools or even pointed sticks, as children still do today to dig themselves snug burrows in the cliffs. Or the tools may have been discarded by campers on the canyon floor during an early interglacial period and marine transgression, with an estuary of the sea handy to the mouth of the canyon. The lithic evidence could have been successively mixed, exposed and washed about by floods, reburied and disturbed by rodent burrows until no sign of a living floor can now be found.

In recent years it has become apparent that Buchanan Canyon is far from unique, and that the same massive but still undatable tools are scattered over the coastal zone from the sea to the foothills in a broad band about ten miles wide. They are among the cobbles of many canyon bottoms, weathering out of cliffs and cutbanks, and on or just below the surface of the mesas and ridges themselves.

Richard Cerutti, an active and gifted avocational archaeologist and paleontologist, has mapped dozens of localities in the coastal region which contain the heavy choppers, scrapers and cores of this enigmatic industry. Although he has discovered no primary sites or living floors in the area, nor have finite dates been produced, comparison with similar artifacts in the Old World insistently argues great antiquity for them, and an industry that may have remained substantially unchanged for scores of millennia.

I also continued the search and discovered a number of localities where the massive stone tools could be found, but always redistributed into contexts that defied dating or the gathering of information about the makers other than what could be deduced from the tool forms themselves. But in 1977 a site of enormous promise was discovered in Mission Valley. Richard Gadler, a young man who had been a member of the crew during the excavations in 1973, noticed some elongate bipolar cores weathering out of a cutbank beside a busy interstate highway. He notified Dr. Moriarty, who called me, and we examined the locality with care.

About a mile up the valley from its mouth and extending out from the south wall a quarter of a mile, an area of a few acres in dimension had been preserved as an earlier flood plain remnant and uplifted tectonically about 25 feet above the modern stream level. Bisecting it parallel to the valley wall was the eight-lane interstate freeway, which had been cut down through the raised flood plain, leaving a small, isolated remnant like a miniature mesa to the north. It was the south bank of this island of ancient soils and gravels that displayed the cultural materials that so intrigued us.

Bare of vegetation and varying from four to about twelve feet high, the cutbank ran along beside a public sidewalk for about 200 feet. Clearly visible were three quite different strata — different in both color and composition. The top layer was dark brown and had broken shell and bits of broken rock. It appeared to be typical shell midden soil, common in the coastal zone of Southern California. Below it was a heavy, very hard soil that was almost brick-red in color, and below that was a stratum of coarse gravels to cobble size cemented in hard red clay. It was in the lower or cobble stratum, apparently an ancient abandoned river channel, that the bipolar cores were seen.

The elevated landform had a small house and garage on it, but most of its surface was bare. To the east it sloped down to a small arroyo draining canyons in the mesa to the south, and beyond the arroyo was a spring-fed pond, now covered with a multi-storied office building, where George Carter and I used to shoot mourning doves coming in to water some 50 years ago. The north side dropped steeply down to the level of the modern flood plain 25 feet below, mostly part of a golf course today, while to the west the land had been graded down several feet, producing a level but vacant lot.

The owners of the land, Atlas Hotels, Inc., to their great credit, not only granted permission for an excavation on the site, but contributed generously to the financial support of the project, which became the Charles H. Brown Archaeological Project, named for the company's founder. The work was carried out during the summer of 1977 under the direction of Dr. Moriarty, with University of San Diego students doing the digging under the field supervision of Brian Smith (Minshall 1981). The latter, now a professional contract archaeologist, had also been a member of the excavation crew at Texas Street in 1973. I served the project as a consultant.

A grid of two-meter squares was laid out in a clear space east of the buildings, the area was fenced and the garage converted into a field laboratory. When digging was commenced it was almost immediately rewarded. Recent cultural material of the Kumeyaay, the Indians found on the land by early Spanish colonists, was encountered in the first few inches. This included scrapers chipped from shards of porcelain apparently manufactured in Mexico, copied from Chinese ware and discarded on Spanish rubbish dumps at the San Diego Presidio. Also recovered in the top layer were Spanish coins and Kumeyaay stone arrowpoints, as well as more typical shards of Tezon brown ware.

Below the recent Kumeyaay level, the dark midden soils yielded evidence of a long occupation by La Jolla people, the archaic and sedentary cultures of the Southern California coast. In abundance were food shell, flaking debris, scrapers and milling implements. A hearth constructed of small boulders was also exposed in this stratum. Radiocarbon dates of over 3,000 years before the present were obtained on shell in the upper portion of this horizon; recent in terms of human inhabitance and our quest but approximately the time when the Greeks were attacking Troy.

Below this so-called anthropic stratum, at about 22 inches, a very marked unconformity was exposed, a well-weathered surface of clearly much older soils that was presumed to represent a long period of erosion. At this level some scrapers and a dart point recognized as typical of a desert PaleoIndian culture were recovered, indentifiable because of their delicate craftsmanship and distinctive forms. These San Dieguito people, seemingly more nomadic than the La Jollans, appeared in the coastal region about 9,000 years ago, possibly forced out of their former homes across the mountains by environmental changes associated with the ending of the last glacio-pluvial climate cycle, the Wisconsin. Their relationship to the La Jollans is not well understood, nor is the termination of their culture. Whether they moved out of the area about 6,000 years ago or were simply absorbed into the La Jolla mainstream has not been determined. There are suggestions that they may have moved farther south into Mexico.

Below the unconformity the red, indurated clays of the buried paleosol yielded tools that have been classified as La Jolla I, very coarse and primitive choppers and scrapers but still clearly attributable to the earliest phase of the La Jolla culture. This stratum overlay about three feet of channel gravels varying from pebble to boulder size in a matrix of clay and decomposed granite sand.

The artifacts recovered from deep in the channel gravels were somewhat similar to those seen in profusion at Buchanan Canyon and numerous other localities in the San Diego region, but appeared to be slightly more refined technically. They consisted of unifacial, "horse's hoof" type choppers up to four inches in diameter, several large bifacial chopping tools, six bipolar cores and two blades obviously struck from such cores, and a concave scraper or spokeshave. One of the unifacial choppers and one bifacial chopping tool were so symmetrically flaked as to leave no doubt even in the most skeptical critic that they were the products of human workmanship. (Figure 4)

None of the tools showed evidence of substantial stream transport, having sharp edges and little abrasion. However, the bipolar cores did seem to have been stream-rolled, perhaps because of their generally cylindrical shapes. There were very few flakes and flaking waste in association with the tools, suggesting that the former had either been washed away or the artifacts were not manufactured at the site where they were found.

Approximate or minimum dating of the Brown site was possible by means of both soil analysis and geomorphology. Dr. Roy Shlemon of Newport Beach, California, a professional pedologist, made a careful examination of the exposed stratigraphy and contained soils at the site. In addition to detailed soils descriptions of ten separate and distinct levels, including in each case his bases for assigned ages, Shlemon reported the following conclusions:

"From comparisons with soils of comparable development in coastal Southern California, it appears that the buried paleosol at the C. H. Brown site is in the order of perhaps 25,000 to 40,000 years old; and has formed on old channel gravels and overbank deposits probably laid down during marine isotope stage 4, about 60,000 to 70,000 years ago." (Personal communication).

Shlemon's estimate is well supported by the obvious geological history of the site. The present elevation of the buried and gravel-filled river channel is about 42 feet above sea level, or about 25 feet above the present flood plain of the San Diego River, and a little over a mile from tidewater. It is obvious that either the valley floor was 25 feet higher than now when the channel was active and the gravels and included artifacts were deposited, or tectonic uplift has occurred to account for all or most of its elevation.

Figure 4. Two chopping tools from the lowest culture-bearing stratum of the Brown site, in San Diego's Mission Valley.

A rate of uplift of 11 to 14 centimeters per 1,000 years for the adjacent coast has been estimated by Richard Ku and Philip Kern (1974), who dated corals by uranium series on an uplifted marine terrace at San Diego. This works out to about 22 feet over the last 60,000 years. Drilling records have shown that alluvial fill under the present valley floor is over 100 feet thick. In the maximum stage of the last glacial advance, the sea level was lowered over 300 feet, or 50 fathoms. Today the 50 fathom contour is over five miles offshore, while the elevation of the valley floor five miles upstream is only 60 feet. Clearly, abandonment of the river channel at the Brown site must have occurred very early in the Wisconsin as the sea level fell. A major stream in a pluvial climate period, carrying the kind of abrasive material seen in the Brown site channel, and working on unconsolidated sands from earlier valley fills, would soon have cut down far below the elevation of the site and current flood plain as well on its journey to the lowering sea.

Post-glacial valley filling over the last 10,000 years, adjusting itself to the rising sea levels of the Holocene or Recent period, has raised the valley floor to its present level, while the whole coastal zone continues to rise more slowly, probably at the rate proposed by Ku and Kern. But it seems obvious that stream deposits well above the present level of the flood plain must predate the last major excavation of the valley floor, which commenced about 70,000 years ago.

Two alternate explanations for the elevation of the Brown site have been proposed, but neither can be substantiated. It has been suggested that the site has been uplifted by recent seismic action rather than the slow tectonic process described above, and is therefore far younger than has been determined by the investigators. But far older geological strata on the adjacent valley walls are horizontal and undistorted, and no known faults traverse the area.

The other suggestion of recency is even less tenable. It is to the effect that the gravel-filled channel is not a river channel at all, but part of an alluvial fan formed at the mouth of a nearby canyon, and thus of a more modest age. Since the matrix of the channel is weathered granite sands, including chunks of rotted granite so decomposed that they can be pulverized simply dropping them on a hard surface, the origin of the alluvium is obvious. The nearest source of granite is some six miles upstream on the San Diego River, while the adjacent San Diego block is composed solely of sedimentary soils without granite. Thus the materials in the channel fill can only have been deposited by the main stream before the Wisconsin lowering of the sea level and the valley floor.

While it appears plainly evident that the tools recovered from the riverine stratum of the Brown site cannot be younger than 60,000 years, their true age is still completely unknown and could easily be double that figure or more. Nevertheless, the minimum age demonstrated at the site was the first solid and definite support for my almost intuitive belief in the antiquity of the worn stone core I had held in my hands seven years earlier on the flood-torn floor of Buchanan Canyon.

As the Brown site was being backfilled at the end of the summer's work in 1977, another site upstream and on the north side of Mission Valley was being excavated. This was on an interglacial stream terrace called Mission Ridge, a formation somewhat similar to the Texas Street site. The investigator was Dr. Brian O. K. Reeves of the University of Calgary in Alberta, assisted by Dr. Jason Smith and John Pohl. What appeared to be a cobble fireplace had been seen weathering out of the bank of a roadcut through the terrace sediments. The land was under development for a condominium park, and the contractor allowed Reeves ten days to excavate the site before the inexorable tide of condominiums reached it.

Working furiously, the digging team uncovered the fireplace and recovered a number of quartzite specimens similar to the Texas Street material. Included were a number of elongate cores from which spalls or flakes had been removed. Reeves' opinion was that these were fractured by natural means. Some of the irregularly shaped quartzite specimens were considered by Reeves to have been brought to the site already broken and utilized as tools, while others showed definite signs of human percussive flaking. In some cases quartzite fragments locally dispersed from the same cobble core were recovered, and Reeves felt that this was definite evidence of man's presence, since no geological or biological processes known to him other than human behavior could account for it.

Dating of the Mission Ridge site was not possible. According to Reeves, "The surface on which the site sat is most probably Mid Pleistocene in age, and around 500,000 years old. The quartzite assemblage occurred in the surface 30cm. We also recovered a piece of Blue Willow, a .22 shell and a Coke cap." (Reeves 1986:78)

Reeves feels that the site predates the Brown site, primarily on the basis of the tool assemblage which seems far cruder and more primitive. I agree, for the symmetrically-formed biface from deep in the riverine cobbles of the Brown site is clearly more sophisticated than anything from Mission Ridge, or from Buchanan Canyon or Texas Street, for that matter.

In 1982 Brian Reeves came back to San Diego on a winter Sabbatical, bringing with him an archaeological team from Canada. His aim was to locate and excavate a primary site of the same apparently very early industry; that is, a site where tools and features had been undisturbed, and this time with ample opportunity to do a careful and thorough investigation. Unfortunately he was frustrated; Cerutti took him to dozens of sites, but all were either secondary deposits or the owners refused permission to excavate. In some cases the sites were closed because poorly trained and uninformed young archaeologists had filed Environmental Impact Reports stating that no cultural resources were present, thus clearing the parcels for future development.

Despite these difficulties, the Reeves team made a very valuable contribution to the archaeological record, establishing the fact with their surface surveys that the same early stone industry was present throughout the coastal zone. They dug several secondary sites and collected a substantial assemblage for study, while demonstrating repeatedly the antiquity of the early human inhabitants of the region.

The artifact assemblages from Texas Street, Buchanan Canyon, the Brown site and Mission Ridge, as well as numerous other surface sites in the San Diego region, appear to belong to a very long period of occupation with very little change. The only stratified site we have, the Brown site, suggests a regression during a Wisconsin interstade about 40,000 years ago into what is actually a simpler and cruder stone industry; that of the La Jolla archaic horizon featuring dependence on shellfish and finally seed-grinding. Whether the earlier people depended on shellfish or were occasional shellfish eaters is unknown. What may have once been shell in the more ancient soil horizons has apparently decomposed into unrecognizable nodules of calcium carbonate, although one fragment in the Texas Street terrace could be identified as *Dosinia ponderosa*, a large, warmwater slough clam now extinct in the San Diego region (Carter 1957:320).

While I know of no analogue for very early dependence on shellfish in the Old World, it must be remembered that the large shell middens in both hemispheres dating to the Holocene were undoubtedly accumulated by far more generous populations than existed in the Late Middle Pleistocene.

Shellfish foragers in antiquity would probably have consumed their harvest on the spot, to have the shells obliterated by storm tides or encroaching surf lines.

It seems highly probable that the sites and surface scatters containing Buchanan Canyon-type tools represent occupation only during interglacial stages of high sea stand, and that during the glacio-pluvial climate cycles human bands followed the receding coastline some five miles west of the modern beaches. Their now-drowned and obliterated living sites would not only have given ready access to marine resources, but the low profile terrain would have been favorable for grasslands and herbivores.

No name has been agreed on as yet for this little-known cultural stage. Brian Reeves has described it as follows: "The fractured quartzite complex, as first claimed by Carter, is part of a Mid-Late Pleistocene Pacific Rim quartzite cobble core unifacial flake tradition of coastal zone adapted peoples" (Reeves 1986:78). This seems a little unwieldy. Carter calls it the blade and core stage. Emma Lou Davis has called it the Southern California macrolithic industry, a term which I also favor.

Dr. Alex Krieger of the University of Washington has said:

> In a word, the American assemblage (as yet it has no formal name) compares quite favorably with a generalized Middle Paleolithic stage of immense distribution in Europe, Africa, the Middle East and Asia. . . The Buchanan Canyon site contrasts with all the others in being even simpler in its range of tools and techniques, although the bipolar (stone-on-stone) technique is positively present. That is, the materials consist of very hard quartzite cobbles fractured by very hard blows, often struck from one face only, and with edges naturally so sharp that they cannot be made sharper by so-called retouch. At Buchanan, "prepared cores" and resultant blades are easily recognizd, and in quantity (Krieger 1979:70).

The problems associated with this still dimly seen human presence of so long ago are both complex and challenging. Most archaeologists, both in the Americas and abroad, are unaware of its existence, for it has not been highly publicized. But some of the tools are as obvious and indisputably of human manufacture as flaked spearpoints, and substantial antiquity for the sediments in which they are enclosed is undeniable.

Also undeniable is the fact that humans did not evolve from lower forms in the Western Hemisphere. At some point in the distant past, the ancestors of those primitive makers of quartzite tools must have begun the long and gradual expansion into the Americas without ever knowing that they were traveling at all, or transiting from the Old World into the New. For time intervals lasting thousands of years, during glacial stages when ice lay thickly on many interior regions of Amerasia, the continental shelves around the Pacific rim and along the Atlantic coasts lay exposed; broad, low profile landscapes stretching from Asia to San Diego and far beyond, with climates tempered by the sea and rich marine food resources readily available.

But equally for thousands of years, during the marine transgressions of interglacial intervals, the battering surf lines have inevitably crept inland as sea levels rose. Along the broad coastal margins that had been exposed during the glacial periods, and readily exploitable by very primitive human bands slowly drifting east and south behind the beaches, all evidence of human presence would have been erased. For thousands of miles along the coasts the record has been destroyed as surely as it has been by massive ice advances east of the Cordillera in the Northwest Territory and prairie provinces of Canada.

It now seems not only likely but certain, despite the lack of evidence in those critical areas, that humans did filter into the Western Hemisphere either by way of the coastal zones or up the Yukon and Mackenzie Rivers and most probably both, and at time periods far earlier than has generally been believed. Their discarded tools deep in the continental interiors and far down the Pacific coasts bear silent witness to their former presence. If those tools could be matched with similar industries in East and Northeast Asia, tools with parallel morphologies and technological development, it would appear that valuable progress would be made toward solving the problem of the first peopling of the New World.

CAMEO

Zhoukowdian and Exodus

I t is 415,000 years before the present. One of the great glacial cycles of the Pleistocene Epoch will soon set in, but in Northwest Asia it is a time of protracted drought. The grasslands in North China on the Mongolian Plateau and on the plains below are withering, stunted and smothered in dust. The herds of grazing animals and their attendant predators are forced desperately across the land in search of pasture. A few widely-scattered bands of primitive humans still survive. They are of the species Homo erectus pekinensis, and only a severely-reduced, sparse population will carry on the slowly-evolving human line in this corner of the earth.

Some six miles down the valley from the cave shelter on the bluffs the two shivering figures waited, crouched beside a carefully constructed willow screen beside the silver pond. The sun was a formless blur of fire sliding down into the chilly mist that had hung over the valley all day. Soon a moonless dark would envelop them, and darkness could be deadly, defenseless as they were against the great predatory carnivores that prowled the night.

These primitive humans were day creatures, clever and agile and bold enough when they could see, but lacking the acute night vision needed to move safely and easily about in darkness. They feared the dark. The fires burned all night before their caves and shelters, and they rarely ventured far outside the flickering firelight without blazing torches held high. But they were desperate now and starving.

Of the seventeen individuals; males, females and young who had inhabited the cave at the start of this bitter spring, only ten remained. Of these only the two males at the shrinking waterhole were still strong enough to hunt, and they were becoming so weak and emaciated that every effort was agony. But the powerful instinct they shared, a trait which had allowed these relatively weak and defenseless creatures to survive in the savage world of the Pleistocene, a deeply ingrained feeling of social obligation and conscience, bound them to the listless, dying band.

The catastrophe from which they suffered had been endlessly repeated over the millennia. These were predators; they needed the large amounts of protein only meat provided, in order to survive in the cold climate of North China, and the game was disappearing. The band had delayed too long, foraging for roots, lizards and frogs, expecting more herds of deer, horse or camel to move into the valley. Now they were too weak to travel. That tragic, relentless cycle had been reducing the population of hominids periodically for millions of years, keeping the predators and the game in balance. Thus the human population scarcely changed from one millennium to the next. But as with all other creatures, the strongest and most adaptive individuals often survived the depletion of their environment and moved on, to mate and spread their kind across the earth.

The two hunters by the pond had been impressive physical specimens before their gnawing pangs and listless lack of energy began to hunch them over. Their arms and shoulders were massive by modern standards, with powerful, large hands and stubby fingers tipped with gnarled, claw-like yellow nails. They stood a little less than five feet tall on rather short, bowed legs and splayed feet as tough as shoe leather. Their hides were a deep, mahogany brown, and a light fuzz of black hair covered most of their bodies, grew thickly on their scalps and scarcely at all on their faces. Only their skulls were distinctly different from those of modern races; the thick, forward-thrusting necks, pronounced brow ridges and receding foreheads and chins gave them a decidedly ape-like aspect. Their heads were longer and much narrower than any found in even the most primitive of modern societies, but from under those lowering brows keen eyes looked out at the world with wonder, fear, anger and often with great good humor.

But now the eyes were glazed with pain as their owners crouched there in the mist clutching fire-hardened wooden lances, naked against the chill. Normally they would have been clad in pelt loincloths, and pouches containing chipped stone choppers would have swung from knotted rawhide girdles at their waists, but their searing hunger had led them to devour every scrap of animal hide long since. The older of the two, who might have been close to forty and was steeped in wisdom from having survived so long, tensed suddenly. He touched his companion lightly, nodding his head toward the thicket up the bank. Something was moving toward them.

The younger male, whose lower face had been frightfully disfigured by a great, jagged scar along the jaw, crouched tautly in the blind, his heart pounding like a hammer in his chest. Even in easier times the last excruciating moments of the ambush passed in an atmosphere of almost unbearable suspense. The most experienced of hunters then found themselves breathing in short, painful gasps and shaking violently in anticipation. But now in addition the two were weak and wasted from malnutrition and the desperate efforts to find food, and had never been closer to the dark void of collapse and death, nor had the outcome of an ambush ever been more crucial to survival.

A young red deer picked her way through the tall but dying willows, pausing frequently to nibble at the few remaining dried leaves. Similar to the wapiti of North America, she stood nearly five feet tall at the shoulder, and was not yet fully grown. The coarse, reddish-brown hair bristled along her back, glistening in the mist; her large, sensitive ears trained constantly around, and the velvet muzzle sifted the air suspiciously, sorting out the odors of rotting vegetation, dried and caked mud and the rank smell of the willows. Step by step with tantalizing deliberation she approached the blind until at last she stood, forefeet in the pond and muzzle in the dark water, only a few feet from the hunters.

With a great convulsive effort they leaped to their feet and rushed at the deer. One on each side, they lunged with their short, tough lances and thrust them deep into her belly cavity, the only area soft enough to receive the lances without the chance of being blocked by bone.

The animal gave a bawling cry of terror and whirled to career up the bank and into the willows, dragging the two along in a battering, bruising rush through the clutching roots and branches. In easier times they would have let her go, to follow along at a loping trot until she dropped. But now the gathering dark and their desperate need demanded a quick and certain kill. They hung on grimly to the lances, thrusting them deeper whenever a brief foothold permitted.

Both attackers were soon dislodged, but the weakened and confused creature plowed to a stop with the shafts caught fast in the willows. The old male dashed back to the blind, retrieved his quartz chopper and slipped up beside the panting form of the deer. Raising the massive stone weapon above his head with both hands, he brought it crashing down on the lowered skull of the animal as she thrashed and struggled.

The deer dropped instantly to her knees, then sagged stunned against the branches. The dark figures chopped at her with their sharp implements until the blood poured out in a foaming torrent. They continued hacking and tearing at the flesh of her neck, working fist-sized chunks free and cramming the hot, bloody fragments into their mouths until at last they could feel their pinched bellies swell and tighten. They sank back exhausted among the crimson-spattered leaves.

The young man felt pleasure surging through his veins like warm water from sun-touched shallows, pleasure as sweet and thick as honey from a bee tree. But now there was hard, dangerous work to do. Muttering occasionally in guttural grunts which relied on pitch more than mouth shaping for communication, they began to butcher the carcass of the deer. For this they both carried ingenuous stone tools, developed by uncounted generations of hunters. Flaked from split quartz cobbles, they were kidney-shaped, about five inches long, and wedge-shaped in cross-section. The convex edges were sharp cutting blades, the back edges were rounded for a solid grip, and they could be used like a knife to cut through hide and flesh, like a skinning spud or wedge to separate the hide from the carcass, or like a hammer, blunt end down, to break through joints and smash small marrow bones.

Tonight there was no time for careful skinning. It was already full dark, they were far from shelter, and torches were out of the question. They had brought neither smoldering moss nor fire-making tools on this desperate, floundering effort to make a kill and survive. Without their rawhide pouches the stone tools and lances had been burden enough.

The game was cut up then without skinning except for a few strips off the belly to serve as straps. The head and body, saving only the liver and heart, were abandoned to the jackals; the four quarters were lashed into two bundles of over 150 pounds apiece, lances and tools were retrieved and the hunters were ready to leave. They walked down to the pool and drank, belching and blowing resoundingly; splashed away the crusted blood from their faces, hands and chests, and heaved up the heavy packs with gasping grunts of effort. Still weak and shaky from starvation, they reeled under the grinding weight as the old one led the way to the dusty, well-beaten trail up the valley, staring fearfully into the threatening dark.

As he staggered along under the weight of his burden the younger male could see in the distance a pinpoint of flame twinkling like a star on the bluffs at the head of the valley, but even as he watched, the fire faltered and died down to a red glow in the mist. Alarmed, he tried to move faster up the trail but the towering load seemed to press his feet into the powdery dust and constrict his lungs with hot, grasping claws. His old companion struggled along seemingly unaware of the dying fire.

For the weak, emaciated young hunter the march became a nightmare journey. The same highly developed brain which could comprehend the use of weapons, tools and fire was already capable of vivid imagination. To him the crowding darkness seemed alive with menacing, savage creatures, crouching as he had crouched, ready to leap and strike with the same merciless fury. The wooden lances, blunted now from the tough hide of the deer, would be useless now against the sudden rush of a charging cat or the lumbering, crushing power of the bear. Straining to hear the first hint of nearby danger, he heard murmurings and whispers on every hand, vague blurs of sound produced by his own laboring, pounding pulse and lungs.

Now the busy, tormented mind of the returning hunter began to paint pictures of tragedy at the hearths yonder, in response to the dying flames. He saw the helpless females and young, the fumbling, wasted aged beset by the hyenas who lurked always just beyond the firelight, waiting. He saw the scuttling, furtive scavengers advancing into the living place with grinning fangs and glowing eyes, heard them snarling and jabbering over the feebly struggling forms. He groaned aloud in an agony of worry and frustration.

The beacon flames had disappeared completely, and the tough old male in the lead finally stopped and lifted down his load. He stared up the hill through the darkness, straining to see the sheltering cave entrance, but it was almost a mile away and over the brow of the bluff, a black and shapeless mass against the misty night sky. He rubbed a gnarled hand through his grey-streaked mane, considering, then motioned to his companion to put down his unwieldy burden and run on ahead. The young man sprinted up the path like a fallow deer.

As he scrambled up the steep slope, bellowing to arouse the camp and frighten away the hyenas, his worst fears were realized. Several dark shapes skulked away, just touched by the pinkish glow from the dying coals. Beyond the dimly lit fire ring the tortured forms sprawled out, not relaxed in peaceful sleep but distorted like corpses on a battlefield. The slight, twisted carcass of an aged female had been dragged almost to the brow of the hill by the animals; he stumbled over it as he approached. The throat and part of the abdomen had already been torn away and devoured. The young male she had borne opened his mouth and his anguish poured out in a great, racking shout of pain.

As he crawled from one form to another he found only two still alive, a fully grown female and a young one of about seven years. Shuddering and trembling, near collapse from his tremendous exertion and weakened state, unable to rise and build up the fire, the dazed young human lay on his back and stared blankly up at the black void of sky.

At last he roused himself enough to struggle to his feet. He nursed the ring of flames back to leaping health and vigor, then started back down the trail, stumbling and sliding down the slope, yelping and tossing pebbles to discourage the scavengers.

The wiry, stubborn old male was still struggling up the valley, shouldering one load and dragging the other doggedly along through the soft trail dust by its hide strap. Grimacing with pain and exhaustion, he refused to surrender the precious meat which had meant life itself and might still mean survival. He seemed confused and dazed, and the younger man had to force the strap from his hand over a snarl of protest.

Together they climbed to the circle of firelight. The old man's sunken, staring eyes took in the frightful scene, the mutilated corpses, the scattered forms beyond the fire sprawled in bent-kneed agony as death had found them. He saw the surviving females huddled together moaning in a mournful chorus, a wintry background of murmuring like wind echoing through a tunnel. He made no sound but sank slowly to his haunches beside the hearth, covered his face with his cracked and bloody hands and sobbed spasmodically, his shoulders twitching.

At daybreak the gaunt forms of the survivors were shadowed against the drifting smoke and mist as they gathered together tools, weapons and meat, stepping over the sprawling corpses of their relatives there on the floor of the living place. The adults instinctively knew only death waited them here in this cave on the bluff, and they must move on while their bellies were full and a surplus of meat was on hand.

The young man looked around the rock shelter that seemed as much a part of him as once had been the soft, dark comfort of his mother's womb. The ceiling overhead of hard limestone had provided shade on glaring summer days, and kept him warm and dry when icy winds drove hail and sleet across the hilltop. Before the rock-walled chamber and open to the sky the curving hearth, with its flat boulders and smaller rocks for roasting meat, had presented a flaming barrier to the hostile outer world.

The whole inhabited space was paved with rubbish, since everything not consumed was simply tossed onto the ground. Bones, nutshells and fruit pits, scraps of wood, flakes of stone used as cutting blades, and worn-out stone and bone tools formed its slowly rising floor. Over the habitation, and completely unnoticed by those who dwelt in it, rose a powerful, fetid stench composed of the odors of excrement and the stale urine with which the animal skins were treated to loosen the hair and make them soft and flexible.

The boulder walls and the bedrock of the cave had accumulated, over generations of use, a coating of grease and carbon from the drifting smoke which tended to blacken everything that touched them. Thus the objects soon took on a patina of grime, as did the hides of the inhabitants, and it seems remarkable that any survived their wounds and scratches.

Near the hearth and scattered along the rock walls were the little band's store of useful objects. There were stone choppers and picks of various sizes, scrapers and butchering tools, fire-hardened wooden lances and digging sticks in all degrees of usability, grooved wooden slabs and rubbing sticks for firemaking, hollow gourds of many sizes for storing drinking water and the urine for working hides, and splintered bone spits, awls and scrapers.

Before they had been shredded and devoured by the starving humans, hide objects of various kinds had also littered the living place; pelts and ponchos for use in freezing weather, crude pouches of rawhide doubled over and laced to serve as carrying bags for food or tools, strips to wind around the feet and legs, and bolas, the stone-weighted lengths of rawhide that were whirled around and cast at the legs of running animals. These devices, the nearest things these primitive hunters had to projectile weapons other than stones and throwing sticks, would wrap themselves around the legs to trip and hold game on the ground long enough to be dispatched with a wooden club or stone chopper.

The dwellers here had been unaware of the incredibly rich record of man's slow evolution that was scattered through the compacted rubble beneath their feet. Bones of earlier human creatures, bones of their predecessors splintered for marrow 200,000 years before in these same caves and fissures in the cliffs, lay jumbled there among the chipped stone and charcoal and dust of millennia past counting. Bones of their fellow creatures, too, the fallow deer, rhinoceros and camel and many more lay buried and compacted far below the leathery feet of these most recent occupants.

The Pleistocene was an age of slowly fluctuating climates. In times of drought the grass and game disappeared from huge areas of the temperate zone, and so did the predators, including humans, for centuries at a time. Such a cycle was developing now at the end of a long period of mild and moderate weather with adequate rainfall. Repeated and protracted droughts had already destroyed vast grasslands, and the herbivores were gradually moving north.

In some areas, where expanded family bands of humans had settled, the depleted and scattered herds could not support the predators, and while most predators simply followed the herds, humans were not yet sufficiently advanced to do so. Scavengers as well as hunters, they needed other carnivores as well as plentiful prey animals to survive, but also needed the protection of secure shelters for the freezing winter nights. They needed to know where, in the surrounding countryside, they might expect to find berry patches in season, succulent root beds and honey trees. For these ancient foragers, even in the best of times, the hunt for food was a never-ending occupation.

As an evolving line the genus Homo, the human creature, was nurtured in the warm tropics. Here amid teeming life of many kinds the omniverous humans found foraging easy. But the awesome brain development, the formation of cooperative human societies and the mastering of sophisticated tool and weapon technologies; these were primarily responses to a far more demanding environment, that of the cool temperate zone. Challenged by bitter winds, threatened by hunger and violent death, the hardy survivors bred and prospered, shaping and improving the evolving line and the conditions of their lives. But periodically, after generations had followed the same culture and life pattern, the environmental rules and challenges were changed again by forces far beyond human control, and man had either to form new habits, or move on, or die.

The four survivors of the famine at Zhoukowdian slung loads of venison on their shoulders, picked up tools, weapons and a smoldering slow-match of coals and moss wrapped in bark, and walked down the hill. Although they had inhabited the cave since birth, and their ancestors before them, they took the dusty trail down the valley without a backward glance, and walked eastward toward the rising sun.

CHAPTER 2

East and Northeast Asia: Cultural Evidence of Vast Antiquity

It is almost universally believed that the first human inhabitants of the Western Hemisphere sifted into North America from Northeast Asia. The popular conception is of fur-clad Mongoloid hunters armed with stone-tipped spears following herds of reindeer across the so-called Bering Land Bridge from Siberia. But among serious scholars the questions of how long ago they came, what routes they followed and what kind of people they were has long remained in doubt. As recently as 60 years ago and within my own lifetime practically nothing was known of the early prehistory of China and Siberia, and very little about human evolution in general.

The tropical regions of the earth have usually been considered to be the only areas of the world capable of incubating man in his earliest and most vulnerable stages. If this premise is accepted, and since no early trace of human evolution has ever been found in the Western Hemisphere, the only alternatives for human origins would be Africa or southern Asia. But world climates and environments may have changed more radically than we realize in the Cenozoic Era, and the location of the Cradle of Mankind, so to speak, is still uncertain.

In recent years highly important discoveries of fossils of long extinct hominids, creatures that walked erect on two legs and were probably ancestral to man, have been found in South Africa, the Olduvai Gorge, in Kenya and in the Afar Valley of Ethiopia. But the first fossil remains of pre-sapiens man ever found were discovered in Java before the turn of the century. Based on bone fragments, a pre-human ape-man christened *Pithecanthropus erectus*, whose age was guessed at 500,000 years, was postulated. The announcement of this skeleton as the ancestor of man, accompanied by artists' renditions of a shaggy, bestial, ape-like creature, caused the feelings of Bible Fundamentalists as well as those of more moderate Christians to run high.

Java Man had been discovered late in the last century by a young Dutch anatomist named Eugene Dubois. Its classification as proto-human was based on a thighbone, three teeth and some skull fragments, and Dubois and his bones became the center of furious controversy. He was even accused of being a heretic by the religious community, one segment of which still insists today on a literal interpretation of the Biblical account of the creation of man.

It was in the late 1920s and early 1930s that the first fossil remains of very early humans in China were being unearthed at Zhoukoudian, near Peking, and the reports of that discovery caused a similar furor and a sensation in the scientific world. These gradually died down as more and more human fossils and stone tools were recovered. Being employed at the time by the San Diego Museum of Man, I read the accounts of those discoveries with great interest, but of course had no idea then that I would become personally involved in the search in this hemisphere and almost in my own backyard. But the story of Zhoukoudian and the patient, stubborn, years-long probing that ended in success should be an inspiration to all those who are embarked on similar pursuits.

Bordering the broad, flat and fertile coastal plain of North China, the Western Hills mark the edge of the Mongolian Plateau, a vast area of uplifted ancient sea bottom rich in the limestones formed by the deaths of trillions of sea creatures in bygone ages. Dissected now into rolling uplands, its lime has been quarried and burned for centuries, perhaps millennia, by the rural villagers. Seen from some distance out on the plain, the lime quarries along the steep hillsides show up as white scars against the purple slopes.

The village of Zhoukoudian nestles against the hills about 30 miles southwest of the center of Beijing, as Peking is now called. Just behind it a rather steep palisade rises called Longgushan or Dragon Bone Hill. The villagers have always tilled their fields below and quarried lime on the hill. They also used to share a more furtive industry with rural people in many parts of China, the collection of fossil bones. These were sold to bone buyers who in turn sold them to apothecary shops in the towns and cities. There they were ground into powder and marketed as medicine; a powerful elixir which could perform numerous benefits such as the prevention of aging and the restoration of sexual potency. Since these bones brought excellent prices, the sellers tended to be somewhat secretive about their sources.

In most limestone formations the subsurface is frequently honeycombed with caves and fissures, and around Zhoukoudian many of these had been filled with sediments forming a rock-hard clay dating back to the Lower Pleistocene. Scattered through these slowly accumulated beds were the fossilized bones of ancient creatures, covering a time period of over 500,000 years. These were the dragon bones so much in demand by the bone buyers.

A German naturalist, one Dr. Hans Haberer, was the first Westerner to interest himself in the bones shortly after the turn of the present century. He was able to buy a number of them in Beijing and Shanghai and quickly discovered that they were the remains of extinct Pleistocene animals rather than dragons. He set out to stock up on as many as he could get, and managed to acquire a considerable number before he became viewed with such suspicion that he ran out of suppliers. Shipped back to Munich, the fossil collection became the subject of a book called *Die Fosilen Saugethiere Chinas* by Max Schlosser.

In 1914 Dr. J. Gunnar Andersson, a Swedish geologist who was also a paleontologist and archaeologist of considerable accomplishment, arrived in China to work with the Geographical Survey of the Chinese government, locating potential areas for commercial mining development. Dr. Andersson had read Schlosser's book with great interest, and since his work took him to many regions of China, he too began to acquire a respectable collection of dragon bones. His workmen soon discovered his interest and willingness to pay for choice specimens, but they were rarely or never willing to reveal their sources.

Andersson and his colleagues in Stockholm realized that far more could be accomplished if the sources of supply could be investigated. To this end a young Austrian paleontologist, Dr. Otto Zdansky, was invited to take a two year's leave of absence from his post at Upsala University and join Dr. Andersson in China. The latter had managed to locate a number of possibly rewarding sites, among them Dragon Bone Hill at Zhoukoudian.

When his new assistant arrived from Sweden, Dr. Andersson took him and an American friend, Dr. Walter Granger, to Zhoukoudian where they discovered that the vicinity was indeed a rich source of important fossil remains. Dr. Zdansky remained for several weeks and discovered not only the bones and teeth of extinct animals, but also some crudely-chipped pieces of quartz that he believed must have been worked by humans. Dr. Andersson himself had for some time felt a strange presentiment that the caves might reveal not only archaeological evidence but the actual fossil remains of prehistoric humans.

During the next few years Zdansky worked at the caves of Zhoukoudian intermittently, shipping back to Sweden the fossils that were recovered. Often these were still enclosed in a matrix and were not carefully examined before shipment, and it was in Sweden that the first startling discovery was made. The first hominid remains had been found: two teeth that were clearly human.

Now work was intensified, financed in part by the Rockefeller Foundation and supervised by the Chinese Geological Survey and the Canadian Dr. Davidson Black, anatomist at the Peking Medical School. Dr. Birger Bohlin of Sweden directed the excavation at the site. The major effort was begun in 1927, and China was at that time an extremely dangerous place for foreigners. Bandits and petty warlords roamed the countryside, and non-Chinese residents and travelers alike were being seized and held for ransom and even killed. The sound of gunfire could actually be heard at times from the vicinity of the caves. Nevertheless Dr. Bohlin carried on the work, and after five months of careful excavation another tooth was discovered. In 1928 more teeth were found, and then fragments of skulls and a human lower jaw.

In 1929 work was resumed under the direction of Professor Pei Wenzhong. The following is from an account by Dr. Jia Lanpo of the Chinese Academy of Science:

> It happened at four o'clock in the afternoon. The sun had almost set and the light in the hole was getting so poor that candles were called for. In the winter cold, the sounds of hammers and picks did little to cheer up the people at the site. Suddenly archaeological technician Liu Yishan saw a strange object. When it was partially uncovered, Professor Pei Wenzhong took a close look. "An Ape-man's!" he cried, startling everybody around him.
>
> Everybody present was now tense and eager for the whole thing to be freed. The evening grew darker. The other half of the skullcap was still buried in hard clay. Pei Wenzhong thought hard and finally decided to get it out then, instead of waiting for the morning. A year later, when I joined the team, I heard a worker describe that moment, "Who could have borne the agony of a whole night of suspense?" (Jia 1980:22)

Peking man had at last been found!

During the following decade a great deal of work was carried on both at the site and in the laboratories, and many more human fossils, artifacts and evidences of fire were discovered, removed and studied. Fortunately casts were made of the fossils under the direction of Dr. Franz Weidenreich, who had succeeded Dr. Black upon the latter's death. When Weidenreich was forced to leave China by the Japanese invasion at the beginning of World War II, he managed to take the casts out of the country to safety. The actual fossils were crated and turned over to the Marine Guard at the U.S. Legation in Beijing for safekeeping, but on December 7, 1941, the marines were captured by the Japanese Army. The cases were lost in the confusion of war. Their disappearance was surely one of the greatest tragedies ever to occur in the history of archaeological investigation.

After the end of World War II and the Chinese Communist revolution in 1949, scientific activity, including archaeological research, was resumed under the Peoples' Government. The former Cenozoic Research Laboratory was reorganized in 1953, becoming the Laboratory of Vertebrate Paleontology, and later the Institute of Vertebrate Paleontology and Paleoanthrolpology (IVPP) of the Chinese Academy of Sciences, with a staff some 60 times larger than the prewar institution. Since reorganization more than 50 important sites have been discovered, excavated and studied, and the estimated time of human presence in China has more than doubled, with sites at Xihoudu in Shanxi Province and Lantian in Shaanxi Province both considered by the Chinese to be over 1,000,000 years old.

In recent years several excellent and well-illustrated books and journal articles describing the Chinese Paleolithic sites, and particularly the lithic assemblages, have been published in English (Jia 1975:1980; Aigner 1978; Institute of Vertebrate Paleontology and Paleoanthropology 1980; Yi and Clark 1983; Wu and Olsen 1985). This has made it possible for American scholars to acquaint themselves with the technologies, typologies and general morphological characteristics of the early stone industries of China, and particularly with their slow evolution from the massive, crude and steeply trimmed core tools of Xihoudu to the symmetrically flaked small flake tools of the Late Paleolithic.

The Peking Man site at Zhoukoudian has been placed under the jurisdiction of the Chinese Academy, with a paved road and a visitors' center with an excellent small museum displaying many of the artifacts and fossils. Some intermittent work has been done at the site and in the vicinity, and more fossils of early man have been recovered. An upper cave has yielded the skeletal remains and tools of the modern form of *Homo sapiens sapiens*, and the fossil remains of Peking Man are now classified as *Homo erectus pekinensis*. The latter is thought to have visited and possibly inhabited the caves sporadically for over 400,000 years, and as early as 600,000 BP (before the present).

Although the earliest tools used by hominids were undoubtedly simply sharp flakes of naturally broken quartz and fortuitously shaped cobbles, a progression by early toolmakers from massive, frequently amorphous and sometimes bifacial implements to much smaller unifacial flake tools in the Late Middle and Upper Paleolithic industries appears to be typical of developing cultures throughout the world. It is nowhere more convincingly displayed than at Locality 1 of Zhoukoudian, the site of original discovery. This was originally a very large cave whose roof has long since collapsed, so that it is open to the sky. (see figure 5)

The excavated deposits are over 160 feet deep, and have been laid down in 17 distinguishable strata or layers, numbered sequentially from the top. Only Layers 1 through 11 have cultural remains. The latter have been further subdivided into the Early Stage in Layers 11 to 8, tentatively believed to range in age from 660,000 BP to 400,000 BP; the Middle Stage in Layers 7 and 6 between 400,000 and 300,000 years old; and the Late Stage in Layers 5 to 1 believed to have been deposited 300,000 to 200,000 years ago (Zhang 1985).

Figure 5. View of Locality 1, Zhoukowdian, China, as it appears today. A very large cave in prehistoric times, it is now open to the sky.

The great value of the materials in these deposits, which contain thousands of stone tools as well as numerous fossil remains of both humans and the creatures they apparently preyed upon, is in the demonstration of gradually evolving technological skills and traditions, and the slow changes in skeletal morphology and cranial capacity occurring over 400,000 years of human prehistory. For most American archaeologists these changes are of only passing interest since they deal only with Holocene and terminal Pleistocene lithic assemblages, but for those scholars who are aware of what appear to be far earlier artifact assemblages in North America, this panoramic view of human toolmaking progress during the Middle and Upper Pleistocene is critically important. It permits comparative studies leading to far greater insights into the antiquity of the American Paleolithic.

The changing morphologies and technological means of the slowly evolving lithic industries at Locality 1 of Zhoukoudian have been described as follows:

> The lithic assemblage of the Early Stage occupation at Locality 1, comprising Layers 11-8, is characterized by almost exclusive dependence on quartz and sandstone as raw materials. Tools fashioned from cores, pebbles and small chunks of stone outnumber those made on flake blanks. This assemblage is typologically simple, consisting primarily of choppers and scrapers. Points and gravers occur only rarely and are very crudely retouched. *Large tools predominate, forming roughly 70% of the lithic assemblage. . .* Typological classification is more difficult and tools that are apparently multifunctional are more common than those that seem to be task specific. (Italics mine)

(In) the Middle Stage. . . quartz and rock crystal increase in frequency as raw materials, while sandstone is characterized by a dramatic decrease in utilization. The bipolar method of detaching flakes becomes more developed in these Middle Stage strata, and bipolar nuclei outnumber those fashioned through simple direct percussion for the first time in the Zhoukoudian deposits. . . Flake tools predominate over core tools for the first time at Zhoukoudian. . . In all tool types there is a trend toward reduction in size, and implements that measure less than 40mm long and weigh less than 20g constitute over 68% of the total assemblage.

(In) the Late Stage. . . flake tools continue their increase in frequency, now constituting nearly three-quarters of the total, while tools made on nuclei amount to only 26.1% of the assemblage. . . The trend toward reduction in size begun in the Middle Stage deposits continues in the upper strata and this assemblage is characterized by a much higher percentage of typologically classifiable, regularized tool forms. The number of multi-functional tools and implements of uncertain use reaches its lowest point in the Zhoukoudian deposits here (Zhang 1985:168-169).

It is important to note the emphasis placed by Zhang on the steadily diminishing sizes of stone tools over the 400,000-year period of Homo erectus evolution, since very large size is the most characteristic aspect of the undated macrolithic tool assemblages of the San Diego coastal zone, as it is in the Early Stage at Locality 1, Zhoukoudian. The same progression is seen at the Soan River terraces on the border between India and Pakistan. There the highest flood plain surfaces, dating to the Middle Pleistocene, have heavy, massive choppers steeply-flaked on very large quartzite flakes and slabs lying among boulder fields, while increasingly smaller and refined flake tools are seen as one stairsteps down a series of terraces to the modern river level (Movius 1948, Fairservis 1971).

Ash deposits in the Locality 1 sediments contain charred bones and also cracked, broken and discolored stones similar to those at Texas Street which first attracted George Carter's attention almost 40 years ago. There is little doubt that Peking Man used fire, but whether he could light fires or simply captured fire and preserved it is unknown. If he used a wooden fire plow to make fire, as primitive people still do in remote parts of the world, the evidence would have long since decomposed and disappeared.

The earliest suggestions of the use of fire by man has been moved back in time repeatedly by more recent discoveries in northeast China. In 1957 a survey team, dispatched in connection with a reservoir project on the Yangtze River, worked in many parts of China and discovered in Shanxi Province early Paleolithic tools and mammalian fossils in the vicinity of Gehe Village. In 1959 another team carried out a dig at the same locality and recovered more stone artifacts, fossil animal bone and a charred bone tool that suggested the use of fire. In 1960 major excavations were carried out, and 13 sites with early Paleolithic tools and fossils were identified.

The archaeological and geomorphic situation at Gehe was somewhat similar to that at Buchanan Canyon. A deep gully cuts through the village, exposing thick Pleistocene strata along the gully walls. At the bottom is a layer of light brown clay formed of lake sediments in the Lower Pleistocene 1,000,000 to 2,000,000 years ago. The lake had disappeared and been replaced by a river beside which humans lived, hunted and gathered fresh-water clams about 600,000 years ago. A convenient supply of river cobbles, mostly quartzite, provided good material for stone tools and implements.

As at Buchanan Canyon, stone tools were seen redeposited into the bottom of the gully and weathering out of the lower walls. The Gehe assemblages included choppers, scrapers, heavy triangular points, small points apparently not mounted on spears, and stone balls; the latter probably used as bola weights, to be connected by thongs in groups of two or three. These were whirled around the head and cast at game, to wrap around legs or wings and bring it down, to be dispatched with a club or stone chopper.

Similar stone spheroids have been found in many other early Chinese sites, as well as in Africa, Europe and the western United States. Richard Cirutti has found at least a dozen in the San Diego coastal zone. They are said to be in use as bola balls today in western Mongolia and the Arctic for bringing down a variety of game, including flying birds. Indians of the Gran Chaco still employ bolas, and gauchos on the Pampas in historic times used them to capture rheas, the South American ostrich.

A closely related weapon is the slingshot, which also relies on the tremendous velocity that is achieved through centrifugal force by whirling a weighted set of thongs around the head. Whether slingshots were utilized in very early times is not known, since rawhide thongs have not been preserved. But some years ago I saw the efficiency of the simple slingshot, like the one that David used to slay Goliath, demonstrated in Mexico.

An Indian walked slowly and quietly out into a field where a covey of quail was feeding. Seeming to know just how close he could approach them, he stopped about 50 yards from the flock, crouched down and began whirling a leather slingshot with a pebble in the pouch. When he let it fly the stone skipped along over the ground and there was a sudden puff of feathers in the covey. A few quail moved away a short distance, but most went on feeding unconcernedly. After half a dozen casts the quail became alarmed and flew off, while the hunter walked out and collected a handful of birds. I realized I had been privileged to witness a virtuoso performance that might have been repeated over scores and perhaps hundreds of millennia.

While the Gehe Village sites were being excavated, an even older and more important site was discovered at Xihoudu, also in Shanxi Province in the vicinity of Kehe near the east bank of the Huanghe (Yellow River). Xihoudu is a small mountain village in the southwestern foothills of the Zhongtiao Mountains in the southern part of the province. Here exposures of stratified deposits displayed sediments dating from Tertiary to Upper Pleistocene periods, and including a sand and gravel layer of Lower Pleistocene origin containing artifacts and non-human fossils.

The site was discovered in 1959 and excavated in 1961 and 1962 by scientists from the Museum of Shanxi Province. More than 30 stone artifacts were recovered, as well as a generous collection of vertebrate fossils which included burned mammalian ribs, deer antlers and horse dentition. The latter were subjected to laboratory tests that proved they had been burned, suggesting the earliest human use of fire yet found. The fossils represented more than 20 vertebrate species, many of which clearly indicated a Lower Pleistocene antiquity for the site, but "This long cycle of sedimentation is so clearly preserved in the geological section at Xihoudu that the approximate antiquity of the site could be determined on geological evidence alone" (Jia 1985:136).

Preliminary paleomagnetic data have indicated an absolute age for the site of about 1.8 million years BP, but further laboratory tests are needed to corroborate so advanced an age for hominids in Northeast Asia. No hominid remains have yet been found at Xihoudu, not even a tooth, so the proof of human presence rests solely on the artifacts. They are extremely primitive and crude, but judging by the published photographs and drawings of the tools, and particularly a heavy, triangular quartzite point (Jia 1985:139), they are unmistakably manmade.

Published descriptions of the artifacts have a special meaning for us at San Diego, in view of the judgment of some of our colleagues that the bipolar cores recovered at all of our early sites cannot be related to human activity and must have been flaked by some natural means. Again quoting Professor Jia Lanpo: "This is an assemblage of cores, flakes, choppers, scrapers and heavy triangular points. Some of the cores were jagged round pebbles or stone slabs used to strike at flakes along the edges; others were left-overs of oblong rocks placed vertically on stone anvils and struck from the top with a stone hammer to produce flakes. These are, by virtue of their form, called bipolar cores" (Jia 1980:11).

Without human fossil remains, nothing is known about the physical aspects of the inhabitants. The species of animals present suggested a cool climate, and the investigators theorized that the tool makers were incapable of killing very large animals, and lived by preying on smaller animals and by gathering edible plants and ostrich eggs. But the charred bones recovered that suggest the possible use of fire lead to a further speculation: it is my firm belief that as long as humans have had fire, they have scavenged the kills of more effective predators by driving them off with flaming torches.

The lack of human fossil remains at Xihoudu was soon rectified by the discovery of the highly important sites in Lantian County, Shaanxi Province. At Chenjiawo Village near the county seat of Lantian, a complete human mandible was found, the first discovery of *Homo erectus* fossil bone since the work at Zhoukoudian. At Gongwangling Village in the same area a skullcap and upper jawbone and three teeth were recovered. A few meager stone tools were also found in the same stratum that contained the human remains.

At Gongwangling the assemblage included two scrapers, one flake, and four flaked cores, all at a slightly higher position in the same stratum that yielded the skullcap. A large, heavy quartzite point, similar to those recovered at Gehe, was recovered from a comparable stratum nearby. Three years after the initial discoveries, in 1966, an excavation team from the IVPP in Beijing worked the western slope of the Gongwangling site and recovered many mammalian fossils and more artifacts judged contemporaneous with Lantian Man. They included stone cores, utilized flakes, scrapers, large choppers and stone balls. Some charcoal granules were recovered but cannot be considered definite evidence of the use of fire by man.

Dating of the Lantian fossils has been somewhat disputable, with paleomagnetic ages offered by different agencies ranging from 1,000,000 BP to 750,000 BP for the fossil materials from Gongwangling Village and only 650,000 to 500,000 years of age for the Chenjiawo mandible or lower jawbone. However, despite the inconclusive nature of these laboratory dates, it appears that the Lantian fossils are earlier than those of Zhoukoudian, and possibly considerably older. The biostratigraphic evidence supports this view, and suggests a warm, moist, even subtropical climate (Zhang 1985:150).

In 1965 two human teeth and some stone tools were discovered in a gully wall in Yuanmou, Yunnan Province. A geological team had been sent there to do a survey in connection with the projected Chengdu-Kunming Railway. When they asked the villagers if "dragon bones" were to be found in the vicinity, they were directed to Ten Dragon Pass, where the bones of extinct Pleistocene mammals were weathering out of the walls.

The two teeth were upper incisors belonging to an adult individual. They were studied by Hu Chengzhi, paleontologist of the Museum of Geology of the Academy of Geological Sciences in Beijing. According to Dr. Hu, the teeth are big and strong, flat on the buccal surfaces and complicated on the lingual surfaces. They are similar to the teeth of Peking Man at Zhoukoudian in their large size, robust build and complex pattern, but differ in having a broader cutting edge, tapering roots and a more triangular shape than the roughly square form of Peking Man's incisors.

Further investigations at Yuanmou yielded more crude artifacts and quantities of cinders, leading to the suspicion that Yuanmou Man might have been the earliest user of fire yet discovered, since the site was then believed to be nearly 2,000,000 years old on the basis of associated mammalian fossils not known from later periods. Paleomagnetic tests of the deposits in which the incisors were found gave an age of 1,700,000 +/- 100,000 years, about the same age as Louis Leakey's famous *Homo habilis* at Olduvai Gorge in Africa. However, recently acquired data suggest a much younger age for Yuanmou Man, possibly no older than the oldest fossils at Locality 1, Zhoukoudian (Wu and Dong 1985:80). The true age has yet to be determined.

Since only two teeth have thus far been found, nothing is known of the skeletal structure of Yuanmou Man at present, but a great many mammalian fossils have been preserved in the extensive sediments, so that further work there may yet produce human skeletal remains. It would of course be extremely useful for comparative purposes to ascertain the cranial capacity and skull morphology at that level, particularly if the original age estimates should be proven valid.

Because of ample skeletal evidence, it is possible to visualize the physical appearance of Peking Man. Professor Jia Lanpo has offered the following description of the structural features of *Homo erectus pekinensis*, based on the fossils recovered at Zhoukoudian:

All known skulls of Peking Man show marked flattening of the cranial vault and receding forehead. The cranial height, however, is greater than modern large apes', but still lower than of *Homo sapiens*. . . Peking Man's brows are heavily constructed, forming a conspicuous ledge over the eye sockets. The bony walls of the skull are almost twice as thick as modern man's. In contour, Peking Man's skull is an inversion of his modern counterpart, its lower part being larger than the upper part, like an inverted bowl. Peking Man's cranial capacity is nearly 73 percent of that of the average modern man, but is larger than that of the australopithecinae, (a prehuman hominid, or creature that walked erect) whose cranial capacity is only about 56 percent of Peking Man's. In the modern *Homo sapiens*, the tip of the lips and the forehead are on an almost perpendicular line, while Peking Man's lips project way beyond this line. Peking Man's nasal bone is broad, and his cheekbones are high and project forward, suggesting a broad nose and flat face. The most prominent features of Peking Man's mandible (or lower jaw) are its projecting anterior part and the lack of chin eminence. . . Peking Man's teeth are larger, their biting surface more complex than that of the modern man, but smaller in size and simpler in biting surface compared with the great apes.

Peking Man's limb bones are almost indistinguishable from those of *Homo sapiens*. His thigh bone is in the main similar to that of modern man in size, form, muscular attachment and the proportion of parts to each other. However, they still retain some primitive features, such as a small medullary cavity and thick walls. . .

The humerus approximates even more closely to that of modern man, and the only primitive features surviving are the small marrow cavity and thick walls. The structure of the humerus shows that Peking Man could use his arms and hands almost as freely and adroitly as modern man. Peking Man's lower limbs are similar in form to those of modern man, albeit retaining a bit of a crouch stance, but there is no doubt that he could walk upright and even run (Jia 1980:27-28).

From such a detailed framework one can add flesh, skin and hair and make visible to his inner eye the shadowy progenitors of modern populations. Most artists have depicted them as short and broad of stature, with brown skin and eyes, shaggy black hair on their scalps, luxuriant body hair and bulging muscles. They must have had scars and insect bites, leathery soles and long, broken and yellowed nails on feet and hands. Whether they laughed and cried as we do, we will never know.

In addition to the sites mentioned above, a number of other localities in North China have produced evidence of very early man, some contemporary but most of them younger than Zhoukoudian. As might be expected, Upper Paleolithic and Neolithic sites are far more plentiful and richer in materials than the very ancient sites. They are important to the present study because of the marked contrasts in tool morphologies, means of production and refinement between assemblages even 100,000 years old and the macrolithic quartzites of the San Diego coastal zone.

Little work has been done in Korea, but one site is interesting and significant, particularly since it is much closer to the western Pacific coastal margin than the Chinese sites we have been reviewing; only 100 miles from the Sea of Japan. In 1978 a young American soldier named Greg Bowen, stationed in the Republic of South Korea, found some very intriguing rock specimens on an uplifted terrace or flood plain remnant of the Hantan River at Chon-Gok-Ni, about 35 miles north of Seoul.

Before his induction into the Army, Bowen had been a third-year student at the University of Arizona, majoring in anthropology. He appears to have been an unusually apt student, for he recognized the specimens as Early Paleolithic quartzite tools. They were apparently very similar to the artifacts in the Buchanan Canyon assemblage, judging by the descriptions.

Three of the tools were described as bifacially-flaked handaxes, very crude and massive and averaging about five inches in length. There were also a large cleaver, a pointed chopper and a flake tool that he believed was a scraper. Bowen classified the tools as Acheulian, a type named for the place of first discovery in the Acheul District of France, and found in very early sites at Olduvai Gorge in Africa and elsewhere, and he sent a preliminary report to Professor Francois Bordes at the University of Bordeaux in France. He also sent copies to Professors Kim Wonyon at the University of Seoul and Chung Young-Wha at the University of Yeungam, who were immediately interested, conducted surface surveys, four campaigns in 1979, 1980 and 1981, and published the report which I have been fortunate enough to receive from a colleague (Kim and Chung 1979).

Considerable complexity was revealed in the recovered tool assemblages, which included some 50 massive quartzite specimens comparable to the tools found in Europe and Africa from Acheulian industries. Such tools are often crudely flaked bifaces, with a functional or cutting edge all around or nearly all around the periphery. They are often described as large handaxes. Also found in Acheulian sites and at Chon-Gok-Ni are specimens designated as cleavers; large, amorphous tools with sharpened cutting edges across the ends. Both of these types are found in the San Diego coastal zone quartzite assemblages, although possibly in cruder form than those collected at the Korean site. Although the tools are without specific dating, they are estimated to be about 300,000 years old, on the bases both of the geology of the uplifted terrace and the character of the recovered tools as compared to those of dated Chinese sites, although they may be much later.

For advocates of an early circum-Pacific movement of humans along the exposed continental shelves and into the Western Hemisphere during a pre-Illinoian glacial stage, a recently-reported site in Japan is of the utmost importance (Reynolds 1986). This is at Nakamine, Miyagi Prefecture, in the Pacific coastal zone of Northern Honshu, and was excavated in 1983. Here the lowest of five cultural horizons has been dated by thermoluminescence to 368,300 +/- 2,800 BP, by far the oldest industry yet discovered in Japan. Artifacts have been described as including amorphous flakes, some of which were produced by the bipolar flaking technique (cf. Yoshizaki and Masami 1986).

Somewhat closer by land to the warm, sunny canyons of San Diego but far different in climate and environment is Eastern Siberia, where today despite interglacial conditions some of the coldest temperatures on earth have been recorded. Yet here too evidence of very early human occupation, possibly 1,000,000 years ago, has recently been reported, although Paleolithic sites in Siberia have been somewhat controversial both in regard to dating and the acceptance of lithic specimens as humanly altered.

Most of Eastern Siberia today is a thinly-populated wilderness, a rugged land of mixed birch and conifer forest, high mountain ranges, foaming rivers and steppe grasslands. In the north along the shore of the Arctic Ocean there are vast plains of moss and shrub-covered tundra and belts of taiga, the stunted conifers that mark the northern limits of forest vegetation. In the far east, Asia is now separated from North America by the narrow Bering Strait, but in much of the Pleistocene during periods of glaciation and lowered sea level, the continents would have merged into a single landmass. Most of Eastern Siberia would have been indistinguishable from parts of Alaska and the Yukon Territory of Canada.

Some major rivers, among them the Amur and the Lena, and many tributaries drain the rather mountainous region. The Amur winds in huge serpentine bends from west to east, emptying into the Sea of Okhotsk at the head of Sakhalin Island and the Tartarsky Strait. Along much of its length it forms the border between the Soviet Union to the north and Mongolia and the People's Republic of China to the south. The Lena, a broad and rushing torrent in spring freshet, trends east and then north and empties into the Arctic Ocean.

Today, even with an interglacial climate, winters are extremely severe and bitterly cold in Eastern Siberia, although during the Lower Pleistocene conditions may have been more favorable for early man (Dolitsky 1985:364). Despite the clearly far-from-ideal climate in these far northern latitudes, there are indications that humans were living in the Amur Basin, the valley of the Lena and in the Altai region of Southern Siberia in very early times. In 1957 an early site on the Amur River about six miles downstream from the village of Kumara was discovered by an archaeological team under the direction of E. V. Shavkunov (Powers 1973).

What were taken to be crude stone tools were seen on the surface of the gravel beach about 16 feet from the foot of a flanking terrace and along a stretch of about 100 yards. No horizon or stratum in the exposed face of the terrace could be located from which the artifacts might have come. The terrace had a top layer of soil about seven inches thick over some seven feet of yellow loam. The loam rested on the same gravel stratum upon which the tools were found, which was composed of coarse-grained sand and well-rounded cobbles. It was this gravel surface which the investigators felt dated the industry. It was available during the second half of the Middle Pleistocene, or about 350,000 years ago, and the artifacts were tentatively assigned to that period, but there is no finite date.

There were about 20 specimens of which eight were chopping tools and choppers with a worked edge at one end. Of these six had been bifacially worked while the remaining two were unifacially flaked — choppers in the strict sense. Among the rest were quite large pebble cores from which long, irregular flakes had been detached from one side, the opposite side having served as the striking platform. There were also artifacts with points or beaks, and pebbles with crude, flaked facets.

Most of the Kumara I assemblage was excavated from the terrace structure or collected from the gravel beaches under the direction of A. P. Derevianko in the vicinity of Shavkunov's original discovery, during an expedition in 1968. Some of the tools were found directly in the water. Beyond the bank the gravel beds were overlain by more than 30 feet of the sandy loam. Apparently the specimens have been generally accepted by Soviet scientists as the work of man, but the dating is far from conclusive. If they were indeed produced in the latter half of the Middle Pleistocene they would seem, judging by the limited description offered by Powers (1973:19), to be far more primitive than the tools of that period from Zhoukoudian and Chon-Gok-Ni.

Two other localities in the same vicinity, Kumara II and III, were discovered and investigated by Derevianko in 1968. These were also scatters of artifacts and flakes on the gravel beaches of the Amur River, but they are estimated to be much younger than those of Kumara I. Despite the crudity of all the Kumara specimens, and the fact that they were recovered from the gravels of a major river subject to extreme freshet, it appears that, unlike the situation at Buchanan Canyon and Texas Street, no one has attributed them to natural stream breakage. This has not been true at Filimoshki, another early site in the same region.

Located on the Zeia River, a tributary of the Amur, the village of Filimoshki is roughly 150 miles north of the sites in the vicinity of Kumara. The village is built on two terraces of the Zeia. The highest rises about 60 feet above the river level and is composed of finely-laminated light yellow sands that have been described as "lake or dune sands" by Derevianko (Powers 1973:16). The lower terrace, about 30 feet high, has the same yellowish sands over a thick bed of grey, silty sand and loam which in turn rests on gravel beds lying directly on the bedrock. The discoverer was A. P. Okladnikov, a prominent Soviet archaeologist.

The tools were even more primitive in appearance than those of Kumara I, and there has been considerable doubt about their human origin. Derevianko, who enjoyed considerable prestige, accepted them and compared them to the oldest pebble tools of Africa. Powers, who examined some of the specimens, had serious reservations and felt that they might been crushed and shaped by stream action, but also conceded the possibility that they had been shaped by man and then received the crushing, battering and abrasion that made them questionable (Powers 1973:16).

The pieces were described as artifacts with "grooved notches" and large pebbles with flaked points or beaks. The former were cobbles or pebbles with what seemed to be lateral transverse blows on one face, while the latter had points formed by alternate blows directed at both faces. It has long been my personal conviction that such alternate-side flaking is convincing proof of human work, since it is impossible to visualize a natural agency capable of producing such a controlled pattern; that is, turning the piece over after each blow, and striking all the blows with the same force.

The age of the Filimoshki site has been estimated to be the first half of the Middle Pleistocene, or possibly the later half, but the tools are generally believed to be older than those of Kumara I. Age estimates are based on their position in rather than on the gravel stratum, which is believed to have been deposited in the Lower Pleistocene, but reworked early in the Middle Pleistocene. That reworking might be the cause of their battered appearance, which has obliterated those superficial marks of percussive flaking by which archaeologists judge evidence of human work.

Recent work in Siberia suggests that humans may have been living in that now rather forbidding environment for well over 1,000,000 years. An archaeological site at Ulalinka, in the Altai Basin of Southern Siberia, has been dated by thermoluminescence at 1,500,000 BP, within 25% error (Shlyukov 1983, quoted in Dolitsky 1985:364). In the summer of 1983, Soviet scientists discovered a site on the Lena River about 100 miles north of Yakutsk and above the village of Dering-Yuryak that they first estimated to be between 1,500,000 and 2,000,000 years old. Later revised estimates are 800,000 BP.

About 1,500 specimens were recovered that were said to be unmistakably of human manufacture, but no details have been published. The site, situated on a high terrace above the river, was excavated from a thick layer of permafrost by Drs. Yuri Mochanov and Fedoseeva, both of Yakutsk (Mammoth Trumpet 1984).

It is difficult to evaluate the reports on these putative very early Siberian sites from the rather scanty information available. Opinions appear to differ widely on paleoclimates, dates and the significance of lithic specimens. Dolitsky (1985) cites Gromov's (1935) paleontological and Tseytlin's (1979) geological data to the effect that the landscape and geological nature of Siberia, favorable for occupation by early man in the Lower Pleistocene, changed dramatically in the Upper Pleistocene, becoming far more inhospitable, although human settlement occurred on the river terraces. On the other hand, Soviet experts in permafrost concluded, during the operations at Dering-Yuryak, that the average temperature in that district of Siberia 1,000,000 years ago was 8 degrees colder than now.

To scholars of very early man, and particularly to those immersed in the problems of first arrival in the Western Hemisphere, the discovery at Dering-Yuryak is of great importance, regardless of what the age is finally determined to be. It demonstrates that humans could live in extremely harsh and bitterly cold climates far back in antiquity. One of the great stumbling blocks to acceptance of theories of very early presence of man in North America has been the conviction shared by most anthropologists that humans could not survive in an arctic environment until the supposed relatively recent development of sophisticated strategies like sewn clothing.

Another significant aspect of the site on the Lena River is geographical, for it places Lower Paleolithic man within 1,500 miles of Beringia, the now-submerged landmass linking Asia to North America as a single continent. That is less than the distance from St. Louis, Missouri, to the California gold fields, and many an eager gold seeker walked that distance in less than a year. Soviet archaeological exploration has been typically confined to the major rivers in Eastern Siberia, while the more rugged interiors have remained relatively unexamined, so that it is quite possible that more very early sites may be discovered even closer to North America.

In view of the foregoing brief review, it now appears that humans may have been in Northeast Asia as early as 1,000,000 years ago, a prospect unthinkable a generation ago. It is extremely difficult to view such an enormous time span in proper perspective. To us a normal human lifetime seems a very long time indeed; the ancient worlds of Egypt and Mesopotamia lie back in the mists of antiquity, yet these are mere flickers in the space of the human journey up from the world of the australopithecine, and 1,000,000 years are insignificant in geologic time.

It is difficult to believe that primitive humans, capable of expanding over the Asiatic landmass and into such diverse landscapes so long ago, would not have exploited the rich environments of the coastal zones around the North Pacific rim far back in time. These low profile lands behind the beaches, exposed but ice-free during the thousands of years of glacial conditions on the sprawling continent of Amerasia, would have offered almost ideal environments for very early man.

CAMEO

Beringia, A Bison Kill
and Tragedy

*I*t is 390,000 years before the present. A huge area of the earth's surface, *formerly covered by the Chukchi and Bering Seas, has been exposed as low, rolling terrain by the locking up of water in glacial ice on the land. It is called Beringia, and effectively welds Asia and North America into a single landmass, the continent of Amerasia. The coastline of the North Pacific Rim sweeps in a wide arc from the Chutkotski Peninsula south and east almost to the Aleutians and well below the Arctic Circle.*

Grey fog flooded endlessly over the flat, monotonous landscape. The ceaseless wind sent billowing masses rolling across the dun salt marshes; rippled the eel grass and reeds around the channel margins; draped skeins of mist over the low, tough shrubbery that mottled the pale sand dunes.

Beyond the sand stretched the grasslands, vague in the fog and pocked with shallow ponds. Across their wide expanse millions of large animals had grazed. They moved in great herds and droves, and over the millennia they had moved back and forth at random, so that the species were common now to both hemispheres.

Long trains of the great lumbering elephants of the far north, the woolly mammoth, plodded through the mist. Their shaggy, reddish coats and sweeping curves of ivory made them almost impregnable to the predators who hung on the fringes of the herds. They could withstand the bitterest cold; in winter their great tusks swept out masses of shrubbery and frozen grasses from under thick drifts of snow. As they lurched along clouds of steam rose from their heated breath and from the great piles of dung they dropped, and their shrill trumpeting echoed across the plain.

Longhorned bison; huge woolly dark beasts with vicious, rolling eyes and switching tails, wandered across the marshy land behind the dunes and left, as did the Pleistocene musk oxen, churned mud wallows that would become new ponds. Droves of camel and horse, and long files of caribou with white manes gleaming through the fog, packed down the earth over which they passed, inhibiting the growth of vegetation and lacing the land with game trails.

Some mammals formed smaller, mainly familial groups or bands. These were the predators and scavengers preying on the game, and among them were rare bands of humans. Still primitive in appearance, with narrow skulls and heavy brow ridges, their weapons, tools and habits had changed little in 10,000 years. The most significant advances had been intellectual. Their ability to communicate by speech had constantly improved, and with it reasoning power and the sharing of knowledge and opinion, so that the survival of the species was no longer threatened.

Although humans still tended to stay generally in familiar territory, their reliance on the crustaceans and mollusks of the tidal zone caused them periodically to move further down the coast as supplies became depleted. Like the nomadic hunters of Siberia, they now carried the hides and poles for shelters with them. Despite their shellfish diet, they ate gathered foods and meat when available, but their preoccupation with large game centered on the animal by-products as much as meat and marrow. They needed warm bison robes; furs for clothing; large hides for their portable shelters; hide and gut for thongs and a wide variety of uses; bone, antler and horn for tools and weapons.

As most predators do, humans usually sought the easiest game available; the very young, the old, the sick and helpless individuals. Seals and their young were the most readily taken; they could be cut off from the sea and dispatched with clubs or boulders. They robbed other carnivores of their kills when possible, and even trapped and killed large game on occasion.

Elephants were rarely killed except on chance occasions when one was discovered immobilized from old age or injury, or mired in mud and helpless. Wooden spear points would not penetrate the coarse hair and inch-thick hides with enough reliability to make the chance worth taking, and the abundance of easier game made it unnecessary. But the mammoths served them well by providing ample dung for fuel. Dried and carried with them on the travois poles and used sparingly within a hide shelter, it permitted them to live on cold, treeless terrain for long periods in relative comfort.

✳ ✳ ✳ ✳

The woman crouched panting and grunting under the hide shelter. Her black hair, disheveled and ragged, hung across her dark eyes and full-lipped, grimacing mouth, and whipped loosely with the spasmodic, jerking movements of her labor. The dark, mahogany-colored skin shone with sweat; it beaded the sloping forehead and the high cheekbones as the contractions racked her body.

The others in the shelter ignored her. Three other females of various ages sat near the hearth and its tiny fire, chewing hides to soften them for use. This process occupied hours of their time, and would so wear down their teeth that in old age they could scarcely chew their food. Infants and small children sprawled naked on the bare ground playing or simply staring idly at the hide ceiling. An old man toasted strips of meat on a bone spit over the fire, dodging and twisting his head sideways to avoid the curling drift of blue smoke circling toward the bright sky vent. All ignored her.

This would be her second child. The first had been stillborn and almost killed her but she felt no fear, only a kind of instinctive and grim determination to bear and rear a child. This deep-seated drive to reproduce her kind was shared by all living creatures, but augmented by her human awareness and conscious desire to conform. In a society so dependent on the performance of its members barren young women had no place. Male young were especially welcomed, indeed were essential to the survival of parents past their prime.

As her contractions approached the climax, the woman struggled into position on her wide-spread knees, her hands pressing aside the brown thighs. Her back arched convulsively, shook like a tree in a gale with her effort. Her mouth worked now in great soundless gasps. Between her straining thighs the foetal envelope appeared, the head and then the tiny torso wrapped in its membrane.

The mother took the tiny bundle in her hands and stripped it of the placenta and umbilical. She licked it clean as all mothers would, and listened happily to its angry cries of rage at being ejected from the womb. Oblivious of her torn and aching body she fondled and crooned over her little son, and pressed the gasping, wrinkled face to her full breast, cupping the small skull in a gentle brown hand. The crying stopped as he suckled hungrily.

Now the other adults in the shelter appeared to notice the event for the first time, and crowded eagerly around to pat and stroke the exhausted mother and admire her new son. The woman lay stretched on her side with the infant at her breast. She felt the tiny fists pressing and kneading her soft flesh and the avid, small gums nibbling and sucking at her teat. The great ache in her lower torso faded under a swelling tide of exultant joy as she lay half asleep and dazed from her labor.

*   *   *   *

A little over a mile away the infant's sire, a sturdy, mature young hunter of nineteen years and unaware of his mate's travail, toiled with the other young males to dig a pit in the rock-hard soil. This earth, of necessity in the middle of a well-travelled game trail, was pounded and packed by the hooves of generations of heavy animals. It stubbornly resisted the blunted stone hand-picks of the diggers. The tools were of basalt, triangular in cross-section and bifacially flaked, pointed at one end and about three pounds in weight, but they were dulled from use and no stone was available in the vicinity from which new ones might be fashioned.

The pit diggers chopped and flailed at the stubborn soil with their dull tools, grumbling and grunting at the effort. The five men were digging their pitfall at a point where several trails converged. They had marked off a space about five feet wide and eight feet long, with the axis along the trail direction. They needed to dig down at least six feet, leaving perpendicular sides and carrying away all the removed soil in their hide tarpaulins. This was hard, time-consuming labor but the resulting pit would be highly efficient.

The hunters had worked at their trap from dawn to dusk of the preceding day, and now a little after noon it was almost finished. They removed the last of the loose earth from the bottom and refilled the pit with loose, brittle brush and reeds to the surface level. Over the top they strewed handfulls of the sparse, wiry grass that grew in the vicinity. It was scarcely noticeable there in the trail and, unless a mammoth blundered into it, would entrap and hold any game that came along in the fog.

The weary hunters withdrew to a point down wind where they could still see the trail dimly through the mist, and sank down on their haunches to wait patiently and stoically for their quarry to appear. At last they heard the sound of heavy hooves in the fog and the grunting of bison. The dim, shaggy shapes materialized like specters in the gloom, plodding along single file down the beaten track toward the waiting pitfall. The lead bull, a huge animal with heavy, sharp horns at least eighteen inches long, stopped abruptly as the rancid human scent still hanging in the air filled his nostrils. He hesitated and tossed the massive black muzzle in sweeping arcs, seeking the odor's source. The hunters waited tensely, motionless and scarcely breathing.

Satisfied at last that the way was clear, the bull started down the trail. As he approached the pitfall the hunters suddenly leaped up yelping and brandishing their lances. Instinctively the bull broke into a rocking gallop down the trail, his attention on the capering figures in the fog. With a great bellowing and crashing he broke through the thin screen of brush and went thrashing to the bottom of the waiting trap. Only his tossing head and shoulders could be seen above the surface as his churning hooves fought desperately for footing. His roaring stampeded the rest of the herd, which went pounding off to disappear in the chilly mist.

The hunters went leaping up to dispatch their prize. Thrusting their wooden lances repeatedly into the thick neck of the beast, they found at last a vital artery, and the blood gushed out in a steamy torrent. The bison's struggles gradually diminished and at last ceased entirely as he stood passively with drooping head, draining away his life into the dark pool at his feet. With a long sigh he collapsed into the battered brush as though sinking into a pond. Squatting impassively at the brink of the pit, his tormentors waited for him to die.

At last, when the carcass had stopped quivering, one of the hunters, he who had unknowingly become a father that day, climbed down into the pit to begin the difficult job of skinning and butchering the great bulk in that confined space. But as he lowered himself down, the huge head with its wicked, pointed horns suddenly thrashed sideways in a final dying reflex. One of the sharp black points lashed across the man's calf and cut down to the bone, severing the main artery. With blood spurting from his leg, he climbed back out and seized the leg with both hands to stop the pumping blood.

One of his companions pulled up a great wad of grass and clapped it onto the gaping wound to stop the bleeding. They bound it there with a strip of hide when the bleeding would not stop, but he felt weak from the loss of so much blood. He could only lie and watch as they began laboriously to skin the bison, struggling and heaving at the great inert weight to work the precious hide free.

Late in the day, as the light began to fall, the hunting party returned to the camping place. The women and old people who watched for those outside the hide shelter saw four figures emerge from the drifting fog and come striding in, burdened under the great bundles of meat and hide. But the fifth hobbled painfully along in the rear, barely able to keep up and reeling with dizziness as he walked. Gone were his lance and loincloth, and his lower leg was caked with blood below the knotted leather and grass dressing. He crawled slowly into the shelter and lay down by the hearth, weak and panting from the effort and the pain.

His young mate, who had waited so eagerly for his return, felt a terrible pang of terror and foreboding. She laid aside her new-born infant and hurried to his side, but when she loosened the leather thong the blood rushed out, staining the matted grass compress and puddling on the ground. She hastily tightened it again but the truth was obvious to all. The man was doomed.

For the next few days they made him as comfortable as possible beside the fire, but the whole leg swelled and turned a shiny purple and pained almost unbearably. The unmistakable, putrid odor of gangrene hung in the air around him and he lapsed into periods of feverish delirium.

The elders decided the time had come to move down the coast. The hide shelter was dismantled and packed on the travois poles, leaving the dying man sprawled alone by the fire. They placed a gourd of water within his reach and left a small supply of dried dung fuel by the fire. His mate refused to leave his side, and when the women seized her and dragged her from the hearth, she struggled so fiercely to return to him that they relaxed their grip and reluctantly released her, with her tiny child swaddled in furs at her breast.

She sat then by her mate with her eyes fixed hopelessly on his pain-wracked, tortured face. She stroked him and caressed him and crooned over him as to her child. The people trudged stonily away with their eyes averted and disappeared behind the grey curtain of fog.

Hours crept by as the fur-clad form sat there by the fire, adding a bit of the dwindling fuel at times and suckling her infant whenever he awakened and began to cry. The grey light gave way to almost dark and back to grey again. The sick man groaned and twisted in agony and babbled words that had no meaning. At last he suddenly opened his eyes and looked up into her face and she saw with leaping joy that his mind was clear and his pain apparently passed away. He reached up to touch her face tenderly, but his hand wavered and dropped to his side; . . . she saw that he was dead, with the brightness gone from his eyes as a slender torch might wink out in a sudden gust.

She sat there staring and staring. A terrible, lost emptiness yawned inside her body, an ache she would never lose completely. No tears came to her eyes; they felt locked open and hard as pebbles as she touched her mate gently for the last time. She cradled her infant in the fur slung around her shoulders and walked away from the fire and up the trail the others had taken, following the tracks of the travois poles southeastward over the grey-shrouded land behind the dunes.

*   *   *   *

The small, straggling file of humans, some dragging burdened poles and others with bundles on their heads, had been climbing a gentle rise for hours when they finally emerged from the fog into brilliant sunshine. Rolling hills rose nearby, rocky and rather barren but with thin ranks of spruce on the slopes and willows in the draws; far more hospitable than the gloomy flatlands they had left behind. It offered stone and wood in profusion, and rock outcrops for shelter with the beaches only a mile or two below them in the fog. Here they were destined to settle down for a generation or more.

As the humans reached the first meadow above the chilly grey fog, they dropped their burdens. Normally of high spirits, they felt their pleasure swelling within them intolerably at the feel of the warm sunshine and the gentle, crystal-clear air. They chattered and laughed and poked each other in the ribs, the men capering and making elaborate pantomines of lancing game, then switching to burlesques of the game itself, hands sticking out of their shaggy black heads like bison horns or spreading antlers, imitating the creatures that stood always at the center of their lives.

The women stretched out on the ground or sat crosslegged watching the hunters indulgently. They nursed their young and relaxed in the warming rays of the lowering sun. Naked children of all ages raced in circles through the flower-dappled grass, leaping into the air like deer from sheer exuberance.

When they picked up their loads and moved on, the line of dark figures wound upward through a gentle draw to a projecting rock face that would serve to protect them from the bitter subarctic winds of winter, and from wandering carnivores when the fires were lit. Now in late summer it would be a convenient habitation but not a necessity.

The rock face looked out over a wide sweep of country. Below it the flower-decked slopes ran down to a silvery estuary that disappeared in the mist. A rolling sea of fog ran off to the westward under a brilliant blue sky. A child saw it first. A tiny dot had emerged from the fog and was trudging up the slope the way they had come. A shouting cascade of children went streaming down the draw to meet the stubborn young female and her firstborn child.

The adults feigned indifference in spite of the tears rolling down their leathery brown cheeks.

CHAPTER 3

Amerasia and the North Pacific Rim

The great blue curving expanse that we call the Pacific Ocean covers more than half of the planet upon which we dwell. Seemingly a fixed and change-less entity, it has been constantly changing over billions of years; in both minute detail and over its vast and sweeping dimensions. Whole continents rooted to their crustal plates have drifted across its distant reaches. Volcanoes have burst through its floor in great explosions of fiery magma and steam, to tower up into the sky and then at last to die and degenerate into green-clothed islands encircled by black cliffs, and finally to be gnawed and eroded by the sea back down to coral-mantled reefs beneath the surface again.

Huge volumes of the ocean's water at any given time exist as the white, purple-shadowed clouds that drift over its surface, the grey and tattered masses that scud before its gales, and the soft grey mantles of fog that shroud its shores and headlands in its northern reaches. Those same clouds pour across the beaches and high over the lofty ranges of the continents, to spend themselves as rain and snow and find their way back at last to the waiting ocean.

When any of that moisture lies locked and frozen on the land in the form of snow and ice, the great ocean is in that degree diminished. During the glacial advances of the Pleistocene Epoch, for reasons probably related to changes in the earth's orbit around the sun but not well understood, far more snow fell on parts of the Northern Hemisphere, and on higher mountains everywhere, than could melt in summer and run back down the watercourses to the sea. As the glacial conditions persisted for thousands of years, the snow was compacted into ice and spread itself over the land by its own weight, as batter spreads on a hot griddle. On the Laurentian Shield, the vast Barren Lands of Canada, the ice accumulated, and eventually it spread well down into the United States.

The subtraction of such immense amounts of water from the ocean basins inevitably caused profound changes in their physical aspects and dimensions. Sea levels worldwide were lowered over 300 feet, exposing as land enormous areas of former shallow sea bottom and continental shelf. In the regions of the Chukchi and Bering Seas and Bering Strait, much of them today quite shallow, a landmass appeared comparable to most of Scandinavia and hundreds of miles from north to south, effectively changing Eurasia and North America into a single huge, sprawling continent of Amerasia. That broad land linkage and its extension up the valley of the Yukon River and some of its tributaries in Alaska and Canada is called Beringia.

Because of the locations of atmospheric pressure centers over the ocean basins, and the configuration of mountain ranges on the land, some areas of the arctic and subarctic regions remained ice-free throughout the glacial periods, with climates little colder than they are today. The southern coast of Beringia, and coastal zones in the Gulf of Alaska and along the British Columbian shore, may even have been warmer than today, for closure of the Bering Strait connection with the Arctic Ocean would have augmented the ameliorating effect of the Japan Current, flowing clockwise around the North Pacific Basin.

Since most of Beringia remained unglaciated throughout the Pleistocene, including the exposed Bering region and the valleys of the Yukon River and the Porcupine with its tributaries in the Old Crow Basin, it has been called the Beringian Refugium. As the milder interglacial climates slowly gave way to glacial conditions in Northern Canada, Alaska and Siberia, the Pleistocene fauna in those regions, including early human populations if present, would have become concentrated in the Refugium, an area of some 300,000 square miles.

Movement to the east would have been blocked by the huge Laurentide Ice Sheet, to the north by the Brooks Range, to the west and south by ice-covered mountain ranges except for relatively narrow corridors, the exposed continental shelves, and of course the Arctic and Pacific Oceans.

The Laurentide ice was in places and at times over three miles thick, and stretched from Eastern Canada to the Western Cordillera, the series of ranges that forms the rocky spine of the continent and runs almost unbroken from Alaska's North Slope to southern New Mexico. At times of maximum glaciation the Laurentide ice is believed to have coalesced with the Cordilleran glaciers, forming an impenetrable barrier to passage by men and animals to the unglaciated south. But at times of partial melting within a glacial period, called interstades, an ice-free corridor may have opened between the Cordillera and the lowland ice, allowing passage of cold-adapted species, including man, into the more temperate regions to the south.

Until recently it was believed that great accumulations of ice on the Coast Ranges of Alaska and British Columbia, which today in many places rise directly from the sea in the form of towering cliffs, would have blocked human passage to the south into the ice-free lands of North America (Haynes 1971:9). There is no evidence to support such a view. The lowering of sea level by glacial subtraction, called *eustasis*, by more than 300 feet or 50 fathoms, would have moved the beaches several miles out to sea, exposing a broad coastal zone of low relief suitable for human occupation and possibly grazing game. If minor ice tongues did reach the sea, they could surely have been crossed by most mammals, including man, but there is no firm evidence of massive ice sheets extending over the coastal zones to discharge directly into the ocean. Frozen fiords and inlets would have been advantageous for pedestrian travel, making unnecessary extended detours inland to skirt around them, but their presence is doubtful.

The great weight of glacial ice on the adjacent mountains of the Coast Range, rather than hampering human passage, would in fact have facilitated it. This is because of a natural phenomenon called *isostasis*, which causes the earth's crust to rise when neighboring areas are depressed, somewhat as the surface of a waterbed reacts when portions are pressed down. It is now recognized that sea bottoms may have risen substantially when adjacent land areas bore enormous loads of glacial ice (Walcott 1970). How much the outer shelves rose and how much additional coastal zone was produced in addition to the eustatic regression of sea level is not known, but an examination of coastal charts will confirm the fact that under such conditions a broad coastal littoral nowhere less than two miles wide must have existed from Northeast Asia to Southern California, even without invoking isostatic uplift (cf. Fladmark 1978:125).

Fladmark's excellent study of the feasibility of human movement down the Northwest Coast of North America concerned itself with conditions during the Late Wisconsin glacial maxima, but since pre-Illinoian glacial advances are thought to have been much less rigorous (Hopkins 1967:468), there is no reason to suppose that his arguments could not be applied to earlier periods of glaciation as well. His views on climate and environment seem particularly appropriate to the present study:

The overall climate of the Late Pleistocene Northwest Coast would undoubtedly have been milder than continental ice-free corridors of equivalent latitude. The north Pacific remained unfrozen during the Wisconsinan Glaciation and there is every reason to suspect that oceanic circulatory patterns continued then, as today, to bring warm, sub-tropical water masses to the edge of the continental shelf off the Northwest Coast. It seems probable that mean annual temperatures at ocean level along the outer coast were above freezing (cf. Heusser 1965) and the fact of ice accumulation in the Coast Range suggests that moisture laden westerlies remained as a dominant or at least significant weather pattern. Warmer temperatures and greater moisture than most other areas of glaciated western North America at the time suggests that terrestrial flora may have been relatively abundant close to sea level in ice-free regions, although positive demonstration of this may never be attained, due to post-glacial submergence of the outer coast (Fladmark 1978:126).

The reduction of world-wide temperatures by only a few degrees during glacial periods caused comparable lowering of deep sea temperatures, except in areas of special circumstances such as the closure of Bering Strait, which probably produced somewhat warmer temperatures in the far North Pacific. Submarine ecologies, highly sensitive to pressures and temperatures, were measurably altered, so that scientists have been able to determine, by examination of deep sea cores containing organisms whose temperature preferences are known, the approximate times of glacial and interglacial cycles throughout the Pleistocene.

The effects of changing average temperatures and lowering tidelines on the animals of most tidal zones would have been minor, since such changes would have occurred so slowly and over such long periods of time. These creatures are among the most adaptable on earth, since they daily experience drastic changes in their environment. But in stretches of coast which are rocky and precipitous today in an interglacial high sea stand, and which would have had sandy beaches well out to sea, shallow bays, and estuaries during the low sea levels of the glacial periods, marine faunal populations would have obviously changed completely in the tidal zones. Nevertheless, it is most doubtful that coastal waters were ever sterile of crustaceans, and more probable that nutrient-rich glacial melt waters would have fostered more extensive populations than are seen today.

It would be impossible to determine the appearance of the coastal landscape during the earlier advances of glacial cycles in different phases of the Pleistocene and over the approximately 6,000 miles of coastline from Japan to San Diego. Even in relatively stable periods like the present, currents, winds and storm tides are constantly changing and rearranging the physical elements of the coast. Currents carry sand and other sediments from river mouths and ocean bottoms and deposit it on the beaches in huge amounts, or drop it to form bars and shallows. Wind and storm tides strip it away, building dunes far inland, eroding cliffs and minor islands, and laying bare underlying rocks and cobbles. Even the chemical reaction between sandstone and the atmosphere peels away the land. Cliffs at Santa Barbara,

California, have moved inland more than 50 feet in the last century as the result of chemical weathering, rain and wind erosion. It is said that some sea cliffs in an exposed location regressed 600 feet in a decade in the eighteenth century.

Such coastal changes, observable in the brief span of a human lifetime, are insignificant compared to the alterations that must have occurred over scores of millennia. In addition to the changes wrought by advancing and receding glaciers on the continents, the earth's crust itself is highly unstable around the North Pacific rim. Throughout the geologically short period of the Pleistocene Epoch, about 2,000,000 years, and for indeterminate millions of years before that, the great crustal plates have been in motion, floating, so to speak, on the fiery, molten magma of the earth's upper mantle. The North American plate has been slowly drifting westward, lifting the land as the Pacific plate grinds past in a northwesterly direction along what is called in California the San Andreas Fault. Thus the coastlines of North America and Asia around the North Pacific have been subjected to massive tectonic uplifts and depressions, chains of active volcanoes and violent seismic action in the geologically recent past.

At San Diego, California, dating of ancient corals on an uplifted, wave-cut bench called the Nestor Terrace has indicated to the investigators a rise over the past 120,000 years of about 50 feet, or between 11 and 14 centimeters per 1,000 years (Ku and Kern 1974). However, episodes of crustal uplift may have been spasmodic in the distant past, and rates may have varied greatly. The Southern California coastal plain or mesa upon which most of the cities stand has been uplifted to heights of between 200 and 1,000 feet above the present sea level during the Pleistocene.

It would seem then that in the present state of knowledge, little can be said about the physical appearances of the North Pacific coastal zones during the Illinoian and earlier glacial advances except that the beaches were surely far out from the present shores, leaving in the critical areas of the Northwest Coast a broad plain of generally low relief several miles wide, over which primitive humans, grazing game and predators might have roamed seldom hindered by difficult terrain.

The great glacial cycles and interglacial periods of the Pleistocene have been recurring in irregular intervals of 40,000 to 60,000 years of glacio-pluvial conditions of varying severity, broken by interstades or climate of lesser intensity, and separated by interglacials, less humid regimes also of varying duration. The most recent advance, the Wisconsin, is believed to have set in about 70,000 years ago, was interrupted by an interstadial period of milder climate from about 40,000 to 25,000 years ago, and ended about 10,000 years ago. These chronologies vary considerably with the estimates of different scholars.

Some years ago it was believed that there had been only four major glaciations: the Wisconsin, the Illinoian, the Kansan and the Nebraskan, named for their maximum penetrations of the United States. Preceding them was a vague and indefinite period called the Villafranchian. Today these names have been generally abandoned, although the Wisconsin and Illinoian are still in general use. Instead the different climate cycles are identified as Ocean Isotope Stage

1, 2, 3, 4, etc., with Stage 1 referring to the present warm interglacial stage and all even numbers representing glacio-pluvial cold stages.

It is clear that humans slowly expanding their territories from Asia into North America, across the Beringian lowlands and down the coastal littoral, or perhaps following the coastal zone from far down the Asian shore and adapted to marine foraging, had thousands of generations in which to complete the journey, regardless of the glacial stage in which they and their progeny existed. Those whose distant ancestors had wandered into the cul-de-sac of the eastern Beringian Refugium could, during a following interglacial, cross the high passes of the Richardson Range, descend into the vast valley of the Mackenzie and follow it into the heart of the North American continent east of the Cordillera. Such a route would have required adaptation to extremely harsh arctic conditions, but the evidence of human occupation at Dering-Yuryak on the Lena makes plainly evident the fact that very early humans were capable of withstanding bitterly cold climates.

The question of human physical adaptation to cold is an interesting one. The first Europeans to visit Tierra del Fuego at the southern tip of South America were astonished to see the Yaghan Indians running almost naked in the bitter cold. At night they simply curled up together on the ground in their huts and slept without any apparent distress.

In 1933 I was fortunate enough to cruise through the narrow, winding channels of Austral Chile for nearly 1,000 miles in the California Maritime Academy training ship "Golden State." We saw Alakaluf Indians naked or nearly so in the icy wind, paddling their plank boats alongside the ship. There were glaciers on the hills above, discharging into the fiords, and small icebergs floating in the channels even though it was midsummer in Chile. We were dressed in warm peacoats and had watch caps pulled down around our ears, yet the Indians seemed perfectly comfortable in the freezing air. Adults, children and dogs all appeared to have open, suppurating sores on their scalps and bodies, perhaps from dietary deficiencies. We offered them clothes but they only wanted whiskey, which we were unwilling to provide.

The southern tip of the continent of South America is comparable in latitude to southern Beringia. Thick forests of southern beech cover much of the Chilean mainland and the multitude of islands on the Pacific side, and in 1933 herds of wild guanacos could be glimpsed on the shore. Steamer ducks, kelp geese and marine mammals were plentiful in the channels, while shellfish proliferated on the rocks in the tidal zone.

In early 1986 I returned again to the same region and cruised up the inland passages from Cape Horn to Puerto Montt. The Indians and the abundant wildlife were almost gone. Some fishermen whom I took to be Alakaluf, wearing heavy clothing and yellow slickers, were operating an aluminum outboard motorboat. In all that passage I saw only one steamer duck in the distance, and guanacos could only be viewed in a national park east of Puerto Natales.

Some scientists have concluded that the last two glacial advances, the Wisconsin and the Illinoian, or Isotope Stages 2/4 and 6/8, were accompanied by much colder climates in the Bering Strait region of Beringia than were earlier glacial stages. Belts of taiga, cold steppe and tundra are thought to have covered the exposed land between Alaska and Siberia in the later glacial stages, producing a rather bleak environment but one in which humans could undoubtedly have survived. However, during the earlier or Stage 10 glacial cycle about 300,000 years ago, core borings near the Alaskan beaches, containing paleopollens, have suggested that a different environment may then have flourished. Mixed forests grew in that part of Beringia, indicating a more temperate climate perhaps comparable to Austral Chile today.

David M. Hopkins, a leading scholar of Beringia, has offered the following views:

> Although the evidence is not yet conclusive, the Quaternary Period seems to have been characterized in Beringia by progressively increasing climatic stresses that reached a climax during the Illinoian Glaciation. The forests were evidently richer in numbers of tree species during early and middle Quaternary time, but after the Illinoian Glaciation they differed little from the modern taiga (Hopkins 1967:468).

Along the southern coast of Beringia, and curving away to the east and south along the Pacific shore, the exposed lowlands would have had a maritime climate tempered by the sea, and perhaps warmed by the Japan Current as suggested earlier. Nevertheless, winter climates during a glacial cycle would have been bitterly cold, and early humans must have had both biological and cultural means of adapting to them.

In view of the examples of the Yaghan and Alakaluf in historic times, humans can obviously develop physical resistance to cold. Much more highly developed subdermal vascular systems than most modern humans possess have been suggested. Diets high in fats and animal proteins would surely have been useful. Very early humans may have had thick growths of body hair, particularly at the *Homo erectus* stage of evolution. Since all we have left are a few bones and teeth, we can never know details like skin color and thickness, hair growth and quality, and whether eyes were brown, grey or blue, unless we find, like the famous Siberian mammoth carcass, a specimen preserved in ice.

As to cultural adaptations, as stated earlier it has been the general consensus in the field of anthropology that human survival in subfreezing temperatures was not possible until the development of sewn clothing and the stone oil lamp, and that these did not appear until the terminal Pleistocene. The recent discoveries on the Lena River of Siberia have now necessitated a great deal of reassessment of such views, and made it obvious that either sewn clothing was not needed, or was in use very early.

Sewn clothing is admittedly convenient and warm, but so are bison hides with the hair turned in and a hole in the middle to be worn as a poncho. Hide strips can be wrapped around the feet and legs and secured easily without needle and thread, but nobody has the slightest idea how early the sewing or lacing and fitting together of cured hides was practiced. We do have solid evidence that humans have been either scavengers or hunters of large game for hundreds of millennia, based on the associations of stone tools and the bones of animals they must have utilized. It would be specious to assume the hides were never put to use.

Stone oil lamps have been in use for many millennia by Eskimos, Aleuts and Laplanders in the far north, and are highly efficient in a small, confined space like an igloo. They are hardly essential for survival. As mentioned earlier, Chinese sites like Xihoudu with its burnt and charred animal bone make evident the fact that humans may have been using fire for more than a million years. Even on the open tundra fuel would have been readily available: mammoth, woolly rhinoceros and giant bison wandered over the Beringian plain, presumably leaving huge windrows of dung to dry under the summer sun.

Some 15 years ago I startled people at the San Diego Zoo by asking if I might have a box of elephant dung. After explaining my purpose up the chain of command to Dr. Griner, then head veterinarian, I was graciously presented with a large box full of spicy manure. Since it was rather fresh and moist, I took it over to the desert to dry out thoroughly. When I finally lit it with a match, it proved to be a marvelous and efficient fuel, containing so much methane gas that it burned almost ten hours with a hot blue flame. It was clear to me that nobody needs stone oil lamps in mammoth country.

The question of shelters from storms and cold is problematical. It seems that such protection would have been essential when blizzards howled in from the sea. Transit across the relatively flat Beringian plain would have had to be accomplished without the snug comfort of caves and rock shelters; the possibilities must rest on speculation and conjecture. Shelters of hides and poles could have been erected, with the great advantage of being portable. They could have been dragged as travois poles with the hide coverings lashed on top in bundles.

Creatures as inventive and intelligent as humans would surely have noticed the mud and stick lodges of the Pleistocene beavers, believed to have inhabited the streams and ponds of Beringia. With a pit hacked out of the permafrost and a roof framework of stunted arctic willow covered with mud, and possibly a smoke hole in the roof and an entrance trench or tunnel, humans could have passed the winter in comfort and security. An adjacent ice cave could have been stocked with meat for the long hours of darkness.

If northern beech and other forest trees did grow on the lowlands of the Bering region when exposed, or even taiga belts of stunted spruce, shelters of tree limbs and branches would have been simple to construct, as any woodsman knows. Little or no technical skill would be required simply to arrange leafy branches into a protective mat of vegetation to shield against cold winds, rain and snow.

Regardless of what kind of architecture we care to conjure up, we are left with the simple fact: humans did move across from Asia to North America in the distant past, and they must have provided themselves with shelter and probably fire over hundreds of generations during the slow expansion from China and Siberia across the lowlands of Beringia and on into the Western Hemisphere.

From the Aleutian Islands south and east along the shores of the Gulf of Alaska and down the British Columbian coast, the environment would have been far less hostile for human occupation and travel. The steep slopes, islands and cliffs of the interglacial shoreline, far back from the beaches now in a glacial stage yet always visible in the distance, could have provided caves and rock shelters that had been cut by the surging currents of the interglacial high sea stands. Heavy rains of the glacio-pluvial climate would have leached the salt from the exposed sea bottoms over the centuries, and promoted the growth of generous vegetation on the slopes.

From close inshore at sea, had we been there to see them, the sweeping panoramas along these coasts might have been dramatic in the extreme. Deep blue sea shading into green in the shallows, dappled and twisted skeins of surf lining the white sand beaches; perhaps a silvery estuary running back from the foreshore guarded by low, rocky headlands; green slopes and rolling hills and rising above like a theatrical backdrop, the mountains of the Coast Range crowned with gleaming icefields against the sky. But this is the purest speculation; no one has seen that landscape in the last 10,000 years.

I recently flew from Germany to Los Angeles over the northern Great Circle route. We crossed the coasts and ice cap of Greenland on a beautiful clear day and looking down fascinated from 40,000 feet, with my nose pressed against the window to the great annoyance of the other passengers who only wanted to watch the movie, I saw the coastal margins still in a glacial stage. I recalled a vivid description written over 50 years ago by Rockwell Kent; artist, author and a man in love with Greenland:

> The Northern scene, besides being illuminated at so low an angle that long shadows cast its forms into singular prominence, besides the stark intrinsic grandeur of those forms, besides the contrast that is present between level ocean plain and towering mountains, has one unique attribute that makes it stirring as no Temperate scene can be: that is its ice. Picture a Temperate sea and mountain view: Clear day, late afternoon in fall; blue sea and golden-purple shadowed land, and pale blond lower sky; purple to gold, pale light to deep-toned madder. Now, into that, like a shaft of sunlight into a lamplit room, like violins and flutes above the bass, high-pitched, ethereally pure, so clean, sharp, dazzling that it almost hurts, see ice appear. The pale-gold sky is somber now; sea, sky and land are of one low tonality against which *sings* that poignant whiteness (Kent 1935:306).

More certain than the physical appearance of the land is the catalogue of food resources that must have been available in the northeastern Pacific coastal zone. Unquestionably the most important were shellfish and crustaceans: clams, scallops and oysters in the bays and estuaries and probably mussels and crabs in tide pools and on rocky ledges. The role these must have played in the expansion of early humans around the North Pacific rim is of critical significance and cannot be overemphasized. Where such food is present and collectable without equipment other than the two hands, it is impossible to starve.

While there is no Old World evidence for very early shellfish consumption by humans, it must be remembered that as sea levels rose and fell over the millennia of the Middle and Late Pleistocene, middens, if they were ever formed in early times, would have been repeatedly destroyed by advancing surf lines everywhere on earth. Most if not all such food collected by very early human foragers would probably have been consumed on the spot, so that the accumulation of large shell middens behind the beaches by limited populations is most unlikely. But huge shell middens dating within the Holocene or Recent period on most coasts of the world and around the shores of many lakes and rivers testify to man's insatiable appetite for shellfish, which have both fat and protein and are in addition sweet and delicious food.

An even more important aspect of reliance on shellfish is the fact that shellfish collectors will inevitably deplete the resource at any given location and be impelled to move a little farther down the coast in search of fresh and more bountiful supplies. While the rate of movement this would produce along the littoral would be governed by the size of the human band and the abundance of the potential harvest, the coastwise movement itself would seem to be as inexorable as the tides.

Excavation of archaic La Jolla middens on the Southern California coast has repeatedly demonstrated that shell sizes, normal for the species in the lower levels, become progressively smaller in higher and later strata until they are so small one wonders how they could have been usable for food. Such small shell concentrations are invariably covered by sterile soils, indicating the forced abandonment of the site.

It is easy to imagine those shaggy-maned primitive foragers shading their eyes down the beach and wondering what lies around the next headland. Even today we humans have the same unquenchable curiosity in strange country, the same need to know what lies around the next bend in the stream or over the next ridge, the same urge to wander a little farther up the trail. If in addition to simple curiosity we were motivated by the need to fill our bellies, and knew that virgin shellfish beds could always be found by moving far enough down the beach, and were encumbered by a minimum of baggage, there is little doubt that we would move along frequently.

Let us suppose that expanded family bands of humans in successive generations of about 15 years, not unusual for primitive people even today, drifted along the North Pacific rim from Siberia east and south along the coast in a glacial stage of low sea level. At a rate of only 30 miles in each generation, less distance than one can see up and down the coast in clear weather, they could have been in the San Diego region in only 1,500 years, busily harvesting mussels from the rocks at low tide.

While 1,500 years may seem a very long time, it is insignificant when compared to the antiquity of human occupation in China and Siberia. And 1,500 years is not offered as an estimate of the actual time, which could have been far greater or far less, a detail which will never be known. All evidence has undoubtedly been swept away and destroyed by the churning surf and storm tides of recurring interglacial marine transgressions.

Destroyed also, decomposed, buried under tons of sediment on the sea floor or masked by undersea growth are the bones not only of human foragers and hunters, but also of the creatures they must have hunted. There is broad agreement early humans were hunters or scavengers or both. A troop of shouting humans, carrying blazing firebrands and hurling boulders, could have driven the most fearsome carnivores off their kills. Analysis of the stone tools left to us makes clear that many of them would have functioned best as butchering and skinning implements, scrapers of heavy hides and spear shafts, breakers of marrow bones and stone balls for bola weights. Many early sites in Asia contained disarticulated and even charred bones of prey animals, and one such site is known in the Western Hemisphere, the Woolley mammoth site on Santa Rosa Island off the coast of Southern California (Berger 1983).

This extremely important site has been generally and unaccountably ignored by anthropologists and prehistorians, and especially by those very conservative scholars who are still waiting fruitlessly for "convincing" evidence of early man in America. But for over 30 years it has been known that charred mammoth bone, disarticulated and in apparently manmade fire pits, was weathering out of sea cliffs at Santa Rosa Island (Carter 1980:50-52). A radiocarbon date of 29,500 +/- 2,500 BP was published shortly after the first discovery by Carter (Carter 1957:6).

The discovery and examination of the Woolley site, named for the owner of the land, produced even more impressive evidence. Dr. Rainer Berger, its discoverer, reported that weathering of the side wall of a gully above the beach in 1975 had revealed the profile of an apparently manmade hearth that contained not only more charred bones but charcoal and indisputably manmade stone tools. No carbon 14 remained in the charcoal found in the hearth, meaning that the site was more than 40,000 years old by some unknown amount.

The validity of radiocarbon dates has been placed in serious doubt recently by retesting samples by the accelerator mass spectrometer method, which has generally produced much younger ages for what had been considered evidence of antiquity in California. Whether the latter are more reliable is questioned by some, but in cases where no C14 can be detected by the conventional method, the no-date result can be considered valid.

The presence of both man and mammoth, a pygmy race only about four feet high at the shoulder, on an offshore island is somewhat puzzling. Santa Rosa is one of four Channel Islands that would have formed one landmass during the Wisconsin lowering of sea level. Today the nearest, Anacapa, is about 15 miles off the coast. 15,000 years ago in the terminal Pleistocene it is believed that a channel over three miles wide would have existed between the consolidated islands and the mainland. 50,000 years ago the same would probably have been true, judging by modern soundings. But given the seismicity of the Pacific coast it is quite possible that in earlier glacial stages the island mass and the mainland were joined.

Dwarfed mammoths are not known elsewhere in the Western Hemisphere, although there is a race of dwarf or pygmy elephants only six feet at the shoulder in the Congo. How long does it take for natural selection in a restricted environment to produce such an effect? Nobody knows, but it would seem to require a very long time indeed. As to man's presence, the simplest of watercraft could have been employed to cross a channel of only three miles, and evidence of early man in Australia suggests that people have used simple watercraft since very ancient times.

We cannot guess how frequently our Paleolithic ancestors ate meat; cracked open leg bones for the sweet, nutritious marrow; processed hides, bones, antlers, sinews and gut for useful objects. We can, however, guess that such pursuits engrossed them. In our consideration of depletable food resources in the relatively narrow coastal zones of the North Pacific, we must include a variety of large mammals. These would certainly include seals and sea lions, easily killed with clubs when they hauled out on the beaches. Probably present would have been many herbivores: deer, musk ox, horse, mammoth and possibly saiga antelope, but species would have been determined by the floral environment: forest, grassland or tundra.

The broader areas of uplifted and exposed continental shelf may have served as glacial refugia similar to that in the Yukon Basin, but would have been restricted enough to cause depletion of game by man and other predators, so creating additional pressures for movement down the coast, ever farther to the south and east. Pressure from following and competing bands of humans is a possibility, but seems unlikely at the extended time ranges being suggested.

These low-lying lands beside the sea would have offered many other and more easily collected food resources than large mammals for foraging humans. Abundant rains surely produced numerous lakes and ponds behind the beaches, as would glacial meltwater. These could have provided frogs, turtles and small fish. Salmon may have been available if sufficient spawning streams remained unfrozen. In early summer breeding waterfowl, flightless in their annual moult, could have been run down and captured on the shallower ponds; their eggs and and nestlings readily available to be snatched out of nests. Sea bird rookeries on the cliffs and sandy islands would have offered the same choice morsels.

When the Spaniards first colonized Southern California, they were disgusted by the eating habits of the native people they found there. The Northern Kumeyaay of Mission San Diego de Alcalá, whom the mission fathers christened "Diegueños," habitually consumed lizards, snails, maggots, grubs, termites and earthworms which they pounded into an indiscriminate paste in their stone mortars. This revolting pâté, actually an excellent source of protein, they apparently considered a great delicacy and ate with relish to the distress of the European onlookers. Australian aborigines are said to do the same, regarding anything that moves as food, and there is no reason to suppose that such customs are not rooted in the distant past.

At the time of European contact in North America, native peoples in areas where agriculture was limited or not practiced harvested dozens if not scores of wild plant foods. While these varied according to latitude and climate, and presumably in quantities available, it seems probable that human bands as well as their hominid ancestors must have discovered and used those plant foods that were locally obtainable, nutritious and edible without elaborate preparation. Berries, nuts, fruits, tender leaves and buds, roots and tubers would surely have been utilized.

In a north temperate climate with ample rain, such as must have prevailed along the coasts of southern Alaska and British Columbia during glacial stages despite the accumulation of ice on the adjacent mountains, plant foods must have been abundant, but exactly what grew there cannot be said with certainty. Undoubtedly included were blueberries and bush cranberries, both common in most northern latitudes and consumed in prodigious amounts in summer and fall by both bears and humans, helping them to lay on rolls of fat against the lean, dark winter months ahead.

Ponds, marshes and estuaries are all reliable sources of edible plants, roots and tubers. Even certain forms of seaweed are usable as food. In Japan today seaweeds are grown for human consumption, and in Southern California kelp is harvested and processed into food additives. All in all, it is perfectly evident that the food resources in the coastal zones of the North Pacific rim, during the glacial stages of the Pleistocene, could have supported adequately and perhaps bountifully a primitive human population slowly expanding along the littoral behind the beaches.

Along with the positive elements arguing for such an early diffusion of the human species must be proposed some difficulties and uncertainties. The most basic necessities appear to have been present: a relatively temperate climate adjacent to the sea; plentiful food resources obtainable by the most rudimentary means; terrain of low relief but offering shelter nearby over most of the route if needed, materials available for tools and implements of stone, bone, wood, antler and ivory, and hides for leather and clothing. A strong motivation for coastal movement has also been suggested: resource depletion in a restricted zone between the mountains and the sea.

Against these advantages must be placed certain obstacles that would have had to be overcome, both physical and geographical. If we are considering, as we are, a pre-Illinoian entry, then we are dealing with *Homo erectus*, a level of human evolution about which we know very little except for his skeletal structure and stone and bone tools. We know that his species was able to spread over vast areas of the world and over strikingly different landscapes; able to survive in the hot, humid tropics and in cold, subarctic environments; and able to control fire and devise sophisticated hunting devices like the bola. But we have no knowledge at all about individual intelligence, except that cranial capacity was about 75% of modern man's.

It seems certain that lives were short and fraught with the danger of sudden death, from encounters with predators like the huge, carnivorous short-faced bear, *Tremarctotherium simon,* the Pleistocene lion or jaguar, *Panthera leo atrox*, and the sabertooth cat, *Smilodon*. Even more deadly would have been infections and disease, against which there could have been few if any defenses, and broken bones, which could cripple and kill without adequate treatment. It is most likely that gangrene would have been a frequent visitor in human camps.

Despite the impression of easy passage that might be gained by looking at maps and visualizing the width of coastal margins during the Pleistocene regressions of sea level, the actual terrain may have been less than perfect for pedestrian travel. In the periglacial environment and in times of partial thawing, rivers of icemelt must have gone thundering down to the sea, effectively blocking the passage of humans and land mammals. Even when not flowing, such rivers would have cut deep canyons in the silts of former sea bottoms, possibly with precipitous sides impossible for humans to scale. In much colder intervals, tongues of glacial ice reaching the sea might have been difficult and hazardous to cross. And certainly with the kind of rudimentary clothing probably achieved by humans in an early Paleolithic stage, protracted blizzards during the long, dark winters must have taken their toll through freezing, starvation or pneumonia.

Today most of the coasts of southern Alaska and British Columbia are fringed with a maze of islands and winding channels, but during the glacial stages these would have been steep hills and relatively flat-floored canyons and narrow valleys. Whether the latter had streams or were choked with glacial ice is not known, but the outer coasts were undoubtedly clear except for the crossing watercourses, which would have been almost impossible to skirt around because of the extremely broken country upstream. In sum, many dangers and difficulties would have had to be overcome for humans to reach unglaciated regions south of the continental ice a quarter of a million years ago or more.

The question of whether they did gradually spread around the shores of Amerasia from China, Japan, and Siberia, and eventually reach Tierra del Fuego scores of millennia later, may never be settled conclusively. The profusion of massive, early Paleolithic stone tools in the San Diego coastal zone strongly suggests that they must have done so, but empirical evidence on the once-exposed continental shelves is lacking and likely to remain so.

It might be supposed that submarine archaeology and particularly the use of scuba diving equipment could be employed to find traces of ancient occupation on the sea floor, especially where rocky bottoms have been swept clear of sediments. Underwater surveys have been carried out in recent years in nearshore ocean waters from Santa Barbara to San Diego, and many prehistoric artifacts have been recovered by divers. These have been mostly stone bowls, perhaps because such objects are easily recognized, and none has been older than a few thousand years at most. But even if they still existed on the sea bottom in a distinguishable form, the recognition of early Paleolithic stone implements would be a very different matter in the best of circumstances, and would require specialized knowledge. In the deserts such tools have lain plainly visible on the surface for millennia, but until recently escaped the notice of sharp-eyed and otherwise competent archaeologists.

On the sea floor stone objects not deeply buried under a protective blanket of sediments would tend to become disguised by the growth of corals, sponges and other sea organisms in a relatively short time. But in the case of stone tools discarded on the continental shelf 200,000 years ago or more, their survival would seem to be absolutely impossible. This is because the surf lines must have moved across them repeatedly as the sea levels rose and fell, reflecting the changes from glacial to interglacial stages, changes so gradual that the artifacts would have remained in the surf zones on sand beaches or rocky shores for long periods of time.

A colleague, Brian Dunne of La Jolla, California, has reported an experiment which persuasively illustrates what happens to stone objects in surf (Personal communication). He placed a number of freshly broken stones in a nylon bag along with a few pounds of sand, and staked out the bag in the surf on a sandy beach at La Jolla. Two weeks later he recovered the bag and examined the broken stones. Their sharp edges had already been severely worn and rounded, making plain the fact that the transition from jagged fragments to smooth pebbles occurs swiftly in the tidal zone — far more swiftly than in stream beds. That is because of the to-and-fro motion of tidal and surf turbulence; somewhat similar to the rocking of sluice boxes in gold mining. All parts of the object subjected to surf action receive abrasion continually, while stones on a streambed are only abraded during periods of freshet and never during normal flow.

The closely-related question of whether stone objects resembling human artifacts can be produced by heavy surf breaking on a rocky beach is more difficult to resolve. The late Dr. Carl Hubbs of the Scripps Institution of Oceanography at La Jolla was convinced that they could be. He delighted in showing a few specimens to archaeologist friends, and asking to have them identified. The stones in question were mainly flat pebbles of basalt that had had flakes or chips removed along one or more edges, and if Hubbs' victim fell into his trap, saying they were clearly crude scrapers produced by the archaic La Jolla people, he was overjoyed. They were, he explained happily, collected from a cobble ramp on a beach in Baja California, and therefore obviously just chipped by the action of heavy surf.

If Hubbs' prospective victims had been forewarned, they had two recourses. First, if the specimens were carefully examined, they would usually reveal flake scars of different generation; some fresh and clearly more recently received than others which were already slightly abraded, immediately ruling out human work. It is perfectly true that heavy storm waves often propel pebbles through the air and onto a rocky shingle at very high velocities, breaking, splitting or chipping them. But only one or two flake scars would likely be produced by one such episode, and the chance of several flakes being removed along an edge by the same storm is exceedingly remote.

If all the flake scars on Hubbs' exhibit were clearly of the same vintage and so placed as to produce a workable edge, the chances are strong that the piece was indeed a human artifact, possibly washed out of a nearby La Jollan midden on the cliffs recently enough to have been preserved from excessive abrasion in the surf. Since archaic populations occupied the coast for thousands of years, their discarded stone tools and shell middens abound along the Southern and Baja California beaches.

Of course here we are back to the same problem discussed earlier in the case of purported Nature-facts in streambeds. It is conceivable that stones in either streams or surf might receive in very rare cases chipping or nibbling along an edge that could be mistaken for human work by uninformed viewers, but neither natural agency could ever manufacture a shaped point, a handaxe or a bifacial chopping tool. The possibility is even more remote that alternate-face flaking to produce a zigzag or sinuous edge could be achieved by storm surf or stream action. Such objects are plainly manmade, and their presence in clearly ancient sediments in Southern California and elsewhere in the Western Hemisphere needs to be explained rather than ignored.

Most of what we know and accept as fact about the prehistoric world has been deduced on the bases of bits of evidence leading to logical conclusions, sometimes faulty. No human has ever seen a dinosaur, but on the strength of some fossil bones; huge, mineral-replaced eggs and footprints in what was once soft mud, we can easily conclude that such creatures once existed, and even fill in the missing flesh and hide from our fertile imaginations. We can almost hear the huge beasts bellowing and setting the marshy ground atremble; smell the spicy odor of their dung in the steamy air.

But we must proceed with some caution. For over a century we have been informed by the most reputable of scientists that all dinosaurs were cold-blooded, as snakes and lizards are today. However, recently certain very plausible arguments have been raised that some dinosaurs were in fact warm-blooded, and were ancestral to birds.

Perhaps a more telling case in point has been the relatively recent discovery and broad recognition of plate tectonics and continental drift. In the early decades of the present century it was universally believed that the earth's land areas have been fixed and immutable since their original formation. But in 1915 a German meteorologist, Alfred Wegener, and others proposed a startling new theory: that the continents have actually been drifting apart over huge distances on the molten magma of the earth's outer mantle over geologic time. The close fit between the east coast of South America and the west coast of Africa, plus many other evidences of drift from different locations on the surface of the earth, seemed to support Wegener's theory. However, it was not until the 1960s with the discovery of the deep sea spreading centers as a mechanism capable of causing crustal migration that widespread skepticism was finally overcome.

So it may be with the almost universally accepted doctrine of recency for human occupation of the New World. That judgment is based on what is called negative evidence, the failure in the past to find, or more properly to recognize, traces of very early human presence in the Western Hemisphere, leading to the logical presumption that none existed. Such presumptions have a tendency to harden into unshakable convictions, so that contrary views and even solid evidence in opposition to the standard doctrine are violently and stubbornly resisted.

Today our view of the Pleistocene world is built on solid and positive observations, even though no human now alive has ever seen it. Advancing and retreating ice sheets have left their record on the land: glacial moraines, deep scoured-out valleys and mountains of glacial till. Fossil bones of extinct megafauna and recovered paleo-pollens can reconstruct the Pleistocene environment. We can visualize the great sweep of Amerasia curving around the North Pacific rim: the broad coastal zones, the vast ocean and its rich resources, the misty lowlands of Beringia. Whole troops of lumbering mammoth and giant bison stream across the screen of our inner vision.

Only the little file of humans with their bundled hides and weapons is still hazy and indistinct!

CAMEO

The Mackenzie

Three hundred and seventy-seven thousand years before the present. The climate in North America is at a full interglacial stage. The great valley of the Mackenzie River in the Canadian Northwest Territory has been free of glacial ice for over three thousand years. A vast green corridor extends almost three thousand miles from the Beaufort Sea to the Gulf of Mexico. An extremely limited population of humans, Homo erectus, has slowly filtered through the high passes of the Richardson Range and established itself in widely scattered small bands on the tundra, near the foothills of the Cordillera.

Reluctantly the winter snows had yielded to the earth's slow turning as the little file of humans cleared McDougal Pass and started down the eastern slope. Spring lay on the land, its green shimmer increasingly apparent as the people walked down over the raw, gravelly soil still furrowed by signs of the melted drifts and the trickles of icy rills.

Spread out before them here was the tundra, laced and braided with channels of the Mackenzie for a hundred miles above its delta. The river itself was a broad, shallow, moving ocean of snowmelt running down to the sea. It was fed by a thousand creeks roaring down from the hills, while the runoff from countless soggy marshes and ponds added their flow to its burden. The main channel that wound itself over the tundra had been repeatedly snuffed out and reborn again by the grinding advance and retreat of the Laurentide ice sheet in the glacial stages.

The piedmont ice of the Cordillera had left rich clays and silts in the tills at the feet of the mountains. Now as the topsoils thawed in the warming sun, the plants sent up masses of new growth thick and flourishing. As the people came down from the pass and wandered south they waded through shoals of flowers and billowing seas of pasture; forded numberless winding sloughs and streams and even broad, shallow rivers sparkling and bright in the arctic air.

Game grazed on the thick moss and lichens, dotting the landscape out to the flat horizon. The herds had been working north and increasing century after century as the climate warmed. Each spring found more animals on the ice-free tundra and the rich grasslands to the south. On the lower Mackenzie were caribou, musk ox and mammoth. In the south where the tundra merged into steppe were horse, camel and bison in vast herds of thousands of animals; droves and legions as far as the eye could see.

Here, in a broad belt along the eastern margin of the Cordillera during the ice-free stages of the Pleistocene, was an environment highly suitable for man at his earlier and more primitive levels of cultural evolution. In addition to the large grazing game of the tundra and grasslands, woodland species were abundant on the flanks of the ranges. In the rain shadows of towering peaks were groves of spruce, fir and hemlock, and rocky canyons where humans could winter without having to flounder about in deep snow. Wood for fires and straight shoots for lances and shelter poles were always at hand. Stone for toolmaking lay in the riffles, berries and fish could be eaten in season, and in summer the people wandered across the tundra as people still did in Siberia and as their ancestors had done in the distant past.

Eventually, after thousands of years had passed, the increasingly bitter climate and accumulating ice of another glacial advance would force their remaining descendants south as the land was locked up again for many millennia. All traces of human presence would be ground away and obliterated.

*   *   *   *

In late spring the treeless tundra all around the world resounded with the clamor of millions of breeding waterfowl, but now in midsummer the great flocks fell silent as their broods were raised and the adult birds began the period of annual moult. As the emerging new feathers pushed out the primary flight pinions of snow geese and whistling swan and black-necked lesser Canadas, the resonant music of the birds was muted. Flightless now, they kept nervous watch on their surroundings, hiding in the fringes of brush and reeds around the shallow ponds when danger threatened.

This was a time the people eagerly awaited, a time for fun and easy forage in which even the children joined. They had feasted already on the rich eggs of the birds, chasing them off the nests and clubbing those that resisted too fiercely, but now it was possible to run them down if one were fleet enough of foot and tireless in pursuit.

The people formed a line a few yards apart and began walking across the still-soggy tundra, splashing through the shallows and thrashing the willow thickets to flush out the geese and swans that might be hiding there, with their long necks compressed and tight against their shoulders. As the shouting humans came too close the big birds burst from their coverts in a flurry of beating wings and honking. Half running and half flying, they could travel at surprising speed just above the surface, and would go frantically drumming off with a hunter in close pursuit.

Amid an uproar of laughing, shouting, flapping and honking the chase went on, crashing through brush and pounding across ponds in great cascading curtains of glittering water. Trying to tackle and bring down a full-grown gander or swan in full career led to some bruising falls, but the hunters were tough and hard to discourage.

Unfortunately, faced with such a plentitude of game, early man displayed a hideous frailty shared by few other predators. Stirred by the excitement of the chase he killed far more geese than he could possibly eat, and left the surplus there to rot, a ghastly glut of carrion on the land. Humans were accustomed to killing for a community instead of just for themselves, and the practice of storing winter meat also developed a penchant for mass killing, so the hunters killed as many as they could regardless of their need, from what must have seemed to them an inexhaustible supply.

As the men and boys came back to their camp, set on a gentle rise overlooking the green and silver plain rolling off into the distance, they staggered under their loads. Their swarthy hides and shaggy black heads were almost hidden by snowy mounds of snow goose and swan. As they dumped the trophies there upon the hill, the piles of white forms grew into a mountain, a great drift of tangled wings and bodies gleaming in the pale sunlight.

The women and children began to pluck some of the fattest birds, and soon a blizzard of white feathers went drifting downwind, sticking like wet snowflakes to every twig and stem. They ripped the feathers from the breast, then pulled the plump fillets off the bone and threw the carcasses aside. Soon the odor of sizzling goose fat rose from the fires and hung over the plain, and the people gorged themselves to repletion.

After a week of feasting the flesh of the birds had become soft and tender, but the smell and taste had begun to sicken the people so they broke camp and moved on, leaving a mountain of rotting carrion untouched except by the scavengers and a swirling, shimmering and droning cloud of flies that covered the piles like a blanket.

*   *   *   *

From somewhere in the dim distance of human evolution the grim practice of intentional disposal of the aged had persisted. Only humans faced the problem; no other creatures could survive into a state of helpless infirmity. In the fixed existence of caves and rock shelters the aged who lapsed into senility or became physically helpless were set aside beyond the fires for the hyenas or dire wolves. Nomadic people on the move simply walked away and left those who could neither travel nor recover. The large, bone-crushing scavengers were quick to move in on sick, wounded or defenseless creatures, and in a time of teeming life forms of every sort the scavengers prospered in proportionate abundance. They patrolled with special diligence the vicinity of human camps and habitations, profitting from man's profligacy and waiting patiently in the dark beyond his fires.

In addition to their large frames and heavily-muscled shoulders, the dire wolves had powerful jaws like the hyenas', able to break down and consume large bones without a trace. Although intelligent and aggressive, they rarely attacked healthy animals, preferring to pull down sick, aged or infirm individuals or unguarded young. They culled weaklings from the herds and thus improved the quality of many species, serving as one of Nature's instruments for selectivity and the survival of the fittest. Because of very voracious appetites and numbers carrion rarely remained long on the land.

An aged human sat on a boulder in the sun and wistfully watched the young hunters go striding off across the tundra. Their supple, well-muscled bodies and springy step proclaimed their vigorous youth and energy. He could see them swinging along far out on the rolling plain in the clear air, heading for a chain of hummocks where caribou often grazed and where the more broken land offered the possibilities of an ambush or a successful stalk.

Now in the camp behind him only the women and small children remained. The adolescent young were gathering firewood and dried animal droppings for fuel, a never-ending responsibility. The fires burned continuously when the band was camped, and fuel was carried with them when they moved unless the country was well wooded. The women worked with their curing pelts, nursed their infants or simply sprawled in the warm sunshine.

This old man had been a powerful hunter in his time, a rather squat giant who could lift a three hundred pound doe to his shoulders and easily carry it in to the camp. Now at fifty-two he was an exceptionally ancient human waiting to die. A mass of wrinkles crinkled the skin of his face and his wispy hair was streaked with grey and white. The powerful barrel chest and massive shoulders had wasted and deformed into a sad, bony caricature of a man, humped and emaciated. But from under the bristling eyebrows and now-ex-aggerated brow ridges bright eyes peered out at the world, clear testimony to a brisk and active mind.

Endowed with the human capability to visualize and reason, the gift that had enriched his life became a curse to haunt him. For his vivid imagination now painted the terrifying spectacle of his own death; both experience and logic told him of its inevitable approach. His arthritic limbs had finally locked and made walking impossible. He would be unable to leave this place where the band was camped, and here he would die.

The old man awaited his looming death with feelings of uncontrollable sorrow and of dread despite his long, full life and mature wisdom. To him the world was a place of rich satisfaction. He was wise enough to take frequent note of its changing beauties and the sensual joys it offered. Even now, above the constant pain he suffered and his aching fear of impending doom, his spirit soared briefly as the tiny children of the band went racing by, leaping and tumbling like colts from sheer exuberance. There in a sense he went himself, reborn and young again, eager to begin the long journey. Several carried his seed, and some perhaps would see the visions and the wonder.

When the hunters returned well burdened with meat and hides, the fires were built up to leaping vigor in the twilight and all feasted on the special delicacies of liver, heart and tongue. The young men babbled and bragged even more loudly than usual and avoided the old man's eyes. It was plain to him that the decision had been made to move on in the morning.

His daughters, well along in life themselves, fed him tender morsels from the coals, and he knew from their misty eyes that they too suspected the bitter truth; his time had come. Waves of panic surged through his body. He had no mental composure or feelings of resignation; no relief at the prospect of physical surcease from pain. His mind raced endlessly and fruitlessly through the long night, the mind that was still vigorous and sound in the worn-out body.

At dawn the people packed their belongings in the hides and lashed them on the poles. They kept away from the old man as though to shield themselves from the corruption of death; in their eyes he had already died. He cowered by the dwindling fire like an animal in a trap. No tradition of dignity in death had been left to him, nor impulse to mask his terror. The people marched away, his relatives included, without a backward glance. The pity they surely felt was hidden and unrevealed.

Now in broad daylight the wolves appeared as if by magic, sensing the helplessness of the gaunt figure by the fire. He roused himself to grasp a tough wooden club in readiness for the struggle. The wolves gathered and moved closer until they ringed the fire, waiting with pale yellow eyes and bared fangs gleaming. The embers slowly smoldered and went out.

All day he faced them down, but darkness came. Now the dim shapes moved in. One, bolder than the rest, slipped up behind the old man and slashed viciously across his shoulder. He screamed and swung his club, losing his precarious balance and sprawling full length upon the ground.

Instantly he was covered with a mass of snarling beasts ripping and tearing at his flesh. His screaming ended in a dark blur of agony and death as his physical presence simply vanished from the earth.

* * * *

For many millennia man had been adapting to life on the arctic and subarctic barrens but few changes and innovations had been necessary. The most notable was the use of the thrown spear instead of the hand-held lance of earlier times, although the spear could be used as a lance in special circumstances. The spear was a weapon made necessary on open plains and grasslands where cover was scant and opportunities to strike from ambush at close range were rare. Objects like stones and cudgels were hurled by hominids always and even some lower primates resorted to such tactics for bluff and bluster, but a well-balanced spear tipped with horn or bone was a sophisticated and deadly instrument. A hunter who practiced with it throughout his life could hurl the heavy shaft with great accuracy for distances of forty to fifty feet and often much farther. It would penetrate many inches of tough hide, bone and muscle.

Working in teams with these weapons the skilled hunters lay prone in the short tundra cover while youngsters herded game in their direction. Covered with loose moss they were almost invisible from forty feet, particularly to animals with all their attention on the yelping, capering beaters. As the game streamed by in panicky stampede the spearsmen leaped up and cast their heavy, twelve-foot shafts, leading the targets a little to allow for time lag. With the weight of their thick arms and massive shoulders behind the delivery, the spears streaked through the air in a relatively flat trajectory, and thudded into the sides of the victims with lethal force. They rarely dropped an animal in its tracks, and still had to follow along behind to finish the quarry off, but in the open country of the tundra this was a simple task.

Born and bred on the tundra the people were hardy and easily withstood the bitter cold but they never enjoyed it. Here the slow, gradual dispersal of the human species did not move like the rings on a pond, but steadily if almost imperceptibly to the south, from the rigorous climate to the more benign. Nomadic people wandering over the face of the earth have an instinct for moving in the right direction. Given a choice they respond like plants, facing the sun and reaching hungrily for it.

A small band of twenty-six humans had been drifting to the south all summer. They would stay in a comfortable campsite, make a kill or two and move on when the meat was consumed or perhaps linger where berry bushes were bearing ripe fruit and eat until they were satiated. In general they moved without goals or conscious direction, simply drifting along where the terrain suggested the easiest passage.

The little file walked steadily across the plain. A September sun was low in the southern sky but the weather was still mild and pleasant. The tundra moss had given way here to the south to long, golden grass, and the stunted willows in the swales and around the ponds were beginning to put on a blaze of color. Soon the band would need to head for higher, more broken country and establish a wintering place under a sheltering cliff. Mountains were visible on both sides as they slowly worked their way south up the valley of the Mackenzie. To the west the Backbone ranges towered over seven thousand feet into the sky, while the more modest peaks of the Franklins loomed to eastward.

As those at the head of the little file went over the top of a gentle rise of land, they came upon a sight so rare as to never before have been experienced in their lifetimes. There below them was a cluster of campfires, and sprawled on the ground were humans like themselves who were completely unknown to them — strangers!

This was a shocking discovery in that distant age. It was comparable to astronauts on the moon suddenly confronting other unknown men. Humans were still so rare a species in North America that no precedent for dealing with the situation had ever been established. In this same period in Asia, while humans had not been common they were encountered at times, and by tradition were to be considered hostile and fair game.

The travelers had always supposed that the few other bands they knew on the tundra of the lower Mackenzie constituted all of humanity. With these they spoke and dealt on friendly terms, and intermarried with their young. All spoke the same basic language. How could they have known otherwise, or even guessed at the earth's great magnitude and alien populations?

So now they had a momentous problem demanding a decision. They carefully withdrew over the low summit and earnestly conferred, squatting in a circle in the dry grass with their long spears prudently lowered to the ground out of sight. They had three options: they might detour around and avoid the strangers, or they might launch a surprise attack on the camp and destroy it, or they might go in peace into the alien camp and fight only if attacked or threatened.

The women waited in the background for the hunters to decide. There were advocates for all three courses, since it was obvious to all that they clearly outnumbered the strangers. Even the most warlike ones had no desire to eat the flesh of the enemy, since cannibalism had never been practiced in their memory. They simply felt a surprise attack was the safest course to follow, for otherwise they might be tricked and destroyed themselves. The mateless young men supported this procedure since they could then select a female from the other camp at their leisure.

But the more moderate counsel prevailed, and they decided to show themselves and walk down the hill to the campfires, keeping their weapons ready. As they loomed against the sky and started down the slope the people of the camp were equally astonished and terrified. The men seized spears and took up defensive positions before their females, who cringed in fear beside the fires.

The newcomers marching down the hill had no idea how threatening they appeared as they walked purposefully toward the fires with their weapons at the ready. Since they had agreed among themselves to go in peace, they somehow expected their reception to be peaceful. But there was no universal tongue that all men spoke, no means of communicating their peaceable intentions. Not even signs and gestures had common currency; if they laid down their weapons they risked their own destruction.

A terrible silence hung over the scene as the travelers drew close. They began to stalk along stiff-legged as dogs do at a first encounter, warily watching for a suspicious move, gripping their weapons fiercely. At last, at the distance of a long spear throw, the intruders stopped and stood, some glaring ferociously, unwilling to attack but uncertain how to proceed. A young hunter by the fire began to draw back his arm stealthily to cast his spear.

But now, when a battle to the death seemed certain, a delightful human miracle occurred. A tiny child of perhaps four years, too young to be aware of such mysteries as emnity and malice, and believing the newcomers to be some of her own people, ran out gaily to the leader and threw her arms around his leg playfully. He stabbed the butt of his spear into the soft earth, reached down and gathered up the child and set her on his shoulder, striding in to the fires with his face wreathed in a broad smile. The tension vanished like a puff of smoke and all began to murmur and to smile.

The people of the camp were now transformed to pleasant, laughing friends, unable to converse in words but eloquent in actions. They drew all the visitors in to the hearths and offered treats of marrow. The two bands camped together for several days, exchanging ideas haltingly as they began to comprehend each other, admiring infants, gear and weapons. Each group tried tentatively the spoken sounds of the other and there were gales of laughter, none on either side having ever heard anything so ridiculous. When the wanderers moved on, their numbers had increased; the two unmated young men having persuaded girls from the camp to lie with them and chew their mittens and mukluks and beget them sons.

CHAPTER 4

Interior America:
Penetration of the Continents

Today Alaska's Seward Peninsula and the Chukotski Peninsula of Eastern Siberia thrust themselves toward each other like belligerent bulldogs or gamecocks, separated by the narrow Bering Strait; separated into East and West, the Old World and the New, by sparkling blue water, the grey shroud of fog or the glittering white of pack ice. From Potato Mountain on the American side, on the rare days of clear weather, one can look past the stark silhouettes of the Diomede Islands in mid-channel and see the vague loom of Asia 50 miles away.

During the low sea stands of the glacial stages, for thousands of years during the Pleistocene Epoch, the great landmass of Beringia appeared, nearly 1,000 miles from north to south, joining and unifying the continents of the Northern Hemisphere. Spawned by ice but ice-free throughout the Pleistocene, Beringia was a wide and varied boreal domain. Beyond the lowlands formed by the bared bottoms of the Bering and Chukchi Seas and the Strait itself, the coastal shelves and beaches trended off to the southeast and southwest, while near the midriff of the exposed landmass the broad valley of the Yukon River led far back into the interior of North America, terrain similar to that of the Soviet Far East but free of glacial ice.

For humans in a very primitive cultural stage, and possibly unaccustomed to diverse environments, the lowlands of Beringia must have served as a sort of crossroads. Those adapted to a coastal and marine economy would undoubtedly have followed the coastal zones and tidal margins down the edges of the continent of North America, utilizing mollusks and crustaceans, marine mammals, sea bird concentrations and their eggs and fledglings, as well as plant foods and game of opportunity.

It would seem logical to suspect that the first humans to arrive in the Western Hemisphere might have followed this route, probably originating in China, Korea and Japan, and possibly at time ranges even earlier than are here being contemplated. The food resources in the coastal environments, as we have suggested, could have sustained the most primitive of humans; humans lacking highly developed hunting skills and equipment. Maritime climates would have been far less severe than conditions in the continental interiors at the same latitudes, far milder than those at the sites on the Lena River in Siberia, and would have required far less sophisticated cultural adaptations. In short, humans at almost any stage of evolution could have survived and prospered as they slowly and gradually expanded around the rim to regions south of the glacial ice.

How far along the coast the earliest meager trickle of human foragers might have drifted cannot be known in present knowledge or even guessed. We do know that the most primitive people with the most archaic skull structures found in the Americas by the Spaniards at first contact were in a geographical location where they could go no farther south: the Pericu at the southern tip of Baja California. Their skulls have been described as of pyramidal form; high, long and narrow, perhaps the narrowest of any human population known (Rogers 1966:8).

Whether the ancestors of the Pericu found their way out of the Baja California cul-de-sac and followed the coast all the way to Tierra del Fuego in the distant past may never be known, but heavy, massive choppers similar to the California macrolithic tools were recently shown to me from the Atacama desert of Chile, tools thickly coated with desert varnish. They were found on now hyper-arid landforms well back from the coast. In the case of the California coastal zone, such tools have only been reported from the San Diego region, where they are of course lacking in desert varnish.

The presumed absence of macrolithic tools in other localities on or near the California coast can be explained in a number of ways. One reason might be that coastal movement by early humans occurred primarily during glacial periods when low sea levels exposed the continental shelves and vastly broadened the coastal littoral. The rising sea levels of following interglacial marine transgressions would have eliminated all traces of human occupation except in a few favored locations like San Diego, now extremely arid zones of relative stability in Chile, and perhaps other localities yet to be discovered.

Another somewhat less plausible possibility is that very early foragers followed the Northwest Coast down to points south of the major glaciation and then wandered up the river valleys of the Columbia and the Snake during interstadial periods between glacial maxima, reaching the rich lake basins east of the Cascade Mountains and the Sierra Nevada. Following periods of full glaciation might have eliminated traces of their passage as surely as the rising sea levels and surf lines of interglacial transgressions abraded the tools of their ancestors back down to cobbles again.

Two other explanations for the lack of reported evidence of very early human presence in the coastal zones need to be mentioned. The most obvious is that the coastal movement never occurred, despite favorable climate and terrain, and that the makers of early Paleolithic macrolithic tools at San Diego reached there over an inland route east of the mountains, having been forced to the coast by the onset of arid desert conditions associated with an interglacial stage. And finally we have to recognize that, given the widespread convictions of recency for man in America, evidence in the form of very crude and massive stone implements has been overlooked or not recognized.

The alternative routes into the heart of the continent: up the valleys of the Yukon River and the Porcupine, and over the McDougal Pass into the valley of the Mackenzie; or over the tundra of Alaska's North Slope beside the Beaufort Sea and up the Mackenzie during an interstade or interglacial, would have been far more rigorous. But creatures able to survive in the Siberian winters would obviously find the northern Yukon no more demanding. There are strong suggestions of very early human occupation as much as 150,000 years ago in the Old Crow Basin, far up the Yukon and Porcupine Rivers and some 800 miles east of Bering Strait.

The Old Crow River Basin, just east of the border between eastern Alaska and Canada and about 80 miles north of the Arctic Circle, is surrounded on three sides by mountain ranges which, during the glacial stages of the Pleistocene, shielded the basin itself from glaciation. Today the Old Crow River meanders in tight, exaggerated loops across the uplifted plain of the basin floor, fed by a number of creeks draining the surrounding uplands, and empties into the Porcupine at the Ramparts in the southwest sector, where it cut a new outlet several thousand years ago. Previously, during interglacial periods, the Old Crow River system drained eastward through McDougal Pass into the Mackenzie Basin. However, during the glacial stages, the Wisconsin and the Illinoian and possibly earlier glacial periods, the pass was blocked by the Laurentide ice sheet on the eastern flank of the Richardson Range, causing huge glacial lakes to form in the Old Crow Basin.

During the present post-glacial period, which is to say the past 10,000 years, the river has cut down through the sediments deposited by the glacial lakes, so that a series of strata are exposed in cliffs almost 200 feet high. Fossil bones of ice-age animals, preserved by permafrost, have been washed out and deposited in the river bars by the hundreds, and some seen weathering out of the bluff faces can be roughly dated by their stratigraphic position in the exposed lake sediments.

In January of 1973 two Canadian scientists, W. N. Irving and C. R. Harington, reported in the influential journal Science the discovery six years earlier of what appeared to be an artifact made of bone, with a radiocarbon age of over 27,000 years, from a fossil collecting station on the Old Crow River. Flaked from a caribou tibia, one end had been thinned and given a denticulate or toothed edge. The resulting implement closely resembled fleshing tools for the preparation of hides still in use by the indigenous people of the Arctic. However, recent retesting by the mass accelerator radiocarbon method has resulted in a far younger age in the Holocene or Recent period.

The fleshing tool and a number of less obvious bone specimens believed broken or otherwise modified by man had been discovered in 1966 by Harington and Peter Lord about 20 miles north of the Old Crow's confluence with the Porcupine. The discovery led to repeated expeditions in the basin during following years, the recovery of scores of bone specimens either considered to be manmade tools or showing what appeared to be evidence of human activity; cut marks and means of breakage that could only be attributed to man by the investigators. Between 1975 and 1979 major operations were conducted along a 12-mile stretch of the Old Crow River, primarily by William Irving and his associates of the Northern Yukon Research Program and the Yukon Refugium Project headed by Richard Morlan (Jopling et al.1981; Morlan 1978).

Excavations of the bluff exposures demonstrated the presence of what were described as bone artifacts and utilized cobbles at levels ascribed to the Illinoian Glacial Stage, approximately 150,000 years ago. As might be expected, the identification of these specimens as tools made by man has been highly controversial, since their acceptance as evidence of human presence places man in the New World far earlier than most scholars have believed possible, especially in as demanding an environment as the northern Yukon. Many tests and replicative experiments have been conducted in recent years in the hope of establishing valid criteria by which human alteration of bone can be distinguished from natural breakage and damage caused by carnivores and rodents. Robson Bonnichsen, Director of the University of Maine's Center for the Study of Early Man has been particularly active in that effort, and has published detailed reports of his findings in this regard, which are to the effect that human alteration of bone can indeed be recognized with confidence (Bonnichsen 1978, 1979).

One of the difficulties in studying the flaking and shaping possibilities of bone is the need for fresh or "green" bone from very large animals, such as would have been used by ancient hunters at mammoth or giant bison kill sites. It is believed that tools were made of the bones of the slaughtered animal itself to skin and butcher it. Experiments have been conducted on horse and cattle bones, but these thin-walled materials cannot be properly compared to the massive megafauna bones common in the Old Crow sites, preserved by permafrost.

A golden opportunity to conduct bone-flaking experiments arose in 1978 when Ginsberg, a female African elephant, died in Boston's Franklin Park zoo. She was donated for the "Ginsberg Experiment" to be conducted by Dennis Stanford of the Smithsonian Institution, Bonnichsen and Morlan. This windfall offered the scientists a unique opportunity to study, not only the effects of human breakage on elephant bone while still fresh, but also the efficiency of a variety of stone and bone tools in skinning and butchering, and the preparation of bone tools directly from the carcass of the animal being butchered (Stanford et al. 1981).

Bonnichsen and Stanford visited me in 1981, and I showed them a massive quartzite chopper from Buchanan Canyon that probably weighed ten pounds. When I said that I believed it had been used to break mammoth marrow bone, they instantly disagreed. They had found that to break Ginsberg's leg bones required a boulder weighing at least 20 pounds. This is because green elephant bone is very elastic, and only becomes brittle when thoroughly dried out. Tools of lesser weight simply bounced off.

Numerous other pieces of useful information were gathered at the outdoor butchering site in Virginia and in the laboratory at the Canadian National Museum in Ottawa the following years. It was discovered that green elephant bone could be chipped and flaked as easily as stone of good quality, but could only be worked with stone tools. Bone flakes and blades, simple to produce, proved to be quite efficient for slicing through flesh but were inadequate for cutting through thick, tough elephant hide. Many of the bone tools manufactured by the scientists from Ginsberg's skeleton appeared to accurately duplicate specimens taken from the sediments in the Old Crow Basin.

Stanford and his colleagues concluded that bone tools may have been widely utilized by prehistoric hunters living in grassland environments, and presumably on open tundra where stone would have been scarce. The mobility of the hunters would have been greatly enhanced by not having to carry with them more than the minimum number of stone implements necessary to produce a supply of bone slicing and cutting tools which could be discarded after use at the kill site.

Work is continuing in the Northern Yukon region, with extremely extensive geological and paleontological studies and excavation of ancient lake sediments being conducted. Specimens considered to be bone artifacts are being encountered at the lowest levels attributed to the Illinoian glacial stage, and 150,000 BP might be a minimum date for man in the region. It is clear that tools found in the silts and clays of lake bottoms must have been manufactured and used before their burial and inundation by the rising waters of the lake. It seems much more likely that the makers of the tools were there in the preceding interglacial stage before Glacial Old Crow Lake was formed, and that the artifacts were discarded at a kill site after use on steppe grassland or tundra and preserved in muck or permafrost before they could become decomposed.

The evidence suggests a very long period of intermittent occupation by limited human populations, down through the last interglacial stage, called the Sangamon, and the most recent glaciation, the Wisconsin; a record of early man's presence over extremely extended periods of time. It is impossible to guess how long ago, if ever, the first inquisitive humans filtered through McDougal Pass and down to the vast lowlands of the Mackenzie District; down to the tundra, steppe and prairies stretching away to the south and east deep into the interior of North America. During thousands of years of interglacial climates, the way was open without any serious geographical hindrances, southeastward through the Canadian Prairie Provinces and south behind the Northern Cordillera and the Rocky Mountains clear to Texas and New Mexico and beyond.

The Mackenzie River rises in Great Slave Lake and runs north for over 700 miles to its delta on the Beaufort Sea. There is no reason to believe it has not done so in previous interglacial climates throughout the Pleistocene, and that in similar climate cycles the physical environment was not much like that of the present. But there must have been one very important difference: the presence of large herds of grazing herbivores: caribou and musk ox on the tundra of the Lower Mackenzie; and mammoth, horse, giant bison and possibly camel on the steppe grasslands and prairies to the south in what are now Alberta and Saskatchewan, and on the high plains of Montana and Wyoming.

During early interglacial stages, large areas of northern Canada east of the Cordillera must have been covered by lakes, as they are today, and may have played the same role as the coastal beaches would have done in an early human diffusion along the North Pacific rim. The lakes would have offered a readily available source of food, while moving human bands along as those resources became even marginally depleted. But the slow drift of humans to the south may have taken thousands of years; south over the great sweep of land in the rain shadow of the Rockies and through them into the Great Basin and Range Province of the western United States.

Although there may have been periods lasting many thousands of years during the glacial maxima when the continental or Laurentide Ice Sheet joined with Cordilleran valley and piedmont glaciers, forming a solid barrier to southward movements of human populations, these periods of closure represented less than 30 percent of the last 500,000 years. The so-called glacial-interglacial timetable, thought of as a giant gate that opened and closed permitting or denying passage to the warmer south, was far more important when it was believed, only a few years ago, that man's first appearance in the Western Hemisphere occurred in late Wisconsin time, perhaps 12,000 years ago.

The problem then was thought to present a paradox: man could only have crossed Bering Strait when land was exposed by the accumulation of continental ice, (although modern Eskimos have been crossing for centuries over the pack ice) but during such a period the way south would have been blocked by that same glacial ice, it was believed. Yet we knew over 50 years ago, from indisputable evidence of human presence at the Folsom and Clovis kill sites in New Mexico, that man was far south of the ice during the terminal Wisconsin. In the far greater time ranges with which we are now dealing, and with recognition of the availability of the ice-free coastal zones during glacial maxima, such problems no longer trouble us.

Human adaptation to harsh arctic and subarctic climates is a matter of interest now rather than a controlling factor in our acceptance of human expansion during what must have been a very primitive cultural stage, for it is clear now that populations did survive, occupy and move through those bleak northern regions. In the case of humans in the Mackenzie District, the rigors of the environment may have stimulated fairly brisk movement following the migrating caribou southward toward the sun as it dipped ever lower in the southern sky. Long, wavering skeins of swans and geese would have emphasized the urgency of approaching winter with their music spilling down over the land, their arrows dissolving and reforming but always pointing to the south down the continent.

If human bands did move down this broad corridor east of the Cordillera a quarter of a million years ago, all traces of their passage will undoubtedly have been erased, the evidence in the Old Crow Basin being a remarkable exception caused by unusual geomorphic circumstances. The preservation even of hard stone artifacts under the grinding abrasion and enormous pressures of repeated advances of the Laurentide Ice Sheet, in places said to have been almost three miles thick, would seem to be doubtful if not impossible. The topography of the land would have been completely resculptured, and stone tools reduced to unrecognizable forms as surely as would those artifacts which lay in the churning surf lines of advancing and retreating sea stands along the North Pacific rim.

Even stone tools discarded scores of millennia ago in the never-glaciated Yukon Valley would now lie fathoms deep in muskeg or would have been exposed long since by erosion and worked downslope into a watercourse to be pecked back down to cobble form again. Thus there is little hope of ever literally following the back trail of those first ancient wanderers; the best we can expect is to deduce their passage on the basis of the few brief glimpses we have had of them, south of the glaciated lands in the interior and behind the interglacial beaches.

One such brief glimpse was an isolated, massive stone chopper on the surface at McDougal Pass, high above the Mackenzie on the threshold of the continent; an enigmatic, silent witness to the passage of humans in the ancient past (Brian Reeves, personal communication). And much more than a casual glimpse was afforded us over half a century ago, but because of still prevalent convictions of recency for man in the Western Hemisphere, it has been almost universally ignored or explained away with a variety of ingenious interpretations. That is a series of surface sites stretching along over 30 miles of the Black's Fork River in southwestern Wyoming, a little over 2,000 miles south of the Old Crow Basin.

The Black's Fork River rises in Utah's Uinta Range and winds across an eroded and dissected plateau, looping to the north and then to the south where it joins the Green River. Here is one of the few areas in the continental mountain chain where the Great Divide is invisible to the eye; a few miles to the east the North Platte flows into the Missouri and the Gulf of Mexico, while to the west passes in the Wasatch Range lead into the Great Basin. From the Pacific Coast the valleys of the Columbia and the Snake could have conducted early wanderers into the Northern Great Basin and western Wyoming, while to the north during interglacial stages the way was open over the prairies all the way from the delta of the Mackenzie.

This is a tawny, semiarid region of stunted sage and meager pasture, a land of scattered bands of pronghorn antelope and golden eagles and vivid blue skies. Flat-topped buttes and mesas dominate the landscape, remnants of an ancient flood plain formed far back in the Pleistocene when enormous rivers of icemelt swept across it from the dwindling glaciers on the high mountains to the south. The Black's Fork River has cut down over the millennia through the tectonically rising plateau, a gentle flow in summer and fall but covering its meager and greatly lowered flood plain when the melting snows of spring freshets cause swirling torrents to surge over its banks.

Eroded terraces and benches flank the gravels and sand bars of the stream, each level representing a past period of climate change, with the highest surfaces, paved with heavy, water-worn gravels, formed in a time far back in the distant past before the rising land and down-cutting of the river left them dry and isolated, immune to further stream abrasion of their cobble components and receptive to thick coats of desert varnish.

In past glacio-pluvial stages, and never glaciated themselves, these periglacial landscapes must have looked far different from the parched and desiccated mesas seen today. Green, rolling uplands probably interlaced with sparkling streams, lakes and ponds, the most striking aspect might have been herds of grazing game; horse, wapiti and bison with perhaps a troop of mammoth in the distance. Waterfowl would have abounded in such a setting, filling the sky with their clamor. It is apparent now that primitive human bands must have shared that primeval landscape.

In 1932 two amateur archaeologists from Colorado, Edison Lohr and Harold Dunning, discovered some stone artifacts firmly wedged into the desert pavement on one of the highest terraces. Despite the heavy abrasion of past stream action on them, and almost black with the varnish of millennia, they still displayed the regular, controlled flaking along their edges that could only be attributed to human work. They showed the specimens to Dr. E. B. Renaud at the University of Denver. A professor of Anthropology there, Renaud was also Director of the Archaeological Survey of the High Western Plains, sponsored jointly by his institution and the University of Wyoming. He was immediately interested and a field expedition was organized for the summer of 1932.

Renaud had been trained in France under the Abbé Henri Brueil, and unlike most American anthropologists then and now, was perfectly familiar with the stone tools of the Old World Early Paleolithic. His party spent a week under very trying conditions in the scorching midsummer heat, examining and collecting specimens from the desert pavements of terrace surfaces along the Black's Fork River between the towns of Granger on the east and Lyman on the west. In January of 1933 the Seventh Report of the Archaeological Survey of the High Western Plains was published, and in it Dr. Renaud reported the presence of a certain number of early Paleolithic tools among the collected specimens, and offered the following conclusions:

> Therefore, the presence of early and late Chellean and early Acheulian coups-de-poing together with early Clactonian flakes is perfectly consistent and would suggest a cultural complex in America similar to that in Europe, and also a possible very great antiquity for these artifacts from our S-W Wyoming sites, as well as the rest of the industry associated with them.

This typological resemblance between Old and New World implements is striking and may be very significant. However, only a systematic geological and paleontological study of the sites could, together with the archaeological diagnosis here presented, reveal the true age of this lithic industry (Renaud 1933).

To Renaud's surprise and bewilderment this statement, according to a following report, was:

> . . . harshly criticized by one of the irreconcilable opponents of the antiquity of man in America, who had seen neither the sites nor the specimens. After such subjective and unfair criticism, the best course to pursue was to do more extensive exploration, to collect more numerous specimens, to study them more closely, and to compare them directly with Old World artifacts of well-authenticated origin and established age and culture, and to obtain the expert opinions of qualified scientists not prejudiced on the subject of the antiquity of man in the New World (Renaud 1938).

These things were done by Renaud and the Archaeological Survey, including the mounting of three more expeditions to the region; the gathering, classification and study of thousands of artifacts; and direct comparison in France and England with similar assemblages from Europe and Africa. Many experts abroad were of the opinion that the Black's Fork tools represented a similar and parallel development in the New World, according to Renaud.

The reaction of American scientists to Renaud's interpretation of the Black's Fork collections as evidences of great antiquity was, and has continued to be for over half a century, one of general skepticism and disbelief, even though probably not one in a thousand archaeologists has visited the site nor seen the artifacts. The latter are explained away as the cast-off blanks and discards of relatively recent people who visited the sites because of the excellent quartzites and cherts available, and who carried away their finished tools. Over the past five decades, thousands of archaeology students have been assured of this by their professors, and have passed along the verdict to their own students without ever questioning its wisdom.

But the artifacts themselves belie their recency. Many show heavy stream abrasion but are fixed in desert pavements on ancient flood plain surfaces that cannot have had streams for over 150,000 years. Tools of pale grey quartzite and green chert have become almost black with desert varnish; rich, lustrous mahogany coatings polished by blowing dust. Their flake scars are pitted and weathered to resemble the tough, outer rind of stream-worn cobbles, and their edges and projections have been worn down and rounded by abrasion in ancient rivers of icemelt. Many on the highest terraces are tool types typical of very early Chinese industries. (Figure 6.)

Some years ago I showed some of the tools to a nationally-known anthropologist of exceptional prestige. He examined them and said, "Oh yes, we find these all over Wyoming. They're archaic," meaning only a few thousand years old. What are such views based on? Never on finite dating, for stone is impossible to date reliably, although many attempts have been made to do so, by hydration in the case of obsidian, and by fluorine penetration in other lithic materials. But weathering over long periods in a variety of environments can remove original surfaces by undeterminable amounts, particularly by blowing sand or dust, so that surface finds are usually subject only to personal interpretations based on geological provenience, typology, technological aspects, individual familiarity with similar industries elsewhere, and what might be called a "consensus" or current doctrine, whatever that might be.

Figure 6. An extremely massive and weathered chopping tool from the highest floodplain surface at Black's Fork, Wyoming.

But the tools at Black's Fork are in a rather unique geomorphic setting, even though they are surface finds being intermittently exposed and covered by wind-borne loess as fine as talcum powder. Their antiquity was supported in 1938 by Dr. E. H. Stephens, a professor of Geology at the Colorado School of Mines, who visited the sites and studied the high terraces and the tools found on them. It was Stephens' opinion that the highest surfaces represented flood plains formed during the Illinoian glacial period, from 125,000 to 190,000 years before the present or possibly even earlier, and subsequently abandoned as the stream cut down to a lower level during a following interglacial stage. On these surfaces two kinds of artifacts were found. Some were moderately polished by wind and dust, but still had relatively sharp edges. The other group was heavily abraded by stream action. Stephens stated in Renaud's report of March, 1940, "All of these weathered and abraded artifacts were found on surfaces lying above the valley train of the Smith's Fork (or Wisconsin) glacial stage, and thus must have been worn by streams earlier than that stage" (Renaud 1940:16).

In many parts of the world throughout the Pleistocene vast areas have been slowly rising through tectonic action of the earth's crust. Where large rivers have cut across extensive plains being subjected to such uplift, they have inevitably cut down through the sediments to compensate for the slowly rising terrain. The Grand Canyon of the Colorado in Arizona is a very spectacular example. In the southwestern corner of Wyoming, when huge amounts of glacial ice were melting on the Uinta Range of Utah to the south, great rivers swept across the plain, carrying and depositing coarse gravels in beds often miles across, where formerly had existed the steppe grasslands of a periglacial environment.

As the interglacial stage advanced and aridity increased, the much narrower river channels gradually cut down through the broad glacial flood plains, leaving flat-topped and gravel-strewn mesas and terraces flanking the lowered stream valleys. Eventually erosion reduced the mesas to buttes or flat-topped ridges rising above the present flood plains, but the deposits of stream gravels on their tops, concentrated by wind and rain into thick desert pavements, still plainly testify to their ancient origins. Lower benches and terraces represent later episodes of glaciation and climate change.

In attempting to determine the age of the artifacts wedged among the cobbles of the highest flood plain surfaces, one must recognize the fact that the obvious and heavy stream abrasion on many of them could only have been produced when the gravel bed containing them was the bed of an active, high energy stream. Once the latter cut down below its flood plain margins and left the gravels and contained artifacts high and dry, no further stream abrasion would have been possible. Abandonment by the stream at, for example, the level of the Stage 9 Interglacial would strongly suggest primary deposit during the preceding Glacial Stage 10, since their position in a streambed would indicate discard during a human occupation previous to the advent of deglaciation of the Uinta Range.

It seems most unlikely that the artifacts could have been redeposited onto the highest flood plain surface at a later time, for in their water-worn condition they would have been useless as tools, and ample supplies of fresh lithic material were always readily available. No agencies other than human intervention could conceivably have moved them from a lower to a higher elevation.

I remember reading in the 1960s arguments tending to discredit the Black's Fork finds, primarily based on vague reports of radiocarbon testing of charcoal found with some of the tools that gave ages well in the Holocene Period. Since there are some 30 miles of sites of various elevations, such tests can hardly be considered useful. The matter of stream versus wind abrasion on the artifacts has caused the most serious dissension. According to Dr. Marie Wormington:

> It is true that many of Renaud's artifacts were found on high terraces and showed definite signs of abrasion. If it could be proven that this was the result of water action it might provide some evidence of age, for a considerable length of time has elapsed since water last reached these terraces. However, if the smoothing was due to wind erosion it provides no evidence of real antiquity although the fact that some artifacts are worn, while others in the same location are not, suggests that there are definite

age differences between the worn and unworn specimens (Wormington 1957:220).

Much of the confusion regarding the abrasion on the artifacts, whether water or wind-abraded, can be laid to an absolutely inexplicable statement by Stephens, quoted above, who later in the report appears to have reversed his first judgment: "In all the specimens examined the wear was by wind abrasion, thus eliminating the possibility of dating them by the time of the abrasion as might have been done if the wearing was by water action" (In Renaud 1940:17). It was this second and contradictory opinion that was seized upon by Renaud's "irreconcilable opponents of the antiquity of man in America."

The confusion need never have existed, for the condition of the abraded artifacts made plainly evident the cause of the wear. The specimens were abraded on all sides, top and bottom, ventral and dorsal surfaces equally. That is extremely unlikely for wind-blown dust to achieve on heavy stone tools lying in heavy gravel but expectable on objects subjected to surf or heavy stream action. Having examined thousands of stone tools lying on desert surfaces, I can testify that all-over wind abrasion is rare under any circumstances, is only present on specimens lying in loose sand and never appears on heavy gravel inclusions.

In the fall of 1974 I was able to visit the Black's Fork terraces near the town of Lyman, Wyoming. I had been directed to the vicinity of the town rubbish dump as being accessible to some of the best sites, and as I parked and got out of the car I saw on the ground, among the tin cans and bottles, a large stone ovate chopping tool, an almost poetic symbol of human continuity. But it was clearly recent and without chemical alteration, and I was searching for antiquity, so I climbed up the slope to the top of the nearest flat-topped ridge. Although Renaud's archaeological teams had removed some thousands of artifacts 40 years earlier, the stream-abraded and heavily varnished stone tools were still scattered among the equally varnished cobbles and boulders of the ancient flood plain.

With the soils reduced by the actions of wind and rain and melting snow, the stone materials had been slowly concentrated into a desert pavement, a mosaic-like surface into which the artifacts had been incorporated as solidly as paveing stones. Drifts of soils as white as snow covered the stone carpet in places, perhaps explaining how substantial areas had escaped the collecting boxes of Renaud's examining crew. I found numerous examples of what were clearly water-worn stone tools, and collected a modest sample of about a dozen pieces, enough to demonstrate to my own complete satisfaction their great antiquity.

The specimens from the highest terrace showed convincing evidence of having been shaped by human hands. On some of them, the controlled and symmetrical removal of flakes along the edges, in many cases from alternating faces so as to produce a sinuous or denticulate edge, could only be attributed to man. Others closely resembled Lower Paleolithic artifacts from the Xihoudu site in North China and tools from the highest terrace of the Soan River Valley in Indo-Pakistan. Their characteristics, steep edge-flaking on very large flat slabs and split cobbles, are typical of some of the earliest known stone industries of the Old World.

In contrast, tools from the lower terraces and the modern flood plain do not exhibit those very primitive qualities, show little or no desert varnish or abrasion, and are similar to stone industries elsewhere that are attributed to the Upper Paleolithic, or in some cases at the lowest levels, to more recent PaleoIndian occupation. That extremely obvious difference makes one wonder how skeptics of the site's antiquity can account not only for the great disparity in knapping skill but also for the almost complete lack of abrasion and weathering on tools at only a slightly lower elevation, if all the Black's Fork tools are to be considered recent. Surely the brisk prairie winds have been blowing with equal vigor over all the terraces impartially, yet even implements on the next highest terrace surfaces are relatively sharp and only slightly polished on their exposed parts.

The fact that on the highest flood plain remnants representing the oldest alluvial deposits, some tools are far more abraded than others does not necessarily mean different ages, as Wormington suggests, but rather the position of a particular tool in the active streambed. Some are inevitably more exposed to wear than others; those buried in the gravels might very well receive no discernible abrasion at all but could acquire, as surrounding soils were washed away by rain and melting snow after abandonment of the stream, thick coats of desert varnish.

These worn and mahogany-colored specimens appear to be among the crudest and most primitive implements presently known from the Western Hemisphere, yet because of the alternately-flaked edges on many of them, they would seem to be indisputably manmade. In order to support the view that they are merely blanks from a recent quarry site, as some have suggested, that alternate flaking from opposite faces would have to be explained. Surely no flintknapper would contemplate the retouching and refining of such a zigzag or denticulate edge. The presence of heavy coatings of desert varnish on both cortices and flake scars equally also rules out recency.

Based on the unique geomorphic situation at Black's Fork, and on the primitive technology and weathered appearance of the assemblage collected from the highest surfaces, it is perfectly obvious that humans must have been in southwestern Wyoming far back in time. Tools from Europe's Early Paleolithic sites, Abbevillian and Acheulian; specimens from China's Middle Stage of Locality 1 at Zhoukoudian; the so-called handaxes of Chongokni in Korea; all are apparently far more advanced and sophisticated than the coarse slabs of quartzite with their alternately-flaked edges that I collected from the ancient and elevated flood plain. On the issue of the tools' antiquity I stand with the late E. B. Renaud, who was decorated by the French Government for his outstanding contribution to the science of Anthropology, but died almost unrecognized in his adopted country.

There have been other suggestions of very early human occupation far back in the interior of the continent, but they have been vigorously debated and are controversial and generally rejected by the academic and professional community. In many cases this is not because their non-human derivation or recency has been proven, but because of insufficient evidence to decisively establish beyond any doubt the time of early human presence at the places in question. Often the evidence is subject to widely differing interpretation, depending largely on the preconceptions of those doing the interpreting — an apparently inescapable aspect of scientific research. Sites in Alabama, Texas, Utah and Arizona among others have been reported as being clearly far older than most anthropologists have been willing to concede. In general they have been less carefully studied than Old Crow, Black's Fork and especially the Southern California desert sites to be reviewed below. One site, however, at the extreme southern end of North America near Puebla in Mexico, presents an enigma that has remained unresolved.

The Valsequillo Reservoir area south of Puebla has long been known by paleontologists as rich in Pleistocene fossil remains weathering out of bluffs surrounding the reservoir. The bones of such extinct creatures as mammoth, camel, horse and bison have been recovered in some profusion, but human bones have been lacking. However, the exposed sediments have also been known for many years as the source of artifacts of flaked bone and stone (Armenta 1959).

In 1962, excavations on the north shore of the reservoir revealed four sites in which stone tools and vertebrate fossils, including extinct Pleistocene megafauna, were in association: El Horno, El Mirador, Tecacaxco and Hueyatlaco (Irwin-Williams 1967). Considerable further work was done at Hueyatlaco in 1964, 1966, 1968 and 1970 (Steen-McIntyre et al. 1981).

The work at Hueyatlaco was apparently carried out with meticulous attention to detail and stratigraphic identification and analysis. The excavations through several distinct strata revealed a typological sequence of stone artifacts there that was perfectly expectable: large and crude edge-trimmed flake tools in the lowest levels and well-made bifacial tools in the upper strata. The difficulty has been in the dating of the deposits, or more properly how to reconcile the dates obtained by several independent methods with the finely-flaked bifaces in the upper levels. The latter are comparable to stone projectile points not known anywhere on earth earlier than the Late Pleistocene, yet fission-track dating of zircon crystals from two of the overlying volcanic ash layers, obsidian hydration studies and uranium series dating of fossilized camel pelvis in association with the tools gave an average age of about 250,000 years. Very careful pedological and stratigraphic investigation appeared to confirm these dates.

The dilemma posed by these dates is a serious one, for few archaeologists have even attempted to explain the presence of highly sophisticated stone tools such as bifacially flaked knives, scrapers, burins and tanged projectile points in a geological context that insistently proclaims so great an age. According to archaeologist Cynthia Irwin-Williams, "These tools surely were not in use at Valsequillo more than 200,000 years before the date generally accepted for development of analogous tools in the Old World, nor indeed more than 150,000 years before the appearance of *Homo sapiens*" (Szabo et al. 1969: 241).

Various explanations have been offered to explain the apparent discrepancy. The Mexican archaeologist J. L. Lorenzo (1967) suggested that the bifaces had been planted by workers, but this allegation has been refuted by many witnesses, including R. S. MacNeish, F. A. Peterson and H. M. Wormington, who testified to having seen them solidly in situ in the matrix before removal (Steen-McIntyre et al. 1981: 14). Virginia Steen-McIntyre believes that such well-made bifaces originated in this hemisphere far earlier than is now recognized; a theory that is certainly not impossible, but few if any scholars can support her view. My own belief is that the upper stratigraphy was misinterpreted, and that the dated camel bone and the artifacts were washed onto the site from different sources, then covered by redeposited mud and volcanic ash.

It is quite possible that the far more primitive appearing edge-trimmed flake tools in the lower strata are indeed extremely old, and represent an early occupation of the region. Unfortunately, by calling into question the analysis of the upper strata, we tend to discredit the dating of the lower levels as well. Investigation of the site is further complicated by the fact that it is submerged annually by the rising waters of Valsequillo Reservoir.

No such uncertainties exist in the case of the very recently reported cave site in northeastern Brazil, the Toca da Esperanca (De Lumley et al., 1988). Situated 435km west of the Atlantic coast, near the village of Central in the state of Bahia, the cave was discovered by Maria Beltrao in 1982. A stone tool and broken bones of extinct Pleistocene fauna, mostly horse bones, were found in association, and two bones were sent to a laboratory in France for dating by uranium series. The first results gave ages of 200,000 and 350,000 years.

In 1987 the floor of the cave was excavated by an international team under the leadership of Henry de Lumley, a prominent French archaeologist. Participating in the investigations at the site and the laboratory analyses were French, Brazilian, Japanese and American scientists. The floor of the cave was stratified, with the lowest stratum, Level Four, yielding positive evidence of very early human presence: flaked tools of quartz and quartzite in close association with horse bones bearing cut marks presumably made by stone tools.

Several of the bones were dated by uranium series in three different laboratories; at Gif-sur-Yvette in France, at the University of California at Los Angeles, and in the U. S. Geological Survey laboratory at Menlo Park, California. The final dates ranged from 204,000 BP to 295,000 BP.

Attribution of the quartzite tools to human activity is considered to be indisputable, since the nearest source of quartzite is 10km away, and only humans could have brought the quartzite cobbles into the cave. As was pointed out in the report of the investigators, these very early dates tend to support other findings of considerable antiquity in the Americas that have been controversial and slow to gain acceptance.

Despite the still limited state of our knowledge, it has become increasingly clear that people penetrated the continents of the Western Hemisphere far earlier than has been generally believed, adapting successfully to a great variety of environments but none more severe than the Old World climates and landscapes over which their even more primitive ancestors expanded.

There must have been repeated waves of slow movement into the Americas during the glacially-generated low sea stands, as people wandered along the coastal margins and perhaps up the great river valleys into the interior. But there is no such thing as nonperishable evidence. Stone tools in most places were moved down into watercourses and pecked and battered into unrecognizable forms again, crushed in glaciers and mudflows and covered by lava flows. They have been buried under alluvial fans and fathoms of lake sediments, entombed by collapsed caves and rock shelters, and swallowed up by muskeg. Only in very rare circumstances have they come to light for our inspection and study.

In Eurasia far more evidence of very early man has been found, dated and studied. In Africa the discoveries of the Leakeys and Johansen are well known, but in the Americas, partly because extremely deep-seated convictions of recency for man, established early in the present century, have persisted, few scholars have found or recognized evidence of very early human occupation.

The destructive forces of rising sea levels after the termination of glacial climate periods have been described in the preceding chapter; they have accounted for major losses in the remanent stone tools and fossils that must have been deposited on the continental shelves during early human expansion down the Pacific coast.

There are at least two serious obstacles to the establishment of very early human presence in the Western Hemisphere. One is the difficulty to prove beyond any doubt that a given lithic specimen was actually altered by man, even though in some cases no natural means of formation can be proposed, as in the case of alternately flaked edges. As soon as we go beyond flaked stone projectile points, which everyone can recognize, we enter an area of personal experience and judgment which is always subject to challenge by the uninformed. Anyone who has examined areas of natural breakage, like talus slopes, can testify to finding some remarkably convincing specimens, but usually there are some small, telltale features lacking that manmade artifacts normally exhibit. Among these are force lines or conchoidal fracture ridges radiating out from the points of impact that produced flake removals, and which reflect much sharper, harder blows than Nature is apt to deliver; and erailleures, small notches where the blows fell. Regular patterns of flake removals as opposed to random patterns of the distribution of flake scars are also significant attributes of human work, as are beta angles, or the angles of flake removal, which are almost always less than 90 degrees in the case of human alteration.

The other and perhaps greater difficulty is the lack of reliable means of dating stone tools. Even though specimens may be accepted as clearly manmade, and suggest by their morphology considerable antiquity, this is completely unreliable in reaching valid conclusions of age. Numerous examples exist of relatively recent but extremely crude and poorly made assemblages. A case in point is the La Jolla culture in coastal Southern California, securely dated at a few thousand years, and preceded by a much older horizon called San Dieguito in the same general area. The latter assemblages include tools and implements of fine, delicate workmanship and are dated at up to 10,000 BP in the region, while the La Jollan material appears crude and primitive.

Unfortunately, dating by geological estimates is a matter of opinion in most cases, although some geomorphic situations are sufficiently obvious to permit general agreement, as at the Brown site at San Diego described above. But such methods are limited to buried materials in good stratigraphic contexts, and the vast preponderance of putative very early tools are surface finds or have been redistributed from elsewhere.

Unless suitable organic material can be found in indisputable association with stone tools, dating by the various radiometric methods is impossible. Even when such samples are available, dates obtained by radiocarbon methods, uranium series, or potassium/argon are regarded with suspicion, and only accepted with confidence when other means of dating agree. Processes like thermoluminescence and protein racemization require special circumstances and are of little help in most archaeological situations.

Having mentioned all these difficulties in placing tools into a reliable time context, it must also be said that very convincing conclusions, if far from indisputable, can still be reached on the bases of probabilities. When stone artifacts are found without geological provenience nor other means of dating, but which exhibit gross characteristics exactly similar to specimens known to be of great antiquity elsewhere in the world, it would seem specious to insist that they must be recent because of convictions of recency for all evidence discovered in the New World.

If the heavy, slab-like choppers of the high terraces at Black's Fork, trimmed by almost vertical flake removals or alternate blows from both faces, closely resemble the tools of Xihoudu, China, dated at over 1,000,000 BP, and do not resemble any known recent assemblage, it would not seem imprudent to assume that they have considerable antiquity. The fact that the massive quartzite tools of the San Diego coastal zone exactly duplicate quartzite tools from Kehe and Liangshan in China, dated at 600,000 BP, should, as a practical matter, imply a cultural stage far earlier than the clearly more recent and well dated local assemblages found in the area.

The foregoing discussion has been offered to help explain what must seem a paradox: if the Yukon, Black's Fork, San Diego and Brazilian sites are as old as being suggested here, why haven't many other purported early sites been discovered between these widely separated regions? Why is there such a large time disparity between very early sites and the generally accepted sites on the order of 12,000 to 15,000 years before the present?

The answer is simple: in view of the difficulties mentioned above, it is a wonder that *any* very early sites have been located and studied. But it is in the desert sites and localities to be described in the following chapter that the evidence of very early human presence is most perfectly preserved, and where human occupation at very early stages is most convincingly recorded.

CAMEO

The Mojave

Two hundred and fifty thousand years before the present. A major glacio-pluvial climate stage is drawing to a close. In the southern part of the Great Basin the climate is becoming increasingly arid although still suitable for warm-adapted species of grazing and browsing fauna. Humans of the species Homo erectus have intermittently occupied the region now called the Mojave throughout the preceding extended period of humid conditions, but are now gradually drifting out of the area through the passes of the Sierra Nevada to the westward and the Transverse Ranges to the southwest.

The evening sun was sinking down toward the trees above the canyon as the file of dark figures came down through the junipers and out onto the open slope to camp. The autumn air was warm and the people were traveling light. The hunters carried long, antler-tipped spears and small burdens of bundled hides; the young boys had smaller spears and bundles; the women balanced nondescript loads on their heads, and two had infants propped on their hips and dozing. The girls took turns carrying the ember-pack, blowing it up to a cherry red again when it faltered. An old man carried only himself, and that with some difficulty.

The cumbersome poles and shelters were not needed here in the mild climate of the southern Great Basin along the Mojave River. A little morning hoarfrost was scarcely noticed by these tough, hardy people, nor were dustings of snow or even slivers of ice on the ponds and lake margins. They simply made camp near water and wood, and wandered along in all seasons through the grassy valleys and draws and up on the hills, stopping for weeks at a time where convenient campsites were found and food was available.

There was still enough rain over the low, scattered ranges of the Great Basin to keep most of the lakes and ponds potable, although they were far reduced now from their pluvial maximums. The grass came up thick and green along the swales and bottoms in the spring, and many of the gently rounded hills and slopes had clothed themselves in juniper, with piñon pines on the higher elevations. On the low-lying flats south of the Mojave the grasslands and ponds had yielded to vast thickets of mesquite as the climate slowly warmed and became more arid.

Herds of grazing game still ranged the plains east of the Rockies, but here in the southern valleys of the Great Basin and Range Province they no longer proliferated and covered the land. Small bands of camel and horse roamed the flatlands, particularly in the vicinity of the larger lakes, where broad reaches of recently exposed playa now supported rank stands of grass and willows. Mammoth, too, were occasionally present, and tapirs inhabited the marshy lake shores, which were surrounded by broad fringes of rippling tules and reeds.

Deer and antelope were common in the junipers and sage, while huge ground sloths and giant armadillos also foraged through the thickets and meadows, and were especially common in the mesquite to the south.

The small band of humans was camping on a low and largely inactive alluvial fan at the foot of the Calico Mountains above Lake Manix. This meadow at the foot of Mule Canyon and in the lee of the higher slopes had been used periodically for centuries and even millennia by similar small family bands of wandering foragers, descendants of those hardy hunters who had crossed the tundra and the high arctic passes far back in the ancient past. The camping place was a favorite one to which they had returned frequently. It was convenient to the lake, and looked out over the blue water and green shimmer of tules and grass.

The clearing and adjacent slopes had another attraction: here excellent stone was available for working into new tools and implements. Cobbles and boulders of chalcedony and jasper, washed down the canyon in earlier times, littered the ground in places. Broken flakes, cores and fragments were strewn in windrows, marking the sites where people had come for millennia to rough out their choppers, scraping tools and blades.

On the higher slopes of the Calico hills piñon trees still grew, but they were slowly dying off, and the crops of pine nuts the people could harvest were more meager each season. The lake, too, was beginning to show ominous signs and portents. Its waters were not yet too brackish for humans and other land mammals to drink, but its shellfish were beginning to disappear as the salt content almost imperceptibly increased year after year. Both mollusks and fish had been getting smaller and more stunted. The old man had taken, in his youth, mussels more than twice as large as any now in the lake. The slow evaporation without equal replenishment had exposed the ledges and shoals where freshwater shellfish had once abounded. After a strong wind had roiled the waters and turned over the muck on the bottoms, heavy fish die-offs were frequent, and the foul stench of decaying flesh drifted often across the countryside.

Smaller ponds had disappeared completely, and where their last remnants had been no grass would grow. Many favorite campsites were abandoned when the people found, instead of the quiet, cool waters and melodious music of blackbirds, only a ghastly white ghost of a pond surrounded by a dusty tangle of cobwebbed, dead tules and willows.

The little group of humans consisted of the old man, an unmated grown son, two daughters whose mates had attached themselves to the band, a barren and virgin sister of twenty-nine, and five older children plus the two infants. There were perhaps six other such family bands within a radius of two hundred miles. They encountered each other from time to time, were able to make limited conversations together, and were on cordial terms. But like the hunters on the Mackenzie, these people of the southern Great Basin believed they were the only humans on earth, which they supposed extended only a short distance beyond the higher mountains they sometimes saw on the skyline.

Here in the meadow the firewood was soon gathered and piled near the well-used stone hearth. The oldest girl blew up her embers in the black remnants of countless past campfires, and soon the flames were leaping and crackling through the piled brush and dead juniper boughs. As the darkness gathered and the nighthawks and bats began flickering over their heads in the twilight, the people gathered around and hunkered down close to the sizzling slices of antelope haunch broiling there on the rocks. They picked up the hot chunks of meat and ripped away mouthfuls with their strong, white teeth. The fat and juices ran down their chins and glistened on the dark skin in the firelight.

Drawn by the odors of juniper smoke and hot fat, a pair of coyotes crept up to the edge of the warm orange glow cast by the flames. They crouched nervously in the shadows, waiting hopefully and with yellow eyes shining. The people ignored them as always and lay down, one by one, in the dry grass by the hearth to sleep. At last the coyotes trotted off down the slope to prospect among the tules.

The humans napped fitfully. All of them except the infants got to their feet occasionally to wander aimlessly around, relieve their bladders, add fuel to the fire, scratch themselves vigorously and lie down again to be instantly asleep. The two mothers cradled their young against warm, full breasts and nursed them whenever they stirred and whimpered. The tiny creatures almost never cried, for they were rarely laid aside until they were old enough to crawl. All during the times when the females were busy, foraging for roots, nuts and greens, gathering shellfish from the lake shallows or even defecating, their infants were held securely under a strong brown arm.

In the first grey light of morning the people were up and moving around the fire, dodging the smoke, grunting morosely and chewing on more of the tough antelope meat. They decided on the day's forays while squatting there at the hearth. The young men would hunt any game they could find on the lake shores, while the women and children climbed up the slopes above them and gathered ripe piñon cones to bring back to camp in hide bundles. The old man, whose joints were too stiff and sore for hunting or climbing, would stay in the meadow, tend the fire and bask in the sun.

The three hunters strode off down the slope toward the flats with their spears over their shoulders and stone cleavers swinging at their waists in looped rawhide. The youngest one, who was still unmated, felt the excitement of the coming hunt surging through his veins, and he stared eagerly through the thin spirals of mist wreathing the bottomlands, hoping to be the first to sight game. As his searching gaze probed the distant willow thickets and clearings, it crossed and returned to a darker shape there in the gloom, almost a mile away. He kept his eyes on it as they walked along. The blur became a camel browsing its way to the water. Then he made out another, and still another behind it in the willows.

Now he pointed out the game to his companions, feeling a flush of pride as they looked and nodded and grunted admiringly at his prowess. The three stalked carefully down the bare hillside to the nearest cover, then spread out with spears lowered and ready to approach the quarry from different directions in the windless air.

The experienced hunters knew that their best chance of success here was to stampede the animals into the black muck of a slough just beyond where they were browsing. Camels were adapted to and preferred dry country, and despite their broad feet were at a serious disadvantage in soft mud. When forced into it they often became panicky, thrashing and miring themselves long enough for the hunters to surround and dispatch them with their long spears.

The intent, brown figures crept noiselessly forward toward the shaggy, dun shapes of the camels, glimpsed at times through the curling mist in the willows. Suddenly one of the long necks jerked up in alarm; the narrow head with its pendulous lips, flaring nostrils and bulging yellow eyes swiveled around suspiciously. A stray wisp of scent or a rustle of brush had been caught, and now the big animal began to crash away through the low shrubbery, followed by two more adults and a young, half-grown yearling.

Instantly the three hunters jumped up yelping and brandishing their spears, trying to head off the escaping camels and drive them into the tule-lined slough. The animals went lurching away; the dark forms of their pursuers followed, leaping over low bushes and scrambling through thickets, running full tilt to force them into the sucking, bottomless trap of the marsh.

The three larger animals, recognizing the danger instinctively, refused to be driven and one after another slipped by the threatening, blustering hunters to disappear in the fog. But the yearling camel dashed straight into the slough, not having had any experience with the treacherous muck, and immediately began to flounder as he sank through the soft stuff to his belly. The men dashed up and threw their spears into his ribs before he could thrash his way clear. As their victim's struggles grew weaker, the youth clambered through the black, blood-stained bog, threw himself on the laboring form of the camel and slashed the extended throat with his sharp stone cleaver. The yearling's life gushed out in a red torrent into the churned mud and water.

Hauling and straining, and at times falling full length into the black slime themselves, the three at last managed to work their trophy out of the clutching, malodorous mud of the slough and onto the bank. The carcass of the camel, although not yet fully grown, already weighed over six hundred pounds. But the men were extremely powerful and energetic, and years of experience had taught them where and how to apply their great strength. Nevertheless, when the bedraggled hulk lay in the clear ready for skinning and butchering, they were exhausted.

The three filthy scarecrows, panting and blowing, left their kill and walked down the slough to the nearest clear water. They were covered from head to foot with a mixture of blood and black, clinging slime, their eyes shown whitely out of hideous dark masks, like owls peering out of holes in a tree. But after splashing and scrubbing and rinsing themselves in the chilly water, they sprawled on the ground in the yellow sunshine and felt the warm, soothing surges of pleasure pulse through their bodies. The youngest knew a keener joy, for he had not only first sighted the quarry but had made the kill also, and the hide would belong to him if he claimed it. But without a woman it would be useless to him, since he could not cure it himself, and in any case hides were far less necessary for survival here in the benign climate of the south.

The meat, bones, organs and entrails were communal property and would be parcelled out among the members of the band as needed. The three hunters skinned the yearling camel and cut up the carcass, carefully removing the heart, liver and kidneys. Their stone blades slashed easily through the tough hide and flesh of the animal, and when the beast was dismembered they piled the parts into three bundles of over one hundred and fifty pounds each, lashed them with hide strings, and heaved the loads onto their shoulders.

Tonight they would feast on the tongue, brains, liver and heart, and perhaps crack open the lower leg bones for the sweet, creamy marrow inside. Over the next two weeks the meat would be completely consumed, adults eating over three pounds a day and the children somewhat less. Wrapped in hide away from the sun it would keep no longer except for the marrow, which would still be sweet a month later.

Despite the weight of their burdens, the hunters trudged up the hill in high spirits late in the afternoon, laughing and calling back and forth to each other, pretending to stagger under their mighty loads, groaning in simulated agony and rolling their eyes in expressive exaggeration. When they reached the camping place the nut harvesters had returned, and exclaimed with pleasure and anticipation when they saw the piles of juicy, fresh meat. The hunters acted out their ages-old pretense of modest indifference.

CHAPTER 5

The Desert Sites:
Vanished Lakes and Fossil Fans

For over 1,500 miles behind the Western Cordillera; the towering crests of the Cascades, the Sierra Nevada and the Peninsular Ranges of Southern California, the deserts of North America lie shimmering in the sun, parched and brown in summer and with brief flashes of ephemeral green after the rare winter rains. From the air the stark white sands of dry, long-vanished lakes, the bleached bones of a once-verdant and well-watered land, can be seen to wander like giant stepping stones down the continent; down through the Mojave and the Colorado Desert and the seared and thirsty plains of Mexico.

These are lonely lands now almost uninhabited except where water is available close to the mountain slopes, or has been brought over miles of aqueducts to make the desert basins fertile. But for hundreds of square miles the only water falls in thundershowers from the sky, lights up the washes and slopes and ridges briefly in bright displays of blooms, then fades again into the dull browns and greys of the muted landscape. Rivers that carry runoff and snowmelt down from the mountains in the spring dwindle gradually and disappear in the sands of ancient lakebeds. Travelers on the roads see wide expanses of cool, blue water dissolve and vanish; mirages in the shimmering air.

Far back in the distant past the lakes existed. For thousands of years during the humid glacio-pluvials of the Pleistocene the inland basins held sparkling fresh water, ruffled with whitecaps in the winds of spring, deep blue under the vivid azure skies. Fringed with tules and shallow marshes, the lakes supported a vast catalogue of living creatures. Shoals of freshwater clams and mussels; fish and frogs and water snakes; waterfowl, herons, gulls and shorebirds and small mammals prospered in and around the cool waters. On the surrounding slopes grasses must have provided abundant pasturage for camel, horse and mammoth and occasional herds of longhorned bison, for we find their fossil remains weathering out of the now-desiccated lake margins.

On the higher slopes and ridges thickets of juniper and groves of piñon trees fed and sheltered deer and peccary, and in the fall the piñon mast attracted enormous flocks of bandtailed pigeons and lesser bands of turkeys. Higher still on the skyline and gleaming in the crystal air were the glaciated peaks of the ranges, bulwarks against the bitter blizzards of winter raging against their western slopes.

But now in the present arid interglacial climate the lakes are gone, and only the vestiges of barren sands and shorelines etched into the solid rock of steep slopes and drifts of cobbles remind us of their past existence. Lizards lie basking on desert pavements of richly-varnished boulders once inter-mixed with soils and vegetation. In these mahogany-colored mosaics on the higher slopes and saddles, overlooking what were long ago blue lakes and fertile marshes, are wedged other vestiges of the distant past, the discarded stone tools and implements of ancient man.

These desert surfaces have undergone successive transformations over many millions of years. Huge lakebeds have been uplifted by pressures below the earth's crust so that now they are mountain ranges. Other areas have been lowered by downfaulting, producing the lake basins that we see today. Over more modest time periods of perhaps 2,000,000 years, recurring glacio-pluvial climate stages alternating with interglacials have successively caused surface changes in the topography of the deserts. During arid cycles lasting thousands of years, the ranges have been severely eroded, with their soils stripped away and moved down the mountainsides and canyons to spread out on the lower slopes and valley floors in the forms of cuestas and alluvial fans, often many miles in extent and hundreds of feet thick.

The process of erosion is undoubtedly promoted and intensified by the lack of vegetational ground cover in arid climates. A single cloudburst can move enormous amounts of soil and rocks downslope through canyons and washes in the form of mudflows, but even more effective and constant in periods of meager rainfall is wind deflation, which removes fine soils without displacing loose rock materials, only lowering and concentrating them into thick carpets of densely-packed rocks at the surface. Such desert pavements, once formed, then become almost immune to further erosion until the next climate change.

With the onset of a humid glacio-pluvial stage the process is reversed. Ample moisture fosters the growth of trees, shrubs and grasses, producing organic soils over the centuries and millennia which bury and disrupt some of the rock pavements. The alluvial fans at the mouths of canyons become inactive and quiescent, covered with soils and vegetation except for minor drainage channels in the form of streams, which cut and dissect the fanglomerate into ravines and minor canyons.

After perhaps 20,000 years another arid cycle returns the vast sweep of countryside behind the mountains to its barren state, stripping away ground cover and soils and exposing the underlying rocks of pavements on plateaus and ridges, to continue the consolidation process and to acquire additional coatings of desert varnish. Canyons in the desert ranges again discharge alluvium onto the fans at their feet, filling the dissected channels and gullies with mud and heavy gravels, so producing cross-sections composed of sediments of vastly different ages; a complex pattern difficult to unravel.

The Calico Mountain Range, named by early miners for the variegated colors and patches on its slopes, rises in a southern area of the Great Basin and Range Province called the Mojave Desert, just north of Barstow, California. Trending roughly southwest to northeast, it overlooks the Manix Basin to the east, the site of a large Pleistocene lake which, in pluvial periods, was fed by the Mojave River, draining the Transverse Ranges to the southwest. Some 20,000 years ago, during the Wisconsin glacio-pluvial stage, overflow from Lake Manix cut Afton Canyon in the northeast sector, causing the lake to drain substantially and probably leaving only marshy areas along the margins of the Mojave River on the basin floor.

During the slow process of mountain building, the Calico mountains incorporated a wide variety of different rocks and minerals, among them volcanics, sedimentary rocks and precious metals, mostly silver for the miners. Important for earlier human exploiters was chalcedony, a siliceous rock derived from silica gels laid down on an earlier lake bottom millions of years ago, compressed and heated into hard, brittle rock when the range was uplifted. Exposed by erosion, outcropping beds of chalcedony were broken up and carried down the canyons in chunks and fragments ideal for the shaping of stone tools by early inhabitants of the Manix Basin.

In the northeast sector of the Calicos, Mule Canyon discharged such rock material onto the huge alluvial fan at its foot, but at some time in the distant past seismic action uplifted the fan, cutting it off from its source of supply. Dr. Ted Oberlander, a desert geomorphologist from the University of California, Berkeley, is convinced that the erosion on the fan must represent at least 200,000 years since the fan was detached from its source area (1983). Very heavy erosion over the millennia since its detachment has reduced what was once a relatively smooth ramp to a complex area of hills, ridges, deep gullies and canyons. Soils analyses of the remaining top surfaces have suggested an age of 80,000 to 125,000 years since aggradation ceased, but some of the top surfaces have subsequently been removed (Bischoff et al. 1981).

Over 40 years ago the late Ritner J. Sayles, a San Bernardino County Museum Fellow in Archaeology, discovered on the slopes and ridges above the Manix Basin, including the inactive and eroded Mule Canyon fan, objects of chalcedony and other chert forms which were clearly man-made artifacts and apparently very old. Sayles brought them to the attention of Dr. Gerald Smith, then Museum Director, and Ruth DeEtte Simpson, then of the Southwest Museum. They both felt that a comprehensive survey should be undertaken through the Archaeological Survey Association of Southern California.

In 1954 the Lake Manix Survey was begun. In addition to more recent sites below the incised shorelines of vanished Lake Manix, the higher slopes disclosed numerous primitive tools including ovate bifaces and chopping tools, large scrapers and workshop debitage or waste material from percussive flaking. No projectile points were seen, and none of the older tools could be found below the highest shoreline of Lake Manix, indicating deposition before the lake drained, or more than 20,000 years ago by some unknown amount.

Dr. Louis Leakey of Olduvai Gorge fame was brought to the area in 1963 and shown the sites by Ruth Simpson. In addition to the surface scatters recorded by the Survey, specimens were seen below the surface weathering out of cutbanks from earlier mining activity on the fan. Since materials discovered below the surface in what could be considered primary or original deposition offered the possibility of dating by geological analysis, and since such materials must have been deposited before the detachment of the alluvial fan from its source, Leakey felt that a major excavation project should be undertaken. Because of his considerable prestige adequate funding could be obtained; the National Geographic Society, the University of Pennsylvania Museum and the Isotope, Wenner-Gren, L. S. B. Leakey and Wilkie Brothers Foundations all provided funds for the work from 1964 to 1970.

Digging was begun in 1964 by both paid crew members and volunteers, the latter being carefully trained by the professionals. In the next six years two very impressive master pits were excavated to depths of over 20 feet, as well as a number of test pits and trenches. The work was directed by Leakey under the field supervision of Ruth Simpson. Tight controls were maintained, and only small hand tools were used; dental picks, hammers and chisels. Specimens encountered and suspected of having been modified by man were carefully triangulated, recorded and photographed before removal, unless discovered in the screens through which all soils were sifted. The sediments were passed through meshes of half inch, quarter inch and window screen before being discarded.

About 300 specimens judged to be stone tools and 3,000 technical flakes, those showing signs of human work, were recovered from the sediments and analyzed in the laboratory, numbers that continue to grow as digging and lab analyses proceed. Epoxy replicas were made of some of the more important artifacts, which were considered too valuable to display publicly.

In 1970 the Calico International Conference was convened at the San Bernardino County Museum and at the site. Nearly 100 distinguished scientists and prehistorians from six continents attended, were shown the site, the stone artifacts and excavated features, and were briefed by Leakey, Simpson, Rainer Berger of the Radiocarbon Laboratory at the University of California, Los Angeles, and Thomas Clements, geologist for the project. During the four days of the conference, they had ample time to examine the evidence and geological context, and to confer and argue among themselves as to whether the project results did indeed represent the presence of early man at Calico.

The great stumbling block to acceptance, in the view of most of the participants, was the apparent great age of the sediments in which the stone specimens were enclosed. Most came already convinced of man's relative recency in the Western Hemisphere, but Clements was proposing an age of 70,000 years. Even more unsettling were the expressed convictions of several geologists that the deposits were far older than Clements' estimate; ages of up to 500,000 years were suggested.

A number of scientists were convinced of man's presence at the site during the time when the sediments were being deposited, regardless of when that time would prove to be. Among them were Thomas E. Lee of Ottawa, John Witthoft of the University of Pennsylvania, Robert L. Stephenson of the University of South Carolina, and George F. Carter of Texas A & M University. Their reasons for acceptance were based entirely on the nature of the lithic specimens and their distribution in the sediments, matters which will be discussed below.

Many of the participants were fence-sitters, unwilling to express their opinions for fear of their colleagues' disapproval and the damaging of their reputations as "prudent scientists." Certainly some were honestly perplexed and unable to reach a conclusion, but the most pronounced and outspoken conservatives did not hesitate to state their opinions that all of the purported artifacts were actually just shaped by percussion in cataracts and pressure in mudflows. Several prominent participants still maintained that view 16 years later at the time of writing.

Because of the negative reactions and expressed skepticism of some of the scientists attending the conference, most of the funding institutions terminated their support of the project, and it has since been continued on a more limited basis, primarily by volunteers. Dr. Leakey's death in 1972 was a severe blow, as was the drying up of funds, but contributions from the public, support from minor foundations, and dues and donations from the Friends of Calico, Inc., as well as valuable assistance from the Federal Bureau of Land Management, has permitted the field and laboratory work to continue.

A third master pit, located between the two original ones, is being excavated by trained volunteer workers. Others are contributing hundreds of hours in the laboratory, examining, classifying and describing the thousands of lithic specimens that have been recovered. Work is underway on a modern visitors' center which will greatly improve interpretive and educational services to the public. Distinguished scientists have contributed time and effort to verify the specimens as humanly produced, to develop finite dates for them, and to understand the complicated geology of the alluvial fan.

In 1975 Clay A. Singer, a graduate student at the University of California at Los Angeles and a specialist in lithic technologies, began a study of wear patterns on the Calico tools, using microscopic examination and photography. The results indicated definite use wear on many of the specimens: battering, crushing, micro-spalling and polishing that could only be attributed to human use (Singer 1979).

In 1981 James L. Bischoff and associates reported a minimum age of about 200,000 years for the artifact-bearing deposits, based on soil analyses, geomorphic stratigraphy and radiometric measurements. Dr. Bischoff, of the U. S. Geological Survey at Menlo Park, California, scraped calcium carbonate or calcrete coatings off of artifacts that had been exposed near the bottom in one of the pits. This white, crystalline material, known to housewives as the white scale that forms on waterpipes, was suitable for dating by uranium series, and was measured by Bischoff in the Menlo Park laboratories, and by Dr. T. L. Ku at the University of Southern California, with the latter using slightly different formulae. Both scientists arrived at the same conclusion: that the tests were reliable and showed an age of 200,000 +/- 20,000 years for the coating on the tools. Dr. Roy Shlemon of Newport Beach, California, estimated after extensive study and examination of the soils at depth that the artifact-bearing lower sediments were on the order of 150,000 to 200,000 years old (Bischoff et al. 1981).

The period of time that passed between the deposition of the tools and the formation of the rind of calcium carbonate that was measured is unknown and could be very extensive. The artifacts must have been deposited during a relatively humid period for the locality to have been occupied by man, and in such a climate the fan would have been inactive except for stream flow. In order to develop the calcium carbonate rinds on tools and cobbles the latter would have had to be buried deeply enough to become subject to ground water action over a very long period in an arid environment.

Other laboratory tests were made in connection with an interesting feature uncovered near the bottom of Master Pit II. This is an arrangement of large cobbles or small boulders placed in a semicircle about two feet across. The stones are roughly the same size and most are tapered with the smaller ends pointing in toward the center and dipping slightly. To most observers the arrangement looks like a fireplace or hearth. It is difficult to imagine how such a feature could have been formed by the random forces of Nature.

In an attempt to test whether the formation had indeed been used as a fireplace, one of the rocks was removed and sliced into one-inch cubes, each labeled as to what part of the rock it came from. These were sent to Dr. Vaslav Bucha of the Geophysical Institute of the Czechslovakian Academy of Science, a specialist in magnetism and magnetic dating. Bucha's tests indicated to him that the rock had been heated in the past, with the end that had been nearest to the center much more highly heated than the rear portion. Control rocks from the same level showed no evidence of past heating.

As might be expected, these results were welcomed by the investigators, but later tests have cast doubts on them. Two other cobbles from the feature were subjected to thermoluminescent testing by Bischoff at Menlo Park. This process measures the radioactivity in the rock, relying on the fact that high heating drives it out, whereupon it is slowly reacquired from the environment at a rate that can be determined. But Bischoff found that his samples were completely saturated with radioactivity, indicating to him that the rocks had not been heated in the past 400,000 years, the time needed for that particular kind of rock to become fully saturated.

So now there are several alternatives to consider. Was the testing flawed in some way? Is the fireplace over 400,000 years old? Is it a man-made feature but never used as a fireplace, or is it simply a natural feature that by incredible coincidence closely resembles a fireplace? The answer to these questions has yet to be determined, but the presence of well-made stone tools in the vicinity and at the same level as the feature makes evident the fact that humans were already present when it was formed.

Most damaging for acceptance of the site as valid evidence of the presence of early man was an article, "The Calico Site: Artifacts or Geofacts?" written by C. Vance Haynes and published in Science, a very influential journal, in 1974. It convinced thousands of archaeologists, anthropologists and prehistorians all over the world that the purported artifacts were simply rocks broken in mudflows and by other natural agencies to resemble tools, and that an age for the lower deposits of over 600,000 years was "in line with current geological estimates."

Scientists in London to whom I showed Calico specimens in June of 1984 were surprised. They had read Haynes' report and were under the impression that the case had long since been settled; there was no evidence for early man at Calico. But if, as Haynes claims, the lithic specimens there were simply broken and flaked by pressures in mudflows and stream battering during transport down the fan, certain plainly evident facts need to be explained.

The specimens identified as artifacts, along with concussively struck flakes and debitage, were concentrated in specific zones or strata within the fan sediments, usually at levels relatively free of heavy gravels and suggesting a humid environment. Since the fanglomerates were all deposited by the same natural forces — flash floods, mudflows, etc., — random breakage should include artifact-like objects from top to bottom of the fan structure, if symmetrical flaking was being produced by natural pressures and percussion. It clearly was not.

The recovered flakes, cores and tools are almost without exception composed of good, selected material, whereas large chunks of poor quality chalcedony and jasper, riddled with holes and irregularities, are common in the fan at all levels. If hydraulic forces or earth pressures were responsible for the breakage and flaking, specimens resembling utilized flakes, cores and tools but composed of the riddled and faulted material should also be present; in fact, would obviously have been the most susceptible to flaking as they were tumbled about. There are other stone materials in the fan, but mostly they do not have flakes removed from them, except for a few soft limestones.

As Leakey pointed out, this high degree of selectivity is something Nature simply cannot do.

Some of the larger chopping tools had been edge-trimmed by striking away flakes alternately from opposite faces along one or more edges, producing zigzag or sinuous effects when seen edge-on. The result is highly symmetrical, with the flake scars of almost identical dimensions, clearly having been produced by turning the workpiece or core over after each blow, striking each blow with approximately equal force and careful, purposeful direction. No means can be visualized by which Nature could have accomplished this even once, yet several such pieces were concentrated in the limited area of the excavations.

The fact that the Calico assemblage closely resembles tool assemblages from very early sites in China, where they are authenticated by the association of human fossil remains, seems highly significant and will be discussed fully in a later chapter. Singer's work on wear patterns has also demonstrated important support for the human origin of the tools, for wear abrasion is always on functional edges or points on the artifacts and not on other parts — again inexplicably selective if attributed to the random work of Nature.

The work at Calico over more than 20 years has suggested rather convincingly that humans were there at least 200,000 years ago, but there are vast gaps in our knowledge. Indeed, the only fact of which we are certain is their presence. The catalogue of what we don't know yet is enormous. We don't even know much about their appearance except by supposition. Even their species is unknown still except by reference to Old World models; best estimates now suggest either a very primitive, transitional form of *Homo sapiens*, the species to which modern man belongs, or a late form of *Homo erectus*, but this is a poorly understood period of human evolution.

The areas exposed by the excavations on the eroded alluvial fan have generally been thought to represent a quarry site, a location where good stone for flaking into tools was available. Great quantities of debitage, the waste lithic debris around a flaking station, attest to the fact that stone tools and implements were produced there. But wear patterns on some of the tools and the presence of a fireplace, if that is what it is, suggest that the site was also a camping place or at least a locality where other objects were processed — objects of wood, bone or ivory; hides for thongs, clothing and pouches. But these have long since vanished into dust or been transported down the fan to lie buried under hundreds of feet of lake sediments.

Even the exact functions of the tools are speculative. Many are designated "choppers" or "scrapers" but exactly what was being chopped or scraped is a matter for conjecture. Implements called "handaxes" by the investigators are especially problematical; their purpose or function is completely unknown. A few tool forms suggest their use; concave scrapers, sometimes called "spokeshaves," usually appear to be the right size and shape for dressing down wooden spear or lance shafts. Round stone balls are almost beyond doubt intended for use as bolas, to be encased in hide, attached to thongs in pairs and whirled around overhead to be cast at running animals, to go spinning off to wrap around their legs and bring them down. Since these are still in use in some parts of the world, we need not question their function.

In 1985 the controversy over the evidence for early man at Calico took a strange turn. Several of the most convincing small flake tools from deep in the excavations were taken to the annual meeting of the Society for American Archaeology in Denver, Colorado, and shown to a number of prominent but adamantly skeptical scientists. The result was surprising, to say the least. The tools were finally accepted as man-made, but now the objection was that they could not possibly have so great an age, even though 200,000 years was modest compared to many of the estimates for the age of the fan sediments offered by geologists at the Conference in 1970, and the greatly eroded and dissected condition of the fan plainly argued extreme antiquity for the formation. One highly respected archaeologist actually suggested that the tools he was shown must have somehow fallen into the excavation from the surface, since flaked tools of such sophistication are not known from anywhere on earth dated to such an early time period. Of course he was just uninformed; almost identical small flake tools have been recovered from the upper levels of Locality 1 at Zhoukoudian, China, and are securely dated at between 300,000 and 200,000 BP, the approximate age of the Calico specimens.

In the fall of 1986 a discovery, still unpublished at the time of writing, was made that is expected to strongly reinforce and support the uranium series dating of the Calico site. Dr. George Carter and Fred Budinger, former Curator of the Calico Project, were examining a cutbank in the vicinity of the former Lake Manix shoreline at the foot of the Mule Canyon fan. This is an area rich in the fossil remains of Pleistocene megafauna, discovered and examined by Dr. George Jefferson of the Page Museum at Rancho LaBrea in Los Angeles. The bones of mammoth, horse, camel and bison, as well as sabertooth and dire wolf, have been found weathering out of lake sediments below a volcanic ash layer that has been securely dated by Potassium/Argon at 185,000 BP.

Ever since discovery of these fossil-bearing sediments, it has been hoped that evidence of human presence might be found in association with the extinct mammal bones. Such evidence has now been found: small stone specimens apparently worked by man and more than 20 feet below the dated volcanic ash stratum at the foot of the Calico/Mule Canyon fan (Carter and Budinger, personal communication), but the site will be excavated and the possibility exists of even more rewarding finds in the form of human fossil material.

The new evidence and dating would seem to corroborate rather convincingly the judgments of Leakey, Simpson and their associates that the antiquity of man in America would eventually prove to be irrefutable. One can always suggest that a single radiometric date is inconclusive, but when two completely independent means of measure agree so closely the possibility of substantial error becomes exceedingly remote. If human skeletal remains can be discovered below the dated ash layer, and can be identified positively as *Homo erectus*, the question of very early human presence will be settled.

There is no reason to suppose that the Calico site is unique, either in the region of the Manix Basin or in the vast sweep of once-verdant lake country behind the mountains. It is simply the site that has been found and excavated.

There is equally no reason to doubt that there are older sites still waiting to be discovered, for obviously people did not leapfrog from Asia to Calico. But it is quite possible that the careful, painstaking nature of the work at Calico will stand as a monument to Louis Leakey, Ruth Simpson and all of the patient, dedicated volunteers who have dug their way far down into the earth with chisels and dental picks.

About 150 miles south of the Calico Mountains lies the Yuha Desert. In the southwest corner of the Imperial Valley and in the rainshadow of the Southern California Peninsular Range, it is hot, dry and sparsely grown to cactus and creosote bushes that are stunted and widely spaced. This is low desert, in places well below sea level, and in the summer months it lies shimmering and baking under the glaring sun. Not many creatures can survive here; a few lizards, snakes, kangaroo rats and coyotes; a few hardy species of birds, but these the traveler rarely sees.

Much of the Yuha Desert is covered by ancient and eroded alluvial fans emerging from the adjacent mountain canyons, and great expanses of cuestas, or slope-washed soils, running for miles out onto the desert floor. These were truncated and incised in the pluvial periods of the Pleistocene by Lake Le Conte, a huge body of fresh water that almost filled the Imperial and Coachella Valley basins. Its ancient shorelines are heavily etched into solid rock at the northern end.

In the southern part of the Yuha Desert, near the border with Mexico, a very old and long-since inactive alluvial fan, eroded and dissected like the one at Calico, enters the valley and is spread far out toward the beachline of the vanished lake. Beside it to the south the modern drainage channel has cut down through the ancient alluvium and formed a desert wash about half a mile across, dry on the surface in normal times but carrying underground runoff from the nearby range. Until recently this nourished on the floor and sloping walls of the arroyo, called the Yuha Pinto Wash, thick growths of ironwood and mesquite.

In the fall of 1976, a tropical storm of unusual intensity, named "Kathleen" by the Weather Bureau, cut its way across the mountains of Baja California near the border. In the United States bridges were destroyed and several people lost their lives. Possibly 12 inches of rain fell on the Pinto drainage, and most of it went roaring down Yuha Pinto Wash, scouring away centuries-old trees, depositing layers of silt up to ten feet thick in places on the floor, and cutting an almost vertical cliff 75 feet high along the northern bank of the wash.

A few days after the storm, when the wash had dried out, the late W. M. Childers, an archaeologist from the Imperial Valley College Museum, went to the wash and examined the exposure. He found what he recognized as a large stone artifact lying loosely on the surface near the base of the cliff. Convinced that it had been washed out of the adjacent cliff, he notified me, and with Dr. Emma Lou Davis of the Great Basin Foundation, we examined the area with care (Childers and Minshall 1980).

Our brief inspection revealed several coarsely flaked chopping tools and scrapers in the matrix near the bottom of the fresh exposure, and two small pieces of bone lying on the surface at the base of the cliff. These later proved to be a human talus bone or ankle bone and a human phalange, one of the bones of the feet. Although they were covered with the same silts as the adjacent buried sediments, they could not be positively associated with it, and thus were undatable.

Permission to conduct limited operations was obtained from the Department of the Interior, since the area was under the control of the Bureau of Land Management. Students from the Imperial Valley College made an inch by inch search of the exposure and collected cultural materials under the direction of Jay von Werlhoff, Curator of Archaeology and Childers, Curator of Paleoanthropology. All specimens were carefully plotted, photographed and recorded before removal. In addition, limited excavation was conducted on the floor of the wash to clarify the geological situation. Excavation into the cliff face was considered too dangerous because of the apparent instability of the vertical and even overhanging wall above.

A surface survey of the area immediately above the wash on the ancient fan surface disclosed evidence of occupation by a PaleoIndian horizon called Malpais which probably dated to the terminal Pleistocene or possibly earlier. These finds, typical stone artifacts and cleared spaces on the desert floor, had no relationship to the crude tools exposed far below at the base of the fan.

The artifacts exposed by the flood were found in a gravel stratum just above the floor of the wash, and directly overlying what is called the Palm Springs Formation; silts, fine sands and reddish clays of the Colorado River Delta considered to be of Middle Pleistocene age, or about 500,000 years old (Woodring 1931). Also resting on this formation was a thick layer of calcrete, a calcium carbonate accretion which suggested the presence of a hot spring at some time in the past. Above the culture-bearing stratum were several layers of different and clearly defined alluvial sediments, some composed of silts and fine sands and others enclosing heavy boulders.

Far down the surface of the fan and miles away, the ancient beachline that truncated the fan has been dated by radiocarbon measurement of fresh-water mussel shell, or rather not dated, for the sample was beyond the range of measure or more than 50,000 years old (Hubbs et al. 1965:90). Comparison with the soils there and those in the vicinity of the Yuha Pinto Wash site showed that the latter were far older on the surface. How much older than surface soils the buried sediments at the base of the fan might be is undetermined, but they could easily be older than Calico.

The stone tools give little indication of their age except by reference to similar but dated assemblages elsewhere, but the Lower Paleolithic stage apparently persisted over long periods of time in some parts of the Old World, notably in China, where the oldest levels at Zhoukoudian have yielded specimens closely resembling those from Yuha Pinto Wash. The assemblage numbers 80 artifacts; choppers, chopping tools, scrapers and utilized flakes. They seem somewhat cruder than the Calico tools, but are difficult to compare because the stone material of which they are made is more intractable; porphyritic andesites and metabasalts as opposed to the fine-grained and brittle chalcedony and jasper of the Calico fan.

Many aspects are similar, however. Both assemblages show obvious evidence of bipolar flaking, as does Zhoukoudian, and some of the tools from both California sites have been bifacially flaked from alternating faces, a maneuver impossible for Nature to perform. But most of the tools from the Yuha Pinto Wash site are generally amorphous; their morphologies dependent on the shapes of cores or flakes from which they were formed. Some chunks and thick flakes from which chopping tools and scrapers have been flaked appear to have been obtained through a process of throwing; hurling cobbles against boulders with great force to explode them into fragments of various sizes and shapes, and frequently producing sharp-edged objects usable without further modification or needing only a minimum of trimming. This also was typical of Early Paleolithic sites in China (Zhang 1985:147).

The artifacts show abrasion in varying amounts. Their edges and contours have been slightly blurred and softened, alteration which suggests polish caused by blowing dust and sand rather than stream abrasion. This would suggest that they had lain on the surface for an extended period of time during an arid interglacial climate stage before being buried in the fan sediments. Since it seems unlikely that early humans could have occupied the low desert during such a forbidding climate regime, they must have been there in a preceding pluvial stage. That humid period was most probably Isotope Stage 10 on the order of 250,000 to 300,000 years ago, or even Stage 12, 350,000 years ago. Both the geomorphology and the nature of the artifacts tend to argue the greater age, for the tools are buried under more than 70 feet of alluvium including heavy boulders, in a fan deposit almost 10 miles long. But these ages are merely estimates and the true time of human presence has yet to be determined.

The clustering of the artifacts in a relatively restricted zone at the Yuha Pinto Wash site suggests that they must have been deposited at that locality or very close by, and this impression is strengthened by their proximity to the spring feature. Unfortunately, failure to be able to excavate the site because of strictures imposed by the Bureau of Land Management has led to the tantalizing suspicion that rich deposits of artifacts and fossil bone lie buried just beyond reach and out of sight. Indeed, one small fragment of bone, unidentifiable as to species but quite possibly related to the recovered human bone collected from the surface, was found weathering out of the matrix with the artifacts.

The advanced ages proposed above were rendered very plausible by a very exciting development in 1988. George Miller, curator of paleontology at the Imperial Valley College Barker Museum and a professor at the college, along with a research team from the college, discovered a mammoth skeleton and excavated it from sediments in the badlands east of Borrego Springs, California. Several of the rib bones had cut marks on them which could only be explained by human activity. The marks are V-shaped in cross section and exactly like marks experimentally produced on green bone by the research team. No animal is known with teeth that could have produced them; only very hard, sharp edges like those of stone choppers could conceivably have left such marks — tools wielded with considerable force. The only stones in the vicinity are tiny, well-rounded pebbles, and very few of those.

No stone choppers have been yet discovered, but if human hunters butchered the mammoth, they must have brought their tools with them and taken them away when they left the scene. The nearest suitable stone for chopping tools is many miles away, so they would have been unlikely to discard them. There is no likelihood that the bones could have been cut by pressure against sharp rocks or shifting and erosion.

The bones are dated at between 300,000 BP and 460,000 BP on the basis of several indications, the most convincing being uranium series on the fossil bone itself conducted by James Bischoff of the U. S. Geological Survey at Menlo Park, California. This yielded an age of over 300,000 years, the limit to which measurement was possible. The finding was supported by Potassium Argon dates on volcanic ash in the same stratum, biostratigraphic evidence (Microtus vole) and paleomagnetic data.

No other sites of comparable antiquity have been excavated in the deserts of the West, but these areas cover thousands of square miles today, and as in similar regions all over the world, the minimal amounts of rain and especially the very low humidity tend to enhance the preservation of most materials. Old shoes and other articles discarded by General Patton's troops, training in the desert for World War II operations nearly a half century ago, can still be found lying on the surface and little changed. The hair and dung of ground sloths believed to have become extinct thousands of years ago have been recovered in desert caves. And ancient stone tools that were deposited far back in the Pleistocene lie on terraces and benches overlooking dry lakes that were once rich and generous environments for man.

In Nevada's Valley of Fire, just north of Lake Mead; on the terraces that overlook Dry Lake Manly in Death Valley; down through the California deserts and far down into Baja California, the mahogany-colored, thickly varnished and wind-polished Lower Paleolithic tools are fixed in the desert pavements: heavy, crude choppers, scrapers and implements of unknown purpose. Undated and inscrutable, they represent scores and possibly hundreds of millennia, and untold generations of primitive foragers. Discarded and mislaid in grassy meadows and the ashes of ancient campfires, they speak of pluvial periods in a greener land, a land of trees and grass and lakes and bountiful food resources for the taking.

In the basin of Pleistocene Lake China, much of it a military reserve and thus virtually undisturbed by pothunters and offroad vehicle activity, Dr. Emma Lou Davis has spent many seasons examining the ancient lake bed and surrounding ridges. Fed by the Owens River draining the Sierra Nevada, a generous lake and marsh environment has been present during the pluvial climates of the past, and both stone artifacts and vertebrate fossil remains are scattered over the surfaces of the lake bed and the adjacent higher land forms overlooking it (Davis 1986).

The materials in the bed of the lake can be dated well into the terminal Wisconsin, about 15,000 years ago, and down into the Holocene. Dart points that Davis considers to be proto-Clovis have been recovered from the present lake bed surface, while far cruder macrolithic choppers have been collected from nearby ridges. The latter have been surface finds without usable geological context for the most part, but an exception has been a series of localities at Basalt Ridge in the northwest sector.

Basalt Ridge is rich in disarticulated, and presumably butchered, animal remains in general association with stone tools. Permission to trench the area was denied by the U. S. Navy, but exposed stratigraphy revealed, according to Davis, "upper dune sands draped over a basalt core. An argillaceous (clayey) paleosol is exposed about halfway downslope over alluvial gravels and a lower calcic paleosol (dated 10,800 +/- 310 B. P.) Beneath that is a sequence of blocky marsh deposits that contain disarticulated remains of extinct animals, including the 42,000 year old mammoth, camel and horse, in addition to coyote, vole, shorebirds and fish" (1986:86).

The mammoth referred to above was a mammoth tooth and two finishing flakes that were considered to be definitely products of human activity. All three objects were embedded in a chunk of marsh mud. They were dated by C. McKinney at 42,000 +/- 3,300 B.P. by uranium series on tooth enamel, considered to be more reliable than bone for uranium series dating. This represents the oldest finite date obtained in the China Lake Basin, but Davis is convinced that there are far older materials in the region (Davis et al. 1981).

Davis' work in the China Lake region has been notable for her use of what she terms remote sensing: aerial surveys from light planes and tethered balloons in order to discover hidden ancient landforms beneath windblown sand. Buried shorelines and former marshes can be located quite readily by this means and then examined at the surface level. Such areas are frequently fruitful since the shorelines and marshes attracted early foragers and hunters as well as the game they sought. The concept of geoarchaeology involves searching out and examining those relict surfaces still available where ancient humans might have lived, as well as trenching depositional surfaces in order to understand and reconstruct past landscapes.

There are many desert surfaces in eastern California, Nevada and Baja California that are relatively undisturbed, remote and obviously stable; that is, neither being subjected to more than minor erosion nor deposition other than wind-borne dust. Most of them are solidly paved with rock materials often including stone artifacts, and the latter are almost without exception covered with coatings of desert varnish varying in both color and amount, from slight traces to extremely dark, heavy coats; dark brown on exposed surfaces and bright red orange on their undersides.

These coatings have until recently been poorly understood, and were generally believed to be the result of high temperatures and wind-deposited pollens, although it was obvious to many workers that long periods of time must be involved in their production. As early as a quarter of a century ago George Carter (1951) pointed out that arrow points in the desert never showed a trace of varnish, nor did late dart points like Folsom and Clovis. Davis' proto-Clovis showed very light coatings as did unifacial flake tools; while the massive bifaces, blades and steep-edge work up on the fans and terraces above the lake basins had heavy coats of varnish.

According to Oberlander (1983), "It should be noted here that the mixed lithology beach cobbles on the 20,000 year B.P. shoreline at Lake Manix (dated by Anadonta shells and tufa) bear only the slightest traces of discoloration, far from anything that would optimistically be called desert varnish." Dr. Theodore Oberlander of U. C. Berkeley and one of his graduate students,

Ron Dorn, have been engaged in intensive studies of the desert varnish phenomena in recent years, and have been able to describe in detail the processes involved in its formation, its constituent parts and times required for its accumulation (Dorn and Oberlander 1981; Oberlander 1983).

Basically this is a film of clays formed from dust in the atmosphere, colored by oxides of manganese and iron from the soil environment, and containing a host of trace elements and many types of bacteria and fungi. Apparently the microorganisms are able to concentrate and utilize the manganese, which is present in much higher levels in the bacteria inhabiting the varnish than in the varnish film itself or the ambient environment. Using a scanning electron microscope, Oberlander and Dorn found that varnish was inhabited by a great many different visible bacteria and fungi. They also discovered that manganese-oxidizing microbes were implicated in the buildup of manganese deposits in non-desert environments such as pipelines, on rocks in alpine regions and possibly in subsurface ore deposits.

Two broad classes of varnish occur in the desert pavements: the brown to almost black manganese type and the orange-red iron oxide coatings. It appears that manganese buildups can only occur in environments that have neutral pH or nearly so. That is, environments that are neither very acidic nor very alkaline foster the accumulation of manganese as a waste product of the metabolic activity of the microbes inhabiting the clay coatings on the rock surfaces.

Varnishes composed primarily of clays and iron oxides, on the other hand, flourish in more arid environments lacking the occasional washing by the weak carbonic acid in rainwater, and are generally alkaline. Thus the undersides of rocks fixed in soils and pavements usually show red-orange iron oxide varnish coatings, while rocks exposed over extended periods of time may have very thin layers of both types alternating and detectable in the laboratory, representing major climate changes from arid to humid and back to arid.

For the purposes of archaeological investigation, by far the most promising and useful development of Oberlander and Dorn's work is its potential for the dating of otherwise undatable lithic specimens on the surface in the desert regions. Their dating process relies on the fact that varnish materials contain a wide variety of major elements and trace elements from atmospheric fallout and surface water. Among these elements are titanium, calcium and potassium. Titanium appears to be retained or to accumulate through time at a slow rate, while potassium and calcium, being soluble, are gradually leached out and lost with time. The investigators have found that the cation ratio between the former and the latter tends to be consistent over regional areas in reflecting the age of the varnish coatings. By measuring the age of volcanic materials in the Coso Mountains using the radiometric Potassium/Argon method, and comparing the ages of the dated specimens with their varnish cation ratio, curves have been produced capable of dating rock varnish over a wide area of the southern Great Basin.

Oberlander has applied this so-called Coso varnish leaching curve to unflaked rocks from surfaces in the vicinity of the Calico excavations, and found their varnish coatings to be at least 100,000 years old, supporting

Shlemon's estimate of 80,000 to 125,000 years for the same surfaces on the basis of soil analysis (Bischoff et al. 1981). He has also visited the extremely arid Atacama desert of Chile, where he collected heavily-varnished and massive chopping tools from old land surfaces in a region having many places where rain has never been recorded. Using his Coso curve on these tools gave ages of 70,000 to 100,000 years, but could not be considered reliable. To date their varnish with confidence would require calibration with Potassium/Argon dates on volcanics in the Atacama region, something still not done, and Oberlander believes the tools are actually much older, since varnish must accrete far more slowly in the extremely arid environment of the Atacama desert than in the Coso Range.

The richest and most remarkable desert surface site known to me is on a series of terraces and gentle slopes overlooking the basin of Pleistocene Lake Le Conte in the Imperial Valley. Its relative inaccessibility by vehicle appears to have protected it from the activities of pothunters and vandals, and those of us who know it are disinclined to describe its exact location, simply referring to it as Imperial 2109. Morlin Childers of El Centro took me there several years ago, and I was astonished at the sheer numbers of obviously man-made tools and implements strewn over the surfaces and fixed in the desert pavements, and at the suggestions of great antiquity presented by almost-black coats of varnish on the artifacts and unflaked rocks equally.

The great concentration of tools is probably the result of generous supplies of a fine-grained chert readily available in the talus slopes nearby. Specimens range from lightly coated unifacial flake tools of modest size, to very heavy and massive chopping tools that have been coarsely trimmed from alternating faces and are almost black with varnish, with most of the other recognizable stages of tool evolution in between. Oberlander visited the locality, collected and tested some of the tools and had this to say:

> The varnish on the Imperial Valley artifacts is extremely hard, thinner than it appears (which implies nothing about age), and difficult to scrape. Cation ratios based on the Coso leaching curve would be in excess of 100,000 years. A second non-destructive method of analysis using the atomic accelerator at U. C. Davis (the proton "beam in air" method developed by Cahil) gave even higher proportions of Ti to leachable bases, increasing the apparent age of the artifacts surfaces even more. Work is in progress to reconcile the contradictory results (Oberlander 1983:6).

The morphology of the older tools from Imperial 2109 is similar to those from the Calico site. Comparison with the San Diego macrolithic quartzites is difficult, primarily due to the difference in lithic raw material, quartzite being extremely intractable, hard and unpredictable while the cherts from Imperial Valley are very easily flaked and similar in quality to the chalcedony of the Calico fan. This makes the former difficult to assess from a temporal standpoint and to place reliably into a scale of evolutionary or developmental toolmaking technological achievement. Such comparisons are only believed to be useful when similar or identical lithic materials are involved, and then only in the broadest terms, since very early tool technologies are thought to have changed slowly and reluctantly and only over scores of millennia.

Clearly change was far more rapid in the Upper Paleolithic, and especially after the appearance of stone projectile points, so that industries containing the latter can often be placed into the proper millennium with confidence. In our own time technological change occurs with breakneck speed, so that future prehistorians, poking through our modern middens, will probably be able to date our rubbish to the nearest decade.

The Buchanan Canyon assemblage of macrolithic tools includes a small percentage flaked from a porphyritic andesite. These appear to be more like the desert assemblages from sites like Imperial 2109; they are mostly bifacially trimmed although far larger than the tools known locally to represent the terminal Pleistocene. Since both andesite and quartzite raw materials are readily available in the region in the form of cobbles, the andesitic tools may well represent a slightly later horizon in the region than the quartzites, which are mostly unifacially flaked; they may also represent an infusion of people with different lithic traditions and material preferences.

We cannot know with exactitude what conditions in the deserts might have been like during the altithermals of interglacial and interstadial intervals, and can only presume they were somewhat similar to the present. As the lakes and marshes dried up and disappeared, juniper and piñon died and vanished from the higher slopes, and grasses were replaced by cactus and creosote bush, it seems reasonable to suppose that humans must have been forced out of the region along with the camel, horse and bison.

Surely the most likely course for human bands to follow would have been westward through passes in the mountains and down to the coastal zone, with its cool breezes and rich marine resources, its sheltering canyons and broad estuaries. Did they behold with wonder the vast ocean around which their distant ancestors had made their way out of Asia so long ago? Or did people even in those ancient times know what lay behind the ranges to the west, and journey back and forth within their own lifetimes, as recent but prehistoric Indians did? There is little likelihood that we will ever know with certainty.

The deserts of southeastern California, and particularly localities like Imperial 2109, offer beyond the slightest doubt irrefutable evidence of the presence of humans in North America far back in the Pleistocene Epoch. On those stable surfaces that have clearly never known streams of more than the most minor energy, have never known mudflows since there is no source from which mud could have flowed, flaked chopping tools and scrapers almost black with successive coats of varnish insistently refute the myth of recency for man in the Western Hemisphere.

Stone tools are all we have upon which to base our views and understanding of the human past in the New World, those and a few bone specimens and features. Unlike the Chinese we lack human fossils of very early periods; no treasure house like Zhoukoudian has appeared in the Americas, although two skulls of what appear to be very early *Homo sapiens* have been reported. One such fossil skull was found by some boys weathering out of a cutbank at Utah Lake. Unfortunately they removed it so that no geological provenience could be assigned to it. It was studied by George H. Hansen, an anthropologist at the University of Denver, who stated, "The Utah Lake skull approaches the upper limit of Neanderthal possibilities" (1934).

The other skull was excavated from a cave in the Lagoa Santa region of Brazil by diggers for H. V. Walter, former British consul in Belo Horizonte. It was examined and photographed by Alan Bryan of the University of Alberta, who reported and described it (1978: 318-320), but the skull has subsequently been lost. Apparently much more primitive than the Utah Lake skull, it had very thick walls and extremely heavy bony protuberances or ridges on the brows, both typical of *Homo erectus*, but because the vault was not notably low, Bryan believes it represents a very early form of *Homo sapiens*. These meager and undated specimens tell us little about the early human arrivals and nothing about their origins and accomplishments, their skill at toolmaking and their lifeways.

To learn more about these matters, we must study the only solid evidence we have: their artifacts of stone and bone, and traces of human alteration on the bones of long extinct creatures. But in doing so, we must not overlook the fact that these were humans who undoubtedly shared with us the rich joys and satisfactions of social exchange and mating; pride and pleasure in adjusting to their environment; and patient resignation to adversity.

CAMEO

Egg-gathering and the
Mating Encounter

*I*t is 285,000 years before the present. The high mountains of the British
Columbian Coast Range are covered with enormous burdens of glacial
ice, while the sea has retreated far out across the continental shelf, leaving
a low and gently-rolling coastal zone west of the mountains. Small expanded
family bands of humans have inhabited the coast for many centuries, gradually and almost imperceptibly extending their territories to the south and
east along the shore. Their physical attributes, customs and lifeways have
changed little in the past 10,000 years.

Like a silver ribbon the estuary wound in great loops through the dark olive green of cord grass and pickleweed, terminating in a broad lagoon behind the dunes. Beyond the blue expanse, ruffled by the fresh ocean breeze, the land sloped gently upward to a belt of heavy timber, fir, spruce and hemlock, which marched up the more precipitous slopes and ridges. High above loomed the shining peaks with their mantles of perpetual snow.

Teeming life was evident everywhere. Herds of grazing game; horse, bison and elk, dotted the grassy meadows and slopes, while occasional troops of mammoth marched ponderously across the landscape. Overhead soared huge black scavengers, the teratorn vultures of the Pleistocene, with wing-spreads of over twelve feet. Their keen eyes could detect sick and dying creatures miles away on the ground, and their sharp, powerful beaks could tear and penetrate the thickest hides of mammoth and mastodon.

Packs of dire wolves, the large, massive-jawed wolf of the Pleistocene in North America, also kept careful watch upon the herds, alert to cut off an unguarded calf or pull down grazing animals showing signs of distress. These powerful creatures, both scavengers and predators, served the same function as the hyenas of the Old World, and could completely devour a large animal in a few hours, leaving nothing but a few small scraps of hide, bone and horn. Most of the larger predators — lion, sabertooth and shortfaced bear, tended to hunt at night and sleep during the daylight hours, but the dire wolves patrolled around the clock.

It was along the beaches, marshes and coastal lagoons that the most activity occurred. The air above these tidal zones was constantly astir with hundreds of flashing wings throughout the spring, summer and early fall. Gulls, terns and pelicans flew above the clear waters of the lagoon and channels, watchful for the silvery glimmer of minnows in the shallows. Shorebirds of many species probed the beaches for sandcrabs, snails and larvae as well as more minute organisms, and at low tide traded across the dunes to cover the exposed mudflats with a restless, twinkling brown blanket.

Waterfowl — geese, swans and bright-plumaged ducks — flew in huge flocks and wavering lines along the coast or fed in the sloughs and estuary, their tipped-up white underparts winking and flashing like signal lights against the dark green of the marsh grass lining the shore.

Two small bands of humans inhabited the region; one on each side of the estuary and lagoon. Both the north group and the south people felt jealously protective of their own territory, and would have fought fiercely to preserve their rights to it. All of the humans in both bands had been born in the region and knew no other. They supposed that the entire world was bounded by the sea horizon, the distant peaks and the dim, blue-violet headlands they could see up and down the coast. They also believed, although none was capable of expressing such ideas in words, that the people in their band and those across the lagoon constituted all of humanity. How could they know other-wise, since none had seen other humans in their lifetimes?

The proximity of the two bands served a highly useful purpose, even though they rarely met and knew each other only as distant figures foraging for clams and scallops on the opposite side of the lagoon. But humans, even at these early stages, tended to mate for life, like geese and wolves. Almost as feuding Hatfields and McCoys, young males in need of mates slipped across the borderline of channels to seek out a willing young female in the opposite camp, despite the disapproval of their elders.

* * * *

The females of the northern family band walked down the trail to the lagoon chattering like magpies. There were three little girls from six to eleven, two mated women in their late teens, an old grandmother of thirty-seven years, and a virgin of sixteen who waited longingly for her life to happen. The young mated sisters each carried an infant astride her hip, and the tiny things dozed patiently despite the jolting motion and the jabbering. Most of the talk was simply noise, and almost meaningless. It was just a patter of words repeated over and over like the chirping of sparrows, intended to express pleasure, good will and companionship more than any clearly-defined idea.

Each of the women and girls had a piece of cured hide over her shoulder in which to bundle the delicacies they hoped to harvest, for now it was spring and the terns were nesting. Tonight there would be feasting and shouting and stamping as the mountain of eggs was devoured around the fire. All eagerly dwelt on the coming celebration except the unmated young woman, whose thoughts turned constantly now in the spring to her mating hunger.

She was long past the age of puberty, but the limited size of the band meant that the pairing off of unrelated couples was often delayed and sometimes unconsumated. In-breeding was now vigorously avoided by humans everywhere, the mature adults being instinctively aware of its dangers. But so powerful was the mating instinct that young males in the spring, or at any time of year for that matter, often roved many miles in search of an unattached female, and when successful usually settled down in her family group. Thus female infants were welcomed almost as much as males in that ancient society, since they would attract sturdy young hunters into the band to support the parents in their old age.

The three little girls were naked; the others wore small pubic aprons attached to rawhide waist girdles, and the three younger women had strings of shell beads slung around their necks and shining against the lustrous, dark fullness of their breasts. The old woman, who was tacitly accepted as the leader of the family band, wore no ornament but had about her an aura of authority that made her station unmistakable. Although the four male hunters made most of the noise around the campfire, she made all the family decisions.

Although fierce and dangerous predators roamed the vicinity of the lagoon, there was little to fear from them in the daylight hours. The women had long since learned to avoid female bears with cubs, and they knew that the big cats hunted mainly at night, and in any case rarely attacked humans unless provoked, finding their rancid odor unappetizing in the extreme. Dire wolves prowled always in the distance, ready to clean up the bloody discards from butchered game, or even snatch an unguarded infant, but the women paid no attention to these familiar and ever-present features of the landscape.

They walked steadily down the trail to the edge of the lagoon, along the shore through knee-high grass and flowers, around a rocky spur or headland, and across the marshy flats toward a distant island. This was a low, flat sandbar which lay offshore about two hundred yards. It stretched for over a mile parallel to the shore, and could easily be reached by wading.

Even before they rounded the rocks the women could hear a shrill splinter of sound that speared across the distance. As they approached the island the noise became almost deafening, and they could only communicate by gestures. Tens of thousands of Caspian terns wheeled in circles or fluttered nearly motionless overhead, screaming in a piercing key that seemed to knife through the eardrums. The clouds of white birds with black caps and fiery red bills covered the sand of the island and filled the air like enormous, whirling snowflakes; a blizzard of birds that raged over the heads of the intruders.

The eggs fairly littered the ground, laid in clusters of three in nests which were no more than slightly smoothed patches of sand. When the harvesters had filled their hide capes with all they could carry, the supply of eggs on the sand seemed undiminished. They ate a few, simply biting holes in the ends and pouring the sweet drafts down their throats in delicious swallows, then sprawled in the warm sand and drowsily watched the whirling motes of silver against the deep blue arch of sky.

The unclaimed young female lay on her back and dozed a little. Half asleep, she felt a shadow fall across her face and sleepily opened one eye, then recoiled in terror and leaped to her feet ready to dash for safety. A dark, shaggy young stranger was standing there staring at her intently, gripping a long spear. He thrust it into the sand and made the universal sign of peace — open hands extended with the palms presented to the front.

Reassured, she stared back at him. They stood facing each other some eight feet apart, and a mysterious but almost tangible current crackled between them. No words were spoken; they could have been neither heard in the screaming din of the terns nor understood, since few words were common to all the human bands on the coast. They stared at each other, and each saw the hunger and desire mirrored in the eyes that stared back. But this was no time nor place for intimacy, and the fires of passion would have to burn unchecked for a time.

The young female dropped her eyes coyly and turned away in confusion; the eager young hunter gathered up her bundle of eggs and his spear, and they splashed off side by side toward the mainland. The rest of the party watched them go, the little girls curious and uncomprehending, and the older ones smiling and nodding to one another in great satisfaction.

When the young man and the woman reached the shore he led her up through the flowery meadow toward some trees that seemed to be waiting for them expectantly. He had not touched her yet, but simply walked off and she followed him as though bewitched, as though a halter had been placed around her neck. Her heart hammered in her chest, and she felt flashes of heat suffusing her cheeks as she followed along with her eyes on the broad, muscular back and shoulders, the trim hips and buttocks swinging along up the meadow.

Now they had reached the deep shade and privacy of the trees. She felt an almost overpowering sensation of dread mingled with bitter-sweet fascination. He stepped close to her and put his hands on her shoulders, and her flesh tingled and burned in response. He gently lowered her down into the fragrant soft grass, and now she felt the warm pressure of his ardent body seeking her. Suddenly she responded fully and completely, and gave herself to him exultantly until at last they lay spent and gasping together in the deep shade beneath the trees.

For a long time they lay together drowsing and murmuring to each other, although little that either said was understood, and it was to take weeks before they were able to communicate more than the simplest ideas to one another. But for the purposes at hand, words were unnecessary; they were welded together for the rest of their lives without spoken vows or ceremony.

The sun hung low in the sky, as though reluctant to take its final plunge into darkness with the earth so fair and green. A pair of mergansers came beating low over their heads in their stiff, labored flight, with their wings gleaming copper and gold in the horizontal rays of the sinking sun. The young man stared after them and then glanced quickly at his new mate. She was staring at him shyly but with plainly evident pride.

At last they gathered up the eggs and moved off up the trail. When at dusk she led him to the fire of the living place in the canyon, the men of the band were back from their day's hunting. All welcomed the brawny young newcomer into the family band with beaming smiles. They offered bison robes and a choice sleeping place, and made the youth feel at home and welcome there among them.

Around the fires that night the men stamped their feet and leaped up and down and shouted with the joy of being alive, while the women and girls clacked sticks together in rhythm, smiling approvingly. The hunters capered, leaping high in the air with fingers forming sprouting antlers, bugling in high falsettos like the bull elk on the frost-touched slopes of autumn. Some put back their heads and turned their faces up to the stars blazing in the crisp night sky; opened their mouths and let their happiness pour out in screaming, bellowing sound. Others put down their shaggy black heads and charged each other, grunting and heaving elaborately like bulls contesting for a harem. Hour after hour the strange spectacle went on, dying down at times as the men crouched at the hearths to draw out sizzling strips of bison tongue or liver and to dribble more eggs down their throats, only to flare up suddenly again as someone leaped to his feet again to stamp and shout.

The pulsing rhythms of their spontaneous, joyful celebration, the stamping all together and the clapping, chanting choruses came as naturally to humans as the beating of their hearts and rhythmic breathing. For rhythm surrounded them and ruled their lives as it does ours and always has. The regular, slow turning of the earth and seasons, the fixed order of the day and night and all the visual patterns of the world were spread lavishly before them. Wind and water rippled across the beaches, the beating wings of waterfowl throbbed across the sky, and the great game herds streamed across the land in undulating, graceful movement accented by tossing horns and flashing legs.

And dancing, too, was never strange to them in times of high excitement. They all had seen the graceful mating displays of cranes and grouse, and the joyful gamboling of young animals in the spring. Sound and movement poured out of the people as freely and unrestrainedly as the liquid music of birdsong pours from the throats of meadowlarks and mocking birds.

The two little boys of the band shouted and stamped with the men, but soon could be seen peacefully asleep amid the tumult, their glistening brown skins crisscrossed and festooned with egg. Finally the last reveller had subsided into silence and slipped away to his sleeping place, and only the trilling of crickets and chirping of frogs could be heard above the distant murmur of surf on the beaches.

Along the wide coastal zones of the North Pacific the people lived their lives for countless generations. Some lived exuberantly and fully, relishing their pleasures and bearing their pains with patience. Others led dull, plodding lives and never saw the wonders all around them. There were tragedy and violence and greed and misery, but there were also the leaping joys of mating and parenthood and safe return from danger.

But slowly and as inevitably as the ocean tides, the trickle of human expansion down the fringes of the continent continued. Eventually and beyond question, it penetrated across the coastal mountains and reached the vast chain of freshwater inland seas and lakes beyond the ranges, waters now vanished into shimmering mirages in the deserts of our own time. Did it merge there with other human currents that had slowly drifted down the interior of the continent over the centuries and millennia?

CHAPTER 6

The Artifacts: Testaments of the Human Journey

Beside me on the workbench as I write are two stone tools, or rather one stone tool and a cast or replica of another. Both objects are discoids exactly six inches in diameter; both are between an inch and an inch and a half in thickness. Both represent large, heavy flakes or thick slabs that have been produced by massive bipolar splitting; both have large and deep eraillure scars on their ventral surfaces where the powerful blow fell; and have been unifacially trimmed by hand-held percussion around their entire circumferences although both show a few small flake scars on the ventral faces.

There are minor differences. Specimen A, a rather coarse quartzite, has larger but more shallow flake scars around its periphery; Specimen B, the original a fine sandstone with almost the same characteristics as quartzite, has smaller and steeper flake scars, although two quite large ones are present. Except for coloring, the replica being a uniform dark grey, one would surely conclude that the two specimens had been excavated from the same site, or at least were products of the same industry.

Specimen A was collected from the bottom of the gully in Buchanan Canyon at San Diego, having apparently been exposed and washed out of an ancient-appearing but undated clay stratum by flood waters in 1970. It is quite typical of the quartzite assemblage from that locality. Specimen B was presented to me by Professor Jia Lanpo in Beijing in 1985. It is cast from a tool excavated from the lowest culture-bearing stratum at Locality 1, Zhoukoudian; the Early Stage believed to range in age from 660,000 B.P. to 400,000 B.P. (Zhang 1985:170). (Figure 7.)

Figure 7. Two very similar discoid choppers. The specimen on the left, an epoxy replica, was excavated from the lowest and oldest stratum at Locality 1, Choukowdian, China. The chopper on the right was exposed by a flood in Buchanan Canyon, San Diego.

The specimen from Zhoukoudian was given to me because of its strong resemblance to Specimen A, which I had shown to the staff of the Institute of Vertebrate Paleontology and Paleoanthropology along with some 40 other artifacts from San Diego and the Calico site. The gift was the culmination of a project undertaken in May of 1985, to be described below.

I had been much impressed by the descriptions and illustrations of artifacts being published in recent years on the Early Paleolithic sites of China, artifacts which seemed to be extremely similar to the tools we were finding in Southern California. Not only the morphologies or appearances of the tools from the two hemispheres seemed to be the same, but the technological means of production, particularly the use of anvil and bipolar flaking, are common to both widely-separated localities. The practice of throwing against boulders to obtain sharp-edged fragments and nuclei was also followed here and across the Pacific, and in the cases of vein quartz and quartzite, is a quick and efficient way to produce very sharp slicing and scraping implements, as well as cores suitable for further trimming by hand-held percussion. It is admittedly impossible to prove beyond question that any given tool was made this way, but it is not uncommon to find in the desert battered boulders with fragments of a different lithology scattered around them on the ground. On the more humid coast, erosion would have long since destroyed such evidence.

Archaeologists frequently remind each other that similar ages cannot be established or even presumed simply by similarities in artifact assemblages, much less by individual tool morphologies, and that seemingly very primitive and crude tool industries can actually be relatively recent. This is well demonstrated in the Southern California coastal zone, where the scrapers and choppers of Archaic gatherers called La Jollans tend to be clumsy and roughly finished, while the earlier PaleoIndian San Dieguito people produced pressure-flaked knives, dart points and other implements of fine workmanship. Thus it would seem impossible to place accurately in time a particular and isolated industry based solely on its characteristics, or to discern a temporal relationship between similar lithic industries separated by thousands of miles and a succession of differing environments.

According to Dr. Alex D. Krieger of the University of Washington, "It is imperative that archaeologists recognize the basic necessity for keeping the problem of cultural or technical similarities separate from those determining age and chronological sequence" (1979: 69). But this does not mean that apparently similar cultural horizons, as reflected by their technological practices and achievements, cannot be usefully compared, leading to broad and general sequential placement in their respective settings of time and space.

In making such comparisons it is important to note both what the assemblages in question contain, and also what they lack, for while some tool forms continued to be made and used with few if any changes over scores of millennia, others, especially tools for the more advanced working of leather, wood and bone, are clearly more diagnostic from a temporal standpoint. The absence of such more refined implements would strongly suggest an earlier placement in any regional sequence where they eventually appeared, but the time of their appearance varied greatly in different environments and geographical areas of the world.

The remarkable sequence of changing tool morphologies and technological means of production at Locality 1, Zhoukoudian, demonstrated over a period of 400,000 years of human cultural evolution, is an invaluable paradigm by which stages of development elsewhere can be identified or at least suggested. While it would be specious to expect that matching up tool industries in California with similar stages in one region of China would produce even remotely comparable dates for the California materials, such an exercise would be very useful in establishing a viable sequence for the California localities: the Calico region, the San Diego coastal zone, and the desert sites in the Colorado River Valley and Baja California.

With this in mind I decided, in the summer of 1984, to make arrangements to visit the Institute of Vertebrate Paleontology and Paleoanthropology in Beijing if possible, and to carry along a representative sample of macrolithic tools from the San Diego coastal zone and some epoxy replicas from the Calico site. In May of 1985, having received an official invitation from the Chinese Academy of Science, I flew to Beijing. At this point it might be useful to describe and discuss briefly some of the most significant specimens that I carried to Beijing.

The largest contingent of tools was from Buchanan Canyon, since the main purpose was to shed light on this mysterious and little understood industry, and place it if possible into a broad temporal framework relative to the better known and more recent California lithic horizons. Categories included choppers, scrapers including spokeshaves, large points, skreblos, bipolar cores and blades. Also taken were specimens that were clearly worked by humans but could not be placed into any of the above types, and whose functions were problematical and possibly multiple.

The largest category of tools collected or observed in the San Diego coastal zone has been choppers and chopping tools, and this is very likely due to the fact that wood needed frequently to be chopped for fires and possibly for clubs and spears and even shelters. But some very heavy specimens have the kind of battering on the edges that my experiments have shown is produced by use on heavy marrow bone.

If chopping implements made on water-rounded stones are to be described as chopping tools if they are bidirectionally flaked, and choppers if unifacial (Movius 1948), it is often difficult to place the Buchanan Canyon tools, and particularly the quartzites, into the proper pigeonhole, for there are no bifaces as the term is usually applied. Most of such tools have had a few large flakes removed from one direction and considerably more from the opposite side, although some very heavy specimens are of the "horse's hoof" type, with a flat ventral plane and all the trimming strokes struck from it. (Figure 8.)

One tool of the latter type was taken to China. It is flaked from a very heavy split cobble, the ventral face is flat and oblong, measuring four by four and one half inches, while the thickness through the domed shape is about two and a quarter inches. The tool has been sharpened by numerous flake removals all around the periphery. This is a common type which seems to have persisted down almost to the present in much smaller versions usually called "scraper planes," but this one weighs two and a quarter pounds and is made of quartzite, rarely employed in later industries. Battering and small step-flakes on its edges suggest use as a chopper rather than a massive scraper, but it could have been used for both.

Several almost identical tools have been recovered from the San Diego coastal zone, including the Charles H. Brown site, but this was the only chopper type taken to China that could not be matched up with an Early Paleolithic specimen there. Two other types of choppers are common in San

Figure 8. Dorsal sides of two heavy "horse's hoof" type unifacial choppers from the San Diego coastal zone. Ventral sides are flat, the pieces having been executed on split cobbles.

Figure 9. Pebble tools from Buchanan Canyon with much of the cortex remaining for a smooth grip.

Diego and appear frequently in the Chinese very early sites: One type with minor variations is a tool made on a very heavy flake or slab and trimmed unifacially or nearly so. Very occasionally alternate-face flaking has been employed, a technique associated with very early sites (Calico, Yuha Pinto Wash, Black's Fork) and tending to disappear in the Upper Paleolithic as in China (Zhang 1985:184).

The other common type of chopper present in both very early Chinese and San Diego assemblages is what is often called a pebble tool, although in the case of these very early industries could more properly be called a cobble tool, for they are sometimes very large. In these a good deal of cortex remains, usually one entire end of the cobble, making them very convenient to grasp in the hand. Some are bifacially and even alternately trimmed, while others are simply sharpened by rough step-flaking from the cortex platform. Replicating experiments have shown that the latter are most easily flaked by the block-on-block method, and their simplicity both of form and means of production suggests that they may have been one of the earliest tool types, along with throwing, to be utilized by the evolving human species. (Figure 9.)

Examples of both types of choppers were taken to Beijing. One of the heavy flake or slab type has been flaked on a large split cobble apparently produced by a massive bipolar blow, and then unifacially trimmed with very sharp, hard blows of hand-held percussion. The specimen weighs two pounds and is six inches long by four inches wide. One end comes to a rather blunt point which is heavily battered, as though it had been used as a stone-on-stone hammer, while the side edges show more modest wear, the kind expectable from use on wood or bone.

One of the pebble chopping tools is made from a cobble of porphyritic andesite. This specimen, also taken to Beijing and also weighing two pounds, is four inches wide, two and a half inches thick and five inches in length. The rear half is rounded, unworked cobble cortex, while the cutting edge has been developed by alternate-face flaking, so that the end-on view has a zigzag aspect. Use wear in the form of tiny step flakes along the functional edges can be seen on this tool.

A pebble chopper included in the group taken abroad, the unifacial step-flaked variety, is almost triangular in profile, its base and elevation being cobble cortex and the hypotenuse represented by the worked face. This piece is ovoid in plan, three inches long and about two and a half inches high. It weighs a pound and a half, and shows 11 large step-flaked removals or scars on the worked face; the rest is cobble cortex. Both of these pebble choppers would be absolutely impossible for Nature to duplicate.

The second most common category of macrolithic tools seen in the San Diego coastal zone is composed of scrapers of various kinds. Many of these are very large amorphous flakes that appear to have been produced by throwing or natural fracturing and spalling, but show symmetrical flake removals along one or more edges or across an end. Many have concavities or spokeshaves worked into an edge; these are almost without exception the appropriate size for working down a spear shaft or lance, and experimental use has shown them to be quite efficient in shaving down surfaces and removing bark from tree limbs of the right diameter. Some specimens appear to have been deliberately roughened in the concave bits to serve as rasps or abrasives.

One of this type, taken to China, is six inches long, about three inches wide and about one inch in maximum thickness. It is a kind of dogleg shape, with the spokeshave cavity worked into the inside bend. It is made of what is locally called "honey" quartzite with a fairly coarse crystalline texture, a roughened bit and tiny step flakes on the concave edge, suggesting vigorous use. One of the straight edges has been sharpened with small flake removals rather steeply executed. (Figure 10.)

Figure 10. Concave scrapers or "spokeshaves" from Buchanan Canyon. The specimen on the left was taken to China, but no tools of this type were seen there.

Figure 11. Large points or picks from Buchanan Canyon. Such tools are very common in the Chinese very early sites.

The large points or picks vary in size from about five inches long to over eight inches, and are usually either triangular or quadrilateral in cross section. They all share characteristically abraded points, almost certainly indicating use as digging instruments, and might have been employed for digging up edible roots and tubers or possibly for excavating caves in the soft limestone San Diego canyonsides. Of several taken to China one is particularly interesting, for it is about eight inches long but curved like the fang of a sabertooth cat. It is a rich brown quartzite, almost the color one associates with fossil bone, and is roughly triangular in cross section with a fairly heavy butt end two by three inches in dimension. One edge has been sharpened for almost its entire length with small, alternating flake removals, and the now-dulled point has been battered and abraded. Of all the tools in the Buchanan Canyon assemblage, this one, perhaps because of its suggestive color and shape, most insistently conjures up for me the vision of a stooped and shaggy maker. (Figure 11)

A very important tool type found in the San Diego region and also in most of the very early sites described above in the western United States, as well as in Siberia and China, is the skreblo, briefly discussed in Chapter I. This is a backed, lunate tool with the curved edge sharpened by either unifacial or bifacial trimming, and usually from four to six inches in length and about half its length in width. The exact meaning of the Russian word "skreblo" is unclear; it has been referred to as a "chopper" and a "scraper" by various writers, but I am convinced that it is a skinning and butchering implement. The same curved and backed blade, now made of steel and backed with bone or antler, is in use today by modern Eskimos, who call it an "ulu" and skin and butcher seals with it. (Figure 12)

Figure 12. Skreblos (left) from Florida Canyon in San Diego and (right) Buchanan Canyon.

The skreblos found in the San Diego coastal zone formed on thick plates or flakes of quartzite would be highly efficient for skinning and slicing game the size of deer or larger; the wedge shape being ideal for separating hide from flesh while the very sharp quartzite edges would cut through the toughest skin, muscle and cartilage. The specimen of this type taken to Beijing is extremely battered on one end, suggesting that in addition to the foregoing functions it may have been used to break bone. It is a little over five inches long and about three inches wide; about one and one half inches at its thickest point. It weighs 1.25 pounds and is made of a light grey-brown quartzite. Although I was shown no similar tools in China, a classic example is pictured in full color from Hubei Province (Institute of Vertebrate Paleontology and Paleoanthropology 1980:25). Judging by the photograph, that specimen is almost identical to the one carried abroad, and is believed by the investigators to date to the early Paleolithic period. It is designated a chopper by the Chinese.

The problem of the bipolar cores and blades, also discussed in Chapter I, is highly controversial and difficult to resolve in the United States. Since most North American archaeologists are unfamiliar with products of the bipolar technique, which can split pebbles without leaving telltale bulbs of percussion, this little-known technology is regarded with skepticism and disbelief. It has been practiced from the earliest times in China, and is perfectly familiar to the Chinese scholars, who have no difficulty in recognizing it.

The most troubling aspect of the problem in the San Diego region is the fact that it now appears that very similar products may have been produced by Nature and by man. Brian Reeves of the University of Calgary, who is a highly competent geologist as well as an archaeologist, studied the bipolar cores in the San Diego region and reached the following conclusions:

> In summary, in our opinion the "bipolar cores" at Mission Ridge can best be explained at this time as a natural phenomenon — the end product of the continuous spalling over tens of millennia of suitably shaped quartzite cobbles exposed by erosion. . . It is an exfoliation process — the earlier stages of which are observable on erosional slopes where spalls are being flung off variously shaped quartzite cobbles. Most likely, it is the result of physical-chemical stresses built up between the weathering cortex and the unweathered matrix, resulting in a spall eventually being thrown off. Stresses along other fracture planes build up and assist in eventual reduction of the quartzite cobble. Salt crystal formation and chaparral fires have played important if not key roles in spall formation.
>
> The origin of the "bipolar cores" is a complex issue. Both Carter and Minshall consider some to be culturally produced. Some may well be the result of human reduction, because Minshall and others have been able to replicate identical bipolar forms. Probably the category includes both natural and manmade forms, and it can be exceedingly difficult to distinguish between them (Reeves 1986:76-78).

My own studies and experiments, including replication, have indicated that while some naturally produced spalled cores might be mistaken for human work, there are certain telltale signs or benchmarks that separate the two categories. A very important one was mentioned in Chapter I: the nature of the flake scars. Most manmade bipolar cores have at least some concave scars; that is, concave in cross section, while naturally spalled cores rarely if ever have, since as Reeves suggests, the weathered cortex or skin of the cobble is being separated from the unweathered matrix. The weathering process extends to the same depth on the cortex, so the cast-off spalls are curved like the cobble surface and are of approximately equal thickness throughout their length. On the other hand, the ventral faces of percussively-struck blades are convex in cross section and bear no formal relationship to the surface of the cobble, although such blades may feather out at the end and leave a skinned look on the distal end of the core, or may terminate abruptly in a hinge fracture.

Manmade bipolar cores are usually pointed and battered at the distal or anvil end, and chisel-shaped at the proximal end. Often the chisel end has a deep indentation in the middle, almost a groove. This is particularly true of bipolar cores from the Calico site. When I began replication experiments I soon discovered the reason: additional but futile attempts to split off one more blade produced the same kind of groove on the exhausted core.

Spalled quartzite cores produced by high heating as in chaparral fires are easily identified, for they are permanently heat-stained a purplish red color, making them immediately suspect. Of course it is quite possible for a genuine manmade core to have been cooked in a hot campfire.

A bipolar core taken to Beijing is quartzite, about five inches long and two inches at maximum diameter and weighs 13 ounces. It is roughly pointed at one end and chisel-shaped at the other. It is polyhedral in cross section, and has seven major flake scars of which three are decidedly concave. One of the latter, the largest one on the specimen, is concave both laterally and longitudinally — almost impossible for a natural spall. No cortex remains on the core. (Figure 13.)

Numerous specimens believed to be bipolar blades have been collected in the San Diego area, and several were included in the assemblage taken to China. Many are triangular or lenticular in cross section, and they vary in size from two to three inches in length and one half to one inch in width. Few have cortex remaining in the total collections and none of those taken to Beijing did so, but dorsal surfaces on such specimens almost always show evidence of previous flake removals.

In addition to the above recognizable tool types, numbers of less readily identifiable fractured cobbles and fragments of quartzite appear to have been used as tools, mostly for chopping and hammering. These amorphous-shaped specimens sometimes show a few deliberate flake removals to produce an edge, frequently dulled by use wear; sometimes the only evidence of human use is extreme battering expectable from stone-to-stone contact over an extended period of time. Many of these are thought to have served as massive mauls for bipolar splitting of cobbles. Although the latter were too heavy to carry in hand luggage, one specimen of this type appears to be an exact

Figure 13. Bipolar cores from the San Diego coastal zone. The one in the center was taken to China.

Figure 14. A massive quartzite hammer or maul from Buchanan Canyon and believed to have been used in antiquity for bipolar flaking.

duplicate of a stone hammer from the Peking Man site illustrated in the Atlas of Primitive Man in China (IVPP 1980:43). By chance I have been using my version of this tool, collected in Buchanan Canyon, for replicative work in bipolar flaking, a function for which it has proved highly satisfactory. It weighs four pounds and is six inches long, while the length of the Zhoukoudian specimen is listed at 146 mm, or almost the same length. (Figure 14.)

In addition to 27 stone tools from the San Diego coastal zone, a suite of 15 epoxy replicas from Calico was carried to Beijing. These were excellent reproductions of mostly larger tools considered important by the investigators, but unfortunately were not truly representative of the Calico assemblage which is composed primarily of small unifacial flake tools. Included in this group were a slab-type chopping tool bifacially flaked from alternating faces, a pebble chopper similar to the San Diego example, a large skreblo, a concave scraper or spokeshave, several specimens designated handaxes, a large point or pick and various less discriminate scrapers and small tools.

For weight reasons many Calico tools and implements could not be carried, since replicas in very light epoxy had not been made of them. High on this list were the stone spheroids believed to be bola balls, of which a number of specimens have been excavated. But there is little or no need to compare them with the abundant Chinese spheroids found in almost all very early sites, since it is perfectly obvious from photographs and descriptions that they are identical.

Seven extremely weathered and heavily varnished implements from Black's Fork, Wyoming, were also taken, but except for one discoid chopper similar to those described earlier from San Diego and Zhoukoudian, no significant parallels could be noted. Although several of these specimens had been alternately flaked, they seemed cruder and more primitive than the Early Paleolithic tools shown to me.

It should be noted here that the Chinese use of the term "Early Paleolithic" very properly refers to a stage in technological evolution rather than a period in time. According to Zhang (1985:147), "Cultural development during the Early Paleolithic in China was a slow, gradual process beginning perhaps as early as 1,000,000 BP and persisting until at least 200,000 BP, although individual localities yielding Early Paleolithic materials may be as young as 100,000 BP."

The technological stage "Middle Paleolithic" in China is generally synchronous with the early Late Pleistocene about 150,000 BP and persists until the "Late Paleolithic" starting around 40,000 BP. These technological and chronological generalities do not preclude great differences in technological achievement within each category, particularly in the Early Paleolithic stage, so that the tools of Xihoudu, thought to be 1,800,000 years old, bear little or no resemblance to the well-made unifacial flake tools of the upper levels at Locality 1, Zhoukoudian.

Clearly, all of the North American tools taken to the IVPP in Beijing would fall into the Chinese classification of Early Paleolithic. When they were laid out on a table at the Institute, the staff gathered around and examined them with great interest, for the prevailing and perhaps only opinion current among the Chinese archaeologists was the same one prevalent in North America: human first arrival in the Western Hemisphere was no earlier than the terminal Wisconsin — perhaps 15,000 BP.

Similar displays had been laid out at archaeological conferences and annual meetings in North America for many years, but since such unfamiliar materials were completely foreign to the experience of most American viewers, they were rarely recognized as the work of man, and routinely attributed to "stream breakage," "pressures in mud flows," or "quarry blanks and discards." I have presided at many such exhibits, and often noticed that most of the archaeologists in attendance demonstrated an extreme reluctance to let themselves be seen even examining such heretical material, almost as though it were obscene. The Chinese scholars, although puzzled, showed no fear of contamination since they had been working with similar materials in some cases throughout their careers.

I delivered a brisk fifteen minute explanatory discourse on the collection, little of which was understood, they later informed me, because I talked too fast. Then the staff began to bring out artifacts from their assemblages to match up with mine. By chance the tools most similar to the San Diego specimens came from Kehe, Shanxi Province Locality 6054 in the Huanghe Valley, the site most like the situation in Buchanan Canyon; that is, both were gully exposures with the tools on the floor and weathering out of the lower strata on the walls. Also contributing numerous specimens was the assemblage from Liangshan, a still-unpublished site in Shaanxi Province near the city of Hanzhong. Its artifacts were almost interchangeable with those of Kehe and San Diego.

These similarities were striking and even remarkable in view of the great distance separating North China and San Diego, some 7,000 miles. The comparisons were considered to be particularly valid because all three assemblages were composed of substantially the same lithic materials: fairly coarse quartzites and a porphyritic andesite that looked exactly like the San Diego volcanics. This lithic correspondence is almost essential in comparing technical achievement and placement on a scale of cultural evolution.

Also remarkable is the fact that both Kehe and Liangshan are estimated by the Chinese scientists to be about 600,000 years old, based on both biostratigraphic and geostratigraphic evidence. This makes them about the same age as the tools in the lower levels at Locality 1, Zhoukoudian, if accurate, but there are no finite dates. What implications might be drawn for the age of the San Diego tools is unclear, but considerable antiquity is certainly suggested, and the problem will be examined in Chapter VII.

Many of the Chinese tools were paired with San Diego counterparts and photographed on a desk top beside an open window. Unfortunately the light was so poor and my photographic skills so meager that the results left much to be desired. However, my experience has been that the best of photographs seldom are able to express completely the more subtle aspects and surfaces of a flaked stone artifact and particularly the nature of edges, nor are line drawings much better at this. As a fairly accomplished and one-time professional artist, I have never discovered a satisfactory way to portray use-wear on edges adequately, especially crushing and battering, in drawings.

Among the artifacts paired with very similar counterparts in China was the quartzite discoid chopper from Buchanan Canyon described at the beginning of this chapter. It was compared to a discoid chopper of the same size and similar quartzite from Liangshan. The latter resembled even more closely the San Diego specimen than did the discoid from Zhoukoudian, partly because of the similarity of lithic material but also because the size and angle of the flake scars were the same. (Figure 15.)

Figure 15. A quartzite discoid chopper from Liangshan, China, compared with a similar quartzite chopper from Buchanan Canyon in San Diego.

Figure 16. Medium size chopping tools from San Diego (left) and Liangshan, China (right). Both are made from very similar porphoritic andesite.

Another almost identical pair consisted of medium-sized chopping tools from Liangshan and San Diego. Both are ovoid core tools made of porphyritic andesite, about three by four inches in plan and one and a half inches in elevation. One edge has been steeply flaked unifacially to provide a comfortable backing, while the opposite edge has been alternately flaked to produce a zigzag and slightly denticulate edge on both tools. The San Diego tool weighs 12 ounces and presumably the Liangshan specimen weighs about the same. Both tools show edge wear in the form of tiny step flake scars and slight crushing; both have small patches of cortex remaining on dorsal surfaces. (Figure 16.)

Figure 17. Scrapers on large flakes from Kehe, China (left) and Buchanan Canyon in San Diego.

The step-flaked pebble chopper with much of the cortex remaining, described above, was matched with several Kehe choppers, this being an apparently common tool in both industries. Common also are the scrapers made on large amorphous flakes of quartzite, but the spokeshave feature, seen repeatedly in the San Diego collections and at Calico, was not represented or at least not seen in any of the Early Paleolithic assemblages of China. Whether this reflects an absence of spear shafts or lances cannot be determined, for such weapons if in use could easily have been dressed down with straight-bitted edge or end scrapers, although less handily. Perhaps we can credit the distant California cousins with an independent invention. (Figure 17.)

Large quartzite points or picks very similar in form to those found at Calico and at Buchanan Canyon are apparently typical of early Chinese sites also, and are considered a diagnostic tradition there (Jia 1980:17). They cover an enormous span of Chinese prehistory. A large point recovered in the Lantian area in a comparable stratum to that which yielded a human skull is dated at possibly 1,000,000 BP, while much younger sites at Dingcun, considered to be in the Middle Paleolithic stage, also have large stone points, although somewhat more sophisticated. One of the San Diego specimens was paired with a Kehe point, while the one from Lantian strongly resembled the epoxy replica from Calico, a likeness completely lacking in temporal significance but suggesting a possible cultural inheritance. (Figure 18.)

Figure 18. Large points or picks believed to have been used for digging up roots and tubers. The one on the left is an epoxy cast from the Calico site in the Mojave Desert, while the pick on the left is from Lantian, China.

An artifact type of very distinctive shape is common in parts of the southeastern California desert and the San Diego coastal zone. It had been called a "ridge-back" by W. Morlin Childers of the Imperial Valley College Museum, who had deduced and replicated its unique means of manufacture (Childers 1977) at least in the desert region. These are unifacially-flaked objects of unknown use in which large flake scars tend to meet at the top of the dorsal surface in a line, a point or a flat-topped ridge, causing the cross section to be triangular. The desert specimens come in a variety of sizes, including huge ones nearly two feet long.

Childers believed the objects were initially flaked from cortex striking platforms on the tops of large boulders partially imbedded in the ground, then detached by a massive blow with a stone punch, accounting for their failure to show bulbs of percussion. If they represent natural fracturing of some kind, no one has been able to propose a rational mechanism; if manmade, as Childers believed, their purpose is equally obscure.

The Buchanan Canyon ridge-backs, on the other hand, although similar in form to the desert specimens, are all four to six inches in length and about two inches wide. They appear to have been formed by more conventional means: bipolar splitting to produce the core, then hand-held percussion from the flat ventral face producing large flake scars which tend to meet at the top.

Edge-wear on them suggests vigorous use as scraper planes, probably on wood. (Figure 19.)

None of the ridge-backs was taken to Beijing, but a very similar specimen, also in quartzite, was included in the assemblage from Kehe. Two such tools are illustrated in the Atlas of Primitive Man in China (IVPP 1980:42) and identified as scrapers of Peking Man.

Figure 19. "Ridge-back" scraper planes from San Diego's Buchanan Canyon. Ventral surfaces are flat.

Figure 20. Heavy ovoid choppers from Kehe, China (right) and the Calico site (left) in the Mojave Desert of California. Compare the waterworn appearance of the Kehe specimen with similar tools from Buchanan Canyon shown in Figure 3, also from gully exposure.

Of the Calico replicas only the large point paired with a very similar specimen from Xihoudu was a very close match, as was the point from Lantien. There were two difficulties with the Calico specimens: they were not really representative of the Calico assemblage, which is primarily well-made small unifacial flake tools, and the critical difference in lithic materials between the Calico chalcedony and the Chinese Early Paleolithic quartzes, quartzites and volcanics made comparisons of cultural and technological achievement rather questionable. The glassy, brittle chalcedony behaves very differently from the coarser quartzite and andesite, being far easier to flake and thus suggesting a much more advanced stage than it may actually represent. A large, ovate flake chopper of quartzite from Kehe, although heavily stream-abraded, shows fewer and larger flake scars than a somewhat similar Calico specimen which has been dorsally thinned and edge-trimmed with alternate-face flaking. (Figure 20.)

The same is true of two small, handaxe-like objects from Calico and Liangshan. The latter is roughly formed with very large flake removals, while the Calico specimen shows a far more intricate pattern of flake scars. This again may be partly due to the very different flaking characteristics of the andesite at Liangshan and the Calico chalcedony, as well as what is almost certainly a vast difference in time and technological progress. (Figure 21)

Figure 21. Small handaxe-like tools from Liangshan, China, (left) and Calico, California (right). Their function is unknown.

Although they could not be directly compared, the small, unifacial flake tools of the Late Stage, Locality 1 levels at Zhoukoudian — gravers, well-made scrapers and reamers — appear to closely parallel the more typical small tools of Calico. The former, being made of good quality vein quartz and rock crystal that more closely approximates chalcedony in flaking characteristics, clearly provide a more reliable index by which to judge the cultural stage of the Calico flintknappers. The fact that the ages of the Zhoukoudian specimens from that level and the Calico assemblage have been estimated to be approximately the same, between 300,000 and 200,000 years, seems highly significant but could be coincidental. It is, however, perfectly apparent that small flake tools of excellent quality were being produced in China and North America somewhat earlier than is generally appreciated by American scholars.

It was an exciting and even an emotional experience for me to visit Zhoukoudian. No place on earth even approaches its importance for prehistorians concerned with the cultural and physical evolution of man. The excellent little museum makes available to the public a panoramic view of human development and progress over a span of almost half a million years. Displays of stone artifacts, human skeletal remains and fossils of their fellow creatures, and life-sized paintings on the walls of *Homo erectus* in various activities, as well as much explanatory material in Chinese (unfortunately unreadable by me) make a visit here an unforgettable event for the thousands of school children and tourists who pass through the museum and wander through the caves on the hill. (Figure 22.)

Figure 22. The visitors' center at Zhoukowdian, China.

The latter are somewhat disappointing, and one needs a powerful imagination to visualize what must once have been the spacious home of Peking Man. The earliest and most important cave of Locality 1, the first to be discovered and excavated, is no longer a cave but a large open pit. The rear wall of the huge excavation that was carried out there is marked off in the various levels representing the different periods of occupation and the different cultural stages totaling over 400,000 years of human development.

Other caves on Longgushan have been excavated and found to contain evidence of somewhat later habitation by *Homo erectus*, while the so-called Upper Cave or Shandingdong (Summit of the hill cave) has skeletal remains and tools of *Homo sapiens sapiens*, the modern human species to which we belong. It is dated at between 20,000 and 10,000 BP. Here were found not only tools but many purely ornamental objects: perforated marine shells and pebbles; beads made of fish bone, bird bone, stone and drilled teeth. Skeletal remains were found resting on beds of red hematite powder, suggesting not only intentional burial but also spiritual beliefs and the practice of ritualistic ceremony (Jia and Huang 1985:221).

In attempting to assess the value and significance of the direct comparison studies carried out in China, the most important outcome appears to me to be the recognition of the fact that, just as humans have gone through definite and measurable physical changes over the past million years, so have their evolving abilities to control and manipulate their material environments. Those changing abilities and increasing skills would have been reflected in many diverse aspects of existence: in hunting and gathering practices, in social adjustments and in the making of tools and implements, but it is only in the latter aspect that they have left records of bone and stone throughout the human journey for us to find and interpret if we can.

We might view the stone tools of Buchanan Canyon, Calico and Black's Fork as scattered and meager units of a jigsaw puzzle, and the far richer and extensive Paleolithic assemblages of China, Korea, Japan and Siberia as a much more complete picture spread out before us on the table and covering most of the definitive stages of toolmaking evolution. China is of course the most useful and complete part of the picture, since we have not only many very early sites there but also, with Zhoukoudian, the longest almost unbroken chain of cultural evolution.

Our problem then, if not simple, is obvious: to drop into the picture our North American pieces where they fit best, regardless of preconceptions and generally-accepted doctrines. It has been suggested that there are certain traits that can be identified as typical of various stages in the evolving picture of man the toolmaker, traits that die out and disappear as cultural development advances. These reflect temporal placement only in the most general way, being sequentially related rather than being tied to definite time periods of the past, particularly in the Early Paleolithic stages. In later periods, as human populations increased, diffusion of ideas would have become more rapid and extensive, so that cultural and temporal factors would have been more nearly parallel in most parts of the world.

The earliest stone tools purposefully shaped by man, beyond those random fragments gained by throwing against boulders, appear to have been large, thick flakes and slabs steeply edge-trimmed either unifacially or by alternate-face flaking. They are usually designated choppers or scrapers and may have served as both, or even slicing tools. Such implements of non-specific type apparently were made by humans over a tremendous span of time, beginning in the Lower Pleistocene or earlier, and extending possibly into the Upper Pleistocene as recently as 200,000 years ago, in isolated pockets of the world. They are known from the highest flood plains of the Soan River in Indo-Pakistan and the Black's Fork River in southwestern Wyoming, as well as from Xihoudu and Lantian in China. The very steeply flaked edges are their most characteristic aspect.

A slightly younger trait of the Asian and North American Early Paleolithic is the mostly bifacial edge-trimming of large cobble core tools, often completely around the perimeter or nearly so, by hand-held percussion. These are generally made of quartzite where available, and are sometimes called "Acheulian" for the district in France where they were first described. Bipolar splitting to produce cores with convenient ventral striking platforms was sometimes employed, and the removal of large thinning flakes from dorsal surfaces is often seen. Such tools occasionally are roughly pointed or given a cleaver edge across one end.

Practically identical tools of this type have been found in the San Diego coastal zone and at Chongokni, Korea, where they are estimated to be about 300,000 years old on the basis of geomorphology but are not securely dated. They are also found in many older sites in China and undoubtedly in parts of Siberia. Their most characteristic aspect is their massive size and rather crude percussive flaking.

The practice of alternate-face flaking, mentioned frequently above, appears in many Early Paleolithic sites in Asia and North America and then disappears completely in the later sites. It is present on chopping tools at Kehe, Filimoshki in Siberia, Black's Fork, Calico, and Yuha Pinto Wash. It is rare in San Diego's Buchanan Canyon, only appearing on tools made of andesite and therefore possibly introduced from the desert areas to the east across the mountains, where it was the preferred technique.

The use of bipolar and anvil-supported flaking techniques for the production of more manageable cores, large flakes and especially in the Middle Paleolithic stage for fine microblades, was common in China almost down to the present, but is mainly, although not exclusively, known from very early sites in the Western Hemisphere. A notable exception is an industry at Avery Island, Louisiana (Gagliano 1967) dated in the terminal Wisconsin and featuring at the lowest levels a bipolar pebble technology.

Block-on-block flaking is also a trait associated with very early sites in both hemispheres. Specifically this is the practice of striking a core sharply against a boulder anvil to remove flakes. The anvils have sometimes been shaped into pointed forms or ridges like the roofs of little houses. Anvil flaking can be recognized by the fact that step or hinge flake scars are normally produced by this method, which was used in the Early Stage at Zhoukoudian, at Calico and at Buchanan Canyon, as well as at Kehe and Liangshan.

Anvil or block-on-block flaking should not be confused with anvil-supported percussive flaking, in which a core is held against an anvil at an angle to steady it as well as to increase the effect of the percussive blow. True bipolar flaking in which the core is held vertically on a stone anvil and struck repeatedly with a very heavy hammer is in reality a form of random flaking little removed from throwing, since the process cannot be adequately controlled. According to Leland W. Patterson, an expert on flintknapping, "True bipolar fracturing, with force rebound from a hard anvil to initiate a secondary fracture plane, may be useful for pebble and cobble splitting, but this technique is not suitable for controlled flaking. Primitive man would soon so determine and preferably use conventional flaking. . . " (Patterson 1983:305). But in China primitive man apparently continued to find it useful for producing sharp blades until relatively recent times.

In considering where in the jigsaw puzzle to drop in our North American pieces, we should look not only at the Early Paleolithic artifacts and assemblages in China that closely resemble them, but also and very importantly what follows sequentially after them in China. We have an excellent model to follow at Locality 1, Zhoukoudian, where coarse, macrolithic core tools in the lowest levels gradually evolve over hundreds of millennia into small unifacial flake tools of discrete types and functions similar to those at Calico. Since the Buchanan Canyon tools in our assemblages closely resemble those at the lowest levels and not at the upper or later ones, the proper sequence or continuity should be easy to establish, but there are two problems, one of them not previously mentioned.

The macrolithic tools from the San Diego coastal zone and particularly from Buchanan Canyon are mostly large and coarsely flaked. But they are almost without exception either surface finds or redeposited from elsewhere. We cannot say with certainty that small unifacial flake tools were not also being made by the same people. They would be far more easily transported, would be more fragile and more easily overlooked; erosional forces would tend over scores of millennia to transport large and small tools to different places. Since some large tools persisted into the Late Stage at Zhoukoudian and are found at Calico, large size may not be after all a decisive feature upon which to base a determination of relative cultural achievement. But the nature of the tools themselves; their relative crudity or sophistication and the technological means of their production should also serve as indices of their position in the Paleolithic sequence, and here we confront the second problem.

The apparently very early tools in the San Diego region that we are investigating are made almost without exception of fairly coarse quartzite and porphyritic andesite. Neither lithic material lends itself to delicate workmanship; fine-grained cherts and quartzes were simply not available in the coastal zone. A fairly fine-grained green andesite, locally called felsite, was available in a few areas of the region in its extreme southern portion and in Mexico, and macrolithic tools made from it seem far more advanced than the quartzites but are probably contemporary. Thus judgments of significant similarity between the San Diego quartzites and the Early Paleolithic tools of Zhoukoudian, made of sandstone, vein quartz and rock crystal, must be made with caution and with due allowance for the flaking qualities of the lithic media involved.

Despite these uncertainties, some of the features of the San Diego tools argue persuasively for placement in an Early Paleolithic technological stage. They are very similar and in fact identical in some cases to the quartzite and andesite tools of Kehe and Liangshan, considered to be contemporary with the earliest levels of Zhoukoudian. They are mostly amorphous rather than typologically uniform, many have been made on split cobbles and randomly-produced cores, flakes and fragments. Prepared striking platforms and secondary retouch are never present, although the flat ventral surface of a split cobble might be considered to qualify as a prepared striking platform of a sort. These features are seen in the tools of the Early Stage at Locality 1, and are not characteristic of following stages, although they are occasionally present.

In the case of the Calico assemblage, no such uncertainties are apparent, for as at Zhoukoudian, all the specimens originally comprising the total assemblage are present, at least in the excavated segments. The flaking media are of comparable quality, the various types tend to conform to established patterns, the ratio of large tools to small flake tools appears to be similar, estimated ages are approximately the same, and in general there appears to be a close correspondence between the two widely separated localities. We can match the Calico pieces with the Late Stage level of Locality 1 with confidence.

The artifacts taken to China from Black's Fork, Wyoming, could not be matched with any industry seen in China or reported from there. One discoid was the same size and allover shape as those described from Liangshan, Zhoukoudian and Buchanan Canyon, but instead of unifacial flaking around the perimeter, this specimen, showing very heavy battering around most of its perimeter, has had seven large flake removals along about one third of its edge, and these have been alternately struck from opposite faces to form the familiar zigzag pattern. The piece is very heavily varnished and weathered, the flake scars having taken on the same texture and appearance as the cortex. The battered edges have vague scallops that may represent extremely abraded flake scars, possibly having been exposed to stream abrasion while the less-worn segment was protected by partial burial in the riverbed. Some of these Black's Fork specimens meet all my criteria for extreme antiquity, have the thickest coats of desert varnish I have ever seen, and are extremely puzzling and difficult to account for. Few anthropologists familiar with the Old World Lower Paleolithic and unaware of their source would reject them from that category, but they remain completely undated, unrecognized and inscrutable.

The foregoing comparative study in China limited itself to the Early Paleolithic sites in Beijing, Shanxi and Shaanxi Provinces, but China is a vast land, and Paleolithic sites are scattered over much of the eastern half. The Zhoukoudian sites have been far more completely studied than those of any other area, excepting perhaps those of the Late Paleolithic and Recent periods. But the situation at Zhoukoudian is not necessarily typical of the Early Paleolithic everywhere in China, and the early tools in Guizhou Province to the south, and particularly Guanyindong, a cave site containing red clay sediments with strata belonging to an Early Stage and a Late Stage, contrast in a number of respects with the industries of North China.

The age of the Guanyindong (Guanyin Cave) has not been determined, but it has been placed in the Middle Pleistocene on the basis of faunal remains. It may be older than the Early Stage at Locality 1, Zhoukoudian, for some of the tools show traits suggestive of greater antiquity. Bipolar work does not appear for the production of flakes, splitting of cores or trimming as it does at Zhoukoudian, and only direct percussion appears to have been used. Even more significantly, working edges are more blunt due to trimming by nearly vertical blows, so that edge angles usually exceed 80 degrees (Zhang 1985:178). As has been pointed out, this steep edge flaking occurs on some of the earliest human stonework, and is characteristic of the tools on the highest and therefore oldest terraces at Black's Fork, Wyoming.

The similarities in tool types and morphologies and the close concurrences in manufacturing technologies (i. e. bipolar work) between the Early Paleolithic assemblages of North China and the possibly very early lithic industries of Southern California are obvious to any observer, but the significance of this close resemblance remains to be worked out. Clearly, many questions and uncertainties remain to be resolved.

CAMEO

Mammoths and Minnows
at San Diego

*I*t is 240,000 years before the present. Humans have inhabited the San Diego coastal zone for thousands of years, but their lifeways and customs have scarcely changed at all since their distant ancestors arrived in the region, having been part of the slow drift of very early people that had moved into the Western Hemisphere along the Pacific rim. The coastal climate is similar to the present; warm and semiarid but tempered by the sea.

The grey veils of rain drifted up Buchanan Canyon from the sea interminably. Water lay everywhere in puddles and ponds and ran in a thousand rivulets down the slopes. It streamed down in steady, whispering curtains from the outcropping that formed the shelter under the rim. The usually cheerful hearths were welters of grey, smoldering ash; their acrid, sour odors intensified by the drumming rain.

The people huddled miserably together under the overhangs. All except a few absent hunters sat or squatted on their heels in the powdery white dust, waiting for the storm to pass. They loathed the rain, and lacked enough grasp of natural cause and effect to appreciate its great benefits to them in this increasingly arid land. They only knew its discomfort. Their fires went out, hides tended to rot in the damp, and mud stuck to everything and made sleep almost impossible, since there wasn't enough room in the shallow cave for all to lie down in comfort.

But at last they began to smile around at each other and to point. Patches of clean-washed cobalt were beginning to show in the west. The downpour changed to a drizzle and then the rain ceased entirely. The children walked out cautiously, staring up at the sky, and soon were splashing in the puddles and throwing mud balls at each other. The adults followed and began poking around the hearths, adding dry tinder and fuel and blowing up the fires again. The sun broke into the clear and bathed the world in an almost blinding shimmer and glitter of light.

Down at the foot of the canyon there was a sudden, shouting commotion. The three hunters that had been off prowling somewhere during the storm were running back up the trail, waving as though they had lost their minds and calling out something over and over again. The five hunters who had remained at the shelters along the rim crowded to the edges of their soaked living places and stared down at the madmen below. At last they understood what the three were shouting: a mammoth was mired in the soft mud of the slough!

All of the males seized spears and rushed off down the canyon. The eight hunters, two old men who rarely ventured forth, and the male young of all ages, able to walk or even to toddle; all streamed down the canyon in a frenzy of excitement. They went careening through the dirty brown flood of the stream, covering themselves with mud. They slid down the slopes and clambered up the banks, bellowing and screaming incoherently.

When the members of this feverish pack came streaming out of the canyon and onto the edge of the salt marsh, they instantly saw the huge creature looming there in the slough. A full grown imperial mammoth was caught in the bog and unable to free himself. Apparently during the height of the storm, the muddy floodwaters coming down the valley had overflowed the banks of the river and spread over the bottomland enough to conceal the edge of the marsh. The usually wary elephant had blundered into the trap of the sucking, soft mud and had sunk too deeply in it to be able to walk out again. Now mired to his belly and exhausted from his struggles he no longer floundered but stood passively awaiting his fate. Already a pack of dire wolves had gathered expectantly around the fringe of the marsh and vultures were circling overhead, ominous symbols of approaching death.

The humans gathered in a knot of dark figures on the muddy bank to discuss the situation and decide on their strategy. It was clear that although the huge beast could not extricate himself, he could wheel enough to threaten attackers from most directions. The great curving tusks and menacing trunk were free and able to sweep the ground, and to approach too closely would invite instant death. But if they simply waited for the creature to die of starvation they risked losing him, for the mud might eventually dry out enough for the mammoth to regain his footing. The only part of the great hairy bulk their spears could penetrate with any reliability was the softer underbelly, but now it rested on the mud beyond their reach.

The hunters and the two elders squatted there racking their brains desperately. While the situation was unusual it was not unique, and mired mammoth had been killed many times before in that valley, but never in the lifetimes of the people gathered on the bank. All that they knew about such momentous occasions was hearsay, handed down to them by old men long since departed, relatives whose memories had been embellished and enriched from vivid imagination.

One of the elders recalled such an exploit recounted to him in his youth; how his intrepid and skillful ancestor had dispatched such a beast in just these same circumstances. The triumphant victor had simply goaded the great creature into struggling and lashing out at him hour after hour until it was so exhausted that it lacked the energy to raise its head. Then the storyteller claimed to have taken a sharp, antler-armed spear and thrust it into the mammoth's eye, plunging it so deep as to reach the brain and kill it instantly.

The tale sounded so logical that they set out to try the method. But the mud around the beast was so soft and badly churned up that they found it impossible to approach the animal or maneuver safely. When they did manage to flounder within ten feet or so, the great bull mammoth reacted with such fury and struggled so violently to attack them that they feared he might succeed in finding his footing and charge them or escape.

So they retreated for another council, sinking down on their haunches and staring at the great mountain of meat and the treasure of rich marrow just beyond their reach. The mammoth glared back at them, raising his trunk to trumpet angrily from time to time.

Several courses of action were suggested and then discarded as impractical. One hunter thought they might carry big boulders down from the canyon to the site and crush the mammoth's skull with them. But it was decided that boulders heavy enough to accomplish the execution could not be hurled onto the animal's huge head, for despite the fact that his legs were buried, the top of the great, blunt forehead towered up over the hunters some eight feet above the ground.

Another strategm called for the setting of burning logs against the hairy body, setting the animal on fire. They could be tossed in from a safe distance. But the mammoth would surely seize the blazing firebrands with his trunk and throw them clear if this were tried, and even if it succeeded the pain might cause the creature to scramble so frantically as to free himself. So that idea too was abandoned.

They decided nothing would be lost by trying to get a spear through the thick pelt and hide, since any penetration at all might produce bleeding and eventually lead to death. So three of the best and strongest spearsmen approached the animal from three different directions, hoping to force him to expose the throat where a vital artery might be opened. But he kept his head prudently lowered, almost as if he suspected their intentions, and the best they could do was to cast at the side of the short neck. All three spears found their mark at this short range, and remained sticking out of the thick hide, but no slightest trickle of blood appeared and it was obvious that the weapons had not penetrated deeply enough to cause any damage or even serious discomfort.

It was now growing dark, and still the men were no closer to a solution. Nothing had worked; nothing more could be thought of to try. The boys ran back up the canyon to the living place for dry wood and embers, and a fire was built on the bank nearby. Everyone gathered around the fire. The great white cumulus clouds of clearing weather went sailing overhead on a steady northwest wind, and the cold winter stars came out to flicker and blink through the ragged holes in the sky.

The men talked incessantly and to no purpose at all. The deep voices rose and fell around the fire. The small boys listened respectfully and shivered with excitement. The mammoth waited patiently in his bog, and now and again he trumpeted plaintively, and tried to find solid bottom with his round, padded feet and tree-like legs. But there was no bottom, only the relentless grip of the churned mud.

One by one the dark figures around the fire lay down to sleep. They napped uneasily and rose often at first to step over and stare at the mammoth's great bulk there in the starlight. But at last all slept, rousing themselves only to relieve their bladders and put more wood on the fire.

In the chilly dawn, the darkness began to pale and withdraw in the east and the first sleepy chirpings of foraging sparrows were heard. One of the hunters stretched himself, yawned cavernously and strolled out to the edge of the bog to look at the mammoth. He stared incredulously, then began a roaring and bellowing that brought the sleepers instantly to their feet, grasping for weapons.

But there was no need for weapons. The mammoth was gone. He had simply found solid footing at last and walked away in the night. The hunters went reluctantly home up the canyon to try to explain the loss to their women.

＊　＊　＊　＊

The young man was puzzled and curious. He had come with several others of the band down to the estuary to collect and eat clams. Most of the band lay sprawled in the sun now, lazily settling their hours-long meal. But this man was more alert and observant than most, and he had seen some strange movements in the shallow tidal channel.

Although humans were aware of fish, they were not part of the normal diet, for no strategy had been devised to take them. Hooks, lines and nets were far in the future, and shellfish were available and simple to collect without any equipment except the two hands and possibly a probing toe. But now the young man saw something shining and flashing gold as it worked up the channel rooting out crabs and snails off the bottom. He waded across the flat to get a closer look and saw the vague shapes of a school of large spotfin croakers moving slowly upstream against the tide. Now and then the bronze back and dorsal fin of a fish at least two feet long broke the surface, and clouds of silt exploded like miniature bombs underwater as the fish probed and sucked out the small crustaceans.

With the hunting instinct always uppermost in male humans, it was inevitable that the youth immediately tried to stalk and capture one of these intriguing and mouthwatering trophies. But the instant he stepped into the channel, where the water was some twelve inches deep, the fish darted away like flashes of sunlight and vanished. When he retreated onto the mud they appeared again after a few minute's wait, glimmering and shining enticingly.

Now the hunter walked back to higher ground, retrieved his spear and began a more careful stalk out to the edge of the channel. The other hunters and small boys, seeing him ready to cast his spear but without any hint of what kind of creature was being hunted, also slipped out to the edge of the winding tidal stream prepared to spear any target they saw. All waited with spears cocked and ready.

Soon a school of spotfins began to shine as they twisted and turned in the clear water flowing over the shell-speckled sand on the bottom. One after another the spearsmen drew back their arms to cast, but always the flickering forms vanished again before they could aim and throw. At last the young man who had seen the first fish made out a vague form about ten feet away and hovering almost motionless. He drove his shaft at the shadow, but it was gone before the tip touched the water. After stubbornly trying several more casts without success, he realized other tactics were needed.

By now the tide was ebbing and the fish were leaving the channel. The young man went back to the bank and squatted there staring fixedly at the mud with his brow wrinkled and creased in concentrated thought. Far back in past ages, earlier folk had built rock and willow weirs to trap trout in the streams of the Rockies, but no knowledge of this could have reached him over the millennia. However, the problem to be solved now was not entirely without precedent, for the humans in the region were accustomed to driving hoofed game into cul-de-sacs and over steep cliffs, and even built brush fences when this would serve to drive game into a trap. It took no unusual perception to realize that the same tactics might be applied to fish in a marsh, particularly when he could see before him an almost dry watercourse in which the creatures would surely be stranded and helpless.

The people were well aware of the rhythmic nature of the tides. Since clams were only available to them when the tide went out, they could even predict by now when, on a particular day, a given stage could be expected. So now a plan of attack gradually took shape in the young hunter's groping mind. He gathered the others together and haltingly explained it, using gestures to reinforce the limited vocabulary at his disposal.

They would wait until the next day when the tide was high. As soon as they saw the school of fish move up the channel, which was about thirty feet wide, they would wade in and block it with brush so that the fish would be trapped and stranded when the tide lowered itself sufficiently. They would then be able to gather up the harvest as easily as picking up a pine cone off of the ground.

The men and boys gathered large piles of brush and stacked them where they were handy to the channel. The next day they came down to the estuary ready to execute the plan. Their women came along to watch the maneuver and share in the feast to follow. All waited expectantly until the tide began to ebb. They strained their eyes to catch the first golden glimmer. No fish appeared. Apparently they were all using a different channel today.

The following day they came again to the edge of the tide flat where they had their brush waiting. This time they saw the same golden flashes again. As soon as the school appeared to have passed them, they splashed out shouting directions to each other and began to set their willow branches in the channel. But they had failed to appreciate the remarkable sensitivity to noise and vibration that all members of the croaker family have, and the spotfins went flashing back past them in a twinkling before the barrier was set and effective. So now they had some more thinking to do, especially since the women were greeting their efforts with increasing giggles and merriment. The next day they went doggedly back to the channel again.

The low tide had been later each day, so that it was almost sunset when they began to see fish in the current. This time they sent a scout far up the channel. He was to wait until the school passed him and then he would signal the others. As soon as he began to wave his arms, they went out and began placing the brush again, driving sticks firmly into the bottom to hold the bundles against the current. As they worked busily in the fading light it was impossible to tell if the school had been trapped. They waded out to wait for the tide to drop and strand their catch.

They waited and waited beside their fire, going out often to see if any fish had been stranded yet. But then it became obvious that the tide was rising, not falling. Without their noticing it the tidal difference had diminished day after day, so that there was plenty of water in the channel at low tide. Soon their brush was submerged and the fish swam down the channel.

It was a week before the tide stages were usable for another attempt, and during that week the hunters had frequently been distressed to hear their mates utter the word for "fish" and then giggle and titter uncontrollably. So now the need to outwit the fish had become an obsession with them. They watched the tides carefully, and as soon as conditions were judged suitable everyone went down to the marsh again. This time the sun was high and everything went well. They saw a large school of spotfins working up the channel, the scout signaled from well up the beach, the men and boys slipped out furtively and placed their brush weir and retreated to the bank. All waited expectantly.

The tide ran out steadily. Suddenly there was a splashing and commotion at the weir, then another. The people all began to shout and point; the hunters whacked each other on the back triumphantly. When the water had drained to a few inches of depth there were big, shining spotfins flopping and croaking all up and down the brush barrier. The men and boys gathered them up and piled them on the sand. Soon they were chopped into pieces with the stone cleavers, exposing juicy, translucent flesh.

The men ate the strange food with grunts of exquisite enjoyment, smacking their lips and rolling their eyes extravagantly. The children ate hesitantly at first but then with pleasure. The women did not seem to care for the flavor or texture and ate with expressions of disgust, although they ate steadily.

※　※　※　※

Spring came rippling over the land on the April wind. The late winter grass was green on the hills and under the pines, and now with the warmer days and the climbing sun the flowers were everywhere. Their sweet fragrance drifted up to the living places; the massed lilac blooms on the slopes of the canyon submerged with their sweet, cloying scent even the rank, fetid smells of the dwelling places.

The people were lured away. They munched happily on the more tender and delicate flowers. The tiny drops of nectar and the green stems delighted their palates, and the touch of sweetness was gratefully savored. Green shoots and crisp new tubers were part of their diet in spring, and the coming of this gentle season after the chilly, grey days of winter made everyone eager to wander.

The family bands travelled together, carried their fire in moss-packs, and camped wherever they found themselves in the evening. Wood and water were everywhere in April and May, but gradually as the summer approached the water sources would dry up and make life more restricted, and the people would return to their canyon and its meager though permanent springs. But now they drifted across the land, feeding on shellfish of various kinds, the eggs of seafowl and green turtles, tender green plant foods and small pigeon fledglings snatched out of nests. The hunters ignored the herds of camel, bison and horse, and draped themselves with garlands of bright blossoms.

The people were camped on the white beach beyond the dunes. While they waited for the tide to go out and expose the hard grey sand where the giant surf clams lay, the men were busy with their toolmaking. They walked down to the rocky beach where a cobble ramp had been uncovered by winter tides. Sorting carefully through the stones, their experienced eyes instantly recognized those quartzite and porphyry specimens which they knew could be split and shaped for their purpose.

The toolmaker set a cobble endwise on a large flat boulder and using the latter as an anvil, he struck the cobble a sharp blow in just the right place with a heavy hammer stone. A long, slender flake, curved and sharp as a knife on its edges, spalled off from the struck stone. The craftsmen kept rotating their cobble cores and striking off blades until they had at least one for each member of the party. These simple tools would be forced between the tightly-clamped shells of the clams to cut the adductor muscles, causing them to gape open. Thus the delicious clam nectar, almost a cupful in each of these succulent giants, could be drunk without spilling a drop.

When the tide had withdrawn far down the gentle slope and the clambeds were reachable in the creaming shallows, the people waded out and probed on the bottom until they felt the smooth, rock-hard shells just under the surface. They were tossed up on the sand until a huge pile had been gathered, then the feasters sat by the fire in the misty evening prying open and devouring clams until everyone was gorged and unwilling to swallow another. They lay sprawled in the white sand luxuriously, flat on their backs with their hands laced across their swollen bellies, belching in contentment.

Hours later, as they drowsed and napped around their fire, one of the children glanced down at the beach, where the tide had reached its crest and was beginning to recede. A nearly full moon hung in the thinly-veiled sky, and gleamed on the snowy breakers and the wet, shiny beach with its rippling counterpane of foam sliding smoothly up the long incline.

The little girl stared in amazement. All up and down the beach, as the hissing curtains of water swept up the slope and withdrew, a shimmering layer of small, silvery fishes leaped and twisted and danced in the moonlight. The child began shouting with pleasure and excitement, and ran down to the glistening sand where the grunion were spawning. The rest of the people, men, women and children aroused by the commotion, ran down too and began to shout.

Stuffed and burdened with clams though they were, the foragers' deeply ingrained instinct drove them to reap this harvest spread so lavishly before them. The children tumbled in the wet sand, screaming with laughter and trying to seize the wriggling, slippery fish, which always managed to slip and squirm out of their clutching fingers. The women, many hampered by infants under their arms, had no better luck with the elusive, dancing creatures. Even the men were hardly more successful.

The stocky, heavy-shouldered hunters, fearsome predators attacking their prey in heavy-browed, scowling concentration, went leaping about the beach on all fours like giant black hop-toads, trying to pounce on the tiny, glimmering fish in the gleaming sand. But the grunion eluded them time after time, and when they did manage to pin one down, it slipped out of their grip and flipped insolently away. The frustrated roars of the hunters echoed far down the beach above the lesser roar of the surf. The females found the spectacle of their shaggy mates' humiliation highly amusing, but soon the strange charade ended and the people wandered back one by one to collapse by the fire again.

The tiny fish danced their elaborate mating ritual unmolested there in the moonlight.

CHAPTER 7

The Harvest: Opinions, Deductions and Conclusions

A profusion of sometimes seemingly unrelated facts has been presented here; bits and pieces of evidence pertaining to a variety of matters, much of it only recently acquired and some of it deduced from new insights into previously puzzling information. Many of the views offered and the conclusions reached are subject to vigorous disagreement, running counter as they do to firmly-held opinions of respected members of the scientific community. But many of those opinions are based on the supposedly wise and authoritative pronouncements of their peers, which in turn are based entirely on negative evidence or, in the case of proposals of very early man in America, the asserted absence of convincing proof of human presence before the terminal Wisconsin about 12,000 years ago.

In this regard, the following quotation from Leo Tolstoy, dated 1898, seems appropriate:

> I know that most men — not only those considered clever, but even those who are clever and capable of understanding the most difficult scientific, mathematical or philosophic problems — can seldom discern even the simplest and most obvious truth if it be such that obliges them to admit the falsity of conclusions they have formed, perhaps with much difficulty — conclusions of which they are proud, which they have taught to others, and on which they have built their lives" (Quoted in New Yorker, 1984:54).

Despite assertions to the contrary, there is now ample evidence for the formulation of a new and updated model for the first peopling of the Western Hemisphere. It will have to be a kind of skeleton model with a few large holes and tentative determinations in it, but it will be vastly closer to the truth than the present widely accepted model of relatively recent first arrival; an account of human prehistory in the New World which simply ignores a substantial and increasing body of solid evidence to the contrary. It would be unreasonable to demand that every aspect of human expansion into North America be known and provable before the new model is presented, for in the present circumstances the current one is obviously flawed and untenable.

Since no pre-human hominid remains have been discovered in the Western Hemisphere, it is presumed that the Australopithecines must have evolved into the genus Homo somewhere in Africa or Asia, and probably the former where their fossil remains have been recovered and described. Some limited discoveries of earlier primate fossils, Ramapithecus and Gigantopithecus, are known in China, but they are not considered to be directly ancestral to man. The Leakeys' *Homo habilis* at Olduvai Gorge in Africa is thought to have evolved into *Homo erectus*, an extremely durable and adaptable species which was able to gradually spread over most of the land areas of the earth, areas which during the glacial stages were interconnected into one great, sprawling landmass draped over the surface of the planet.

By about 1,500,000 BP humans were very sparsely established in parts of China and Siberia during a Lower Pleistocene interglacial stage. At this time conditions were far more suitable for human habitation than in the Upper Pleistocene; the climate was milder and the environment richer in easily collectable food resources. Few hunting skills had been developed and humans were primarily foragers, although scavenging and preying on small game appears to have been practiced. Fruits, berries, roots and tubers composed a large part of their diets, and since men at all stages have apparently preferred to live near lakes, rivers or the sea, mollusks and crustaceans were also harvested.

Tentative evidence for the use of fire — burnt animal bone in close association with stone artifacts — has been found at Xihoudu in China dating to this early period. It seems likely that people may have possessed thick coats of body hair, although there is of course no direct evidence of this. Stone tools were extremely crude and simple: sharp, utilized flakes produced by throwing cobbles or chunks of rock against boulders with great force, large points or picks for digging in the ground, and pebble choppers and thick flakes steeply edge-trimmed probably comprised most of their tool kits. Weapons of wood and possibly bone must also have been employed; such rudimentary equipment as clubs and cudgels, lances and throwing sticks.

Defense against the fearsome predators of the Pleistocene probably consisted of flight into thick cover and climbing trees, barricading cave entrances with boulders and possibly bonfires, and as a last resort the hurling of boulders. The latter would also have been useful in scavenging, as would the brandishing of flaming torches if fire was indeed utilized so early.

Over the following one million years few changes in the physical or cultural evolution of *Homo erectus* have been noted, although the evidence is extremely meager. As glacial stages advanced, people either had to adapt to the colder conditions or be forced out of the boreal regions of Siberia, only to gradually filter back during interstades and interglacials. In China, while changes were substantial they were far less severe, shifting in the southern and central regions from subtropical to cold temperate but unglaciated at all but the highest altitudes. In South China the changing climatic cycles must have had little effect on the human population.

In the period from 500,000 to 300,000 BP, dramatic expansions of human settlement appear to have occurred, eventually reaching into the Western Hemisphere. The reasons for this dispersion are not understood but are probably related to growing populations and increasing technological skills. Based on the archaeological record in China, the centers for this accelerating development seem to have been in what are now Beijing, Shanxi and Shaanxi Provinces, and it can be readily seen in the different levels in Locality 1 at Zhoukoudian, where the character of toolmaking changed more in that period than in the preceding 1,000,000 years. The introduction of small, refined, task-specific flake tools like fine scrapers, awls and gravers suggests a life-style more elaborate than obtained in the earlier horizons. "Although detailed microwear analyses have not yet been performed on this assemblage, our hypothesis is that these small tools were employed in a variety of daily tasks, particularly the processing of animal and vegetal products such as skins, tendons, roots, tubers and bark" (Zhang 1985:161).

The root cause of human expansion into unpopulated areas has usually been the depletion of resources, attributable to a number of different factors. Growing populations in a particular region can strain the hunting and gathering economy; improved technological skills leading to greater efficiency in utilizing available resources can deplete them, as can concentrated heavy use such as the harvesting of shellfish. Drastic changes in the climate and environment can clearly cause the disappearance of traditional food supplies, necessitating major movement into more favored regions.

Scanty as our knowledge is, the recent discoveries of sites and localities in Korea and Japan dated into this period suggest a widening of human settlement reaching the Pacific coast. With the onset of the Isotope Stage 10 glacial period with its falling sea levels and exposure of the continental shelves, the rich marine resources of the coastal zones could have been exploited by very primitive human bands.

Once people became adapted to the coastal environment in a major glacial stage, with its simple shellfish, sea bird and seal economy, a gradual along-shore drift became inevitable, fueled by resource depletion. It is about 6,000 miles along the Pacific rim from the Nakamine site in Japan to Buchanan Canyon in San Diego, 12,000 miles to the Atacama Desert in Chile, and perhaps 13,000 miles across the Isthmus of Panama and down the Atlantic coast to the Toca da Esperanca in Brazil. These are vast distances, but even vaster time periods could be involved. 20,000 years could have elapsed from the first exploitation of marine resources in Japan to occupation of the cave in Brazil by early wanderers; perhaps more but probably less, and the entire movement or drift along the continental shelves could have been accomplished within a single glacial stage of lowered sea levels.

In the undemanding setting of the tidal zones, toolmaking technologies must have remained static, so that the stone implements recovered in Buchanan Canyon and in Chile and Brazil's early sites appear to resemble those of much earlier periods in China; especially those of Kehe and Liangshan, both believed by the Chinese to be about 600,000 years old. While the coastal expansion was in progress, in China's interior change was far more accelerated, probably because of denser settlement and thus more rapid diffusion of technological and other cultural advances. As we have seen, stone industries changed steadily from the massive and amorphous shapes of the earlier periods to smaller unifacial flake tools of specific function — gravers, reamers and perforators or awls — which reflected a steady improvement in the treatment of non-lithic materials.

In addition to the early coastal movement around the Pacific rim, a rather different and probably even earlier human expansion into North America must have occurred. These were very primitive Siberian hunters and foragers who moved eastward rather than north up the Lena during a milder pre-Illinoian glacial stage, out onto the forested platform of the exposed Beringian lowlands and up the unglaciated valley of the Yukon River. In the following warmer interglacial stage they occupied the northern Yukon region, including the Old Crow Basin, and advanced up the Mackenzie Valley and south far into the interior of North America, eventually leaving their crude choppers and butchering tools on the high flood plain of the Black's Fork River in Wyoming.

The Siberian Early Paleolithic industries, judging from reports available, appear to have been more crude and inferior to those of the same periods in North China. This very likely reflects differences in the environments of the two regions: the more demanding the environment, the more time needs to be spent in gathering food and staying alive. It also emphasizes again the importance of keeping separate any judgments of chronological placement from those based upon cultural and material achievement.

If the southward movement continued into the Great Basin and the southwestern deserts, it must have done so during a glacio-pluvial stage when climates and environments became suitable for very early human occupation.

Some have argued that the deserts could have been inhabited at any period in the past, pointing to the desert tribes of the Holocene. But those more recent people had developed means of coping with the harsh desert environment not available to the earlier humans: specifically milling tools for seed grinding and pottery for carrying and storing precious water supplies.

On the other hand the very early sites we have found: Black's Fork, Calico, Yuha Pinto Wash and the San Diego sites as well as most of the early sites in China and Siberia — all have been close to substantial bodies of water, and all have had tools suggestive of dependance on large game, either for meat or hides. In arid climatic cycles in the deserts, lakes and ponds soon become salty and impotable and rivers tend to sink into the sand. Many Navaho families in Arizona and New Mexico today depend on springs so meager that it takes hours to fill a water jar.

While some game today — pronghorn, desert bighorn sheep, peccary and deer — can survive in what are called Upper Sonoran climate zones that include scrub oak and juniper, these are at elevations close to 4,000 feet above sea level, and would have been marginal habitat for early man adapted to foraging in marshes and lake margins, and hunting creatures attracted to such features.

Since the uranium series dating of the Calico site at 200,000 BP would place it in or near the ending of an interglacial climate phase, that would seem a very unlikely time for primitive people like *Homo erectus* to have been present in the Manix Basin in an environment similar to that of today. Even the desert ranges in the vicinity are barren and inhospitable, and early people must surely have sought out more favorable landscapes as grass, water, waterfowl and other creatures disappeared from the region.

The true time of human presence at the Calico site must have been earlier or later than 200,000 BP, and the enormous erosion seen at the Mule Canyon alluvial fan suggests an earlier date, perhaps on the order of 250,000 BP in Isotope Stage 10. However, a date of 180,000 BP is perfectly possible, and would place the occupation of the site in the Illinoian glacial stage. Either date would allow for adequate expansion time south over the high prairies and through the Great Basin during a pluvial period of generous lakes, vegetation and herbivores. It would also allow for cultural advances, and particularly toolmaking, from the more primitive industry on the high plateau of Black's Fork to the far more advanced flake tool industry of Calico.

The movements of Asiatic hunter-gatherers at the *Homo erectus* stage of human evolution into North America, or more properly over the continental landmass of Amerasia, was in no way different from the original distribution of even earlier humans over the vast reaches of the Old World. It was, in a very real sense, simply a continuation of a process or phenomenon begun perhaps 2,000,000 years before, and carried out by people increasingly capable of dealing with their environments.

These movements cannot be thought of as migrations or journeys. They were always extensions of familiar territory. An individual might not have moved farther south or east more than a few miles in his lifetime of perhaps 30 years, but as generation followed generation over the millennia, humans spread gradually over the Western Hemisphere from Beringia to Tierra del

Fuego at the southern tip of South America. These territorial advances also cannot be thought of as the spreading rings on a pond when a pebble is tossed in, for some people undoubtedly remained settled for many generations in favored locations, while other human bands drifted deeper and farther into the continents and down their margins.

Today only meager traces of the original Pleistocene inhabitants of the Western Hemisphere can be seen: a few rock and earth features attributed to them, perhaps a wheelbarrowful of fossil human bone, and thousands of stone and bone tools and implements. Without these bits and pieces that we are able to identify, objects that manifestly proclaim the presence of people far back in the distant past, we would be completely ignorant of their existence. With them we can partially reconstruct the long and sometimes difficult and precarious journey from our earliest beginnings to the present. But we can only do that if we are willing to consider all the pieces, and refrain from ignoring those specimens that do not fit our preconceptions.

The foregoing account represents a personal view of the early peopling of the New World. In the opening paragraph of this chapter attention was called to the fact that many facets of that view are controversial and subject to vigorous disagreement, and arguments will be offered here in support of the above conclusions and opinions. Some have been discussed in the preceding text but need to be reemphasized; others have not yet been mentioned.

One of the most frequently heard objections concerns the absence of the skeletal remains of *Homo erectus* in the Western Hemisphere. If such humans were present for some 150,000 years, and with thousands of archaeologists searching for close to a century, why haven't his bones been found? There are a number of reasons.

First and most importantly one must realize that, although *Homo erectus* is known to have been in China for well over 1,000,000 years and the Chinese archaeologists have been active and diligent, except for the amazing discovery at Zhoukoudian, all the rest of the fossils in China belonging to this species could be carried in a small bucket — mere fragments like jawbones and teeth that could easily be overlooked. In fact, some *Homo erectus* American skeletal parts may have been overlooked or mislabeled, for the postcranial bones are very similar to those of *Homo sapiens*, and unless the sample were datable it would be difficult to identify. Some such fossils may even now be resting, covered with dust, in museum basements, unrecognized and forgotten, for it would not occur to workers convinced of human recency in America that the bones could belong to an earlier species.

Why are such fossils so rare, when those of other Pleistocene creatures are recovered in profusion? Most nonhuman fossils have been found in ancient sediments that had quickly covered them, principally the muds and silts of lake shores and marshes. Some have been preserved in permafrost, where carcasses were quickly frozen. The fossil remains of carnivores are scarcer than their percentage of the total fauna in a normal ecological system would warrant, probably because they are generally more intelligent than herbivores. Humans, being the most intelligent carnivores of all, were unlikely to be swallowed up in mudholes or tar pits or to be drowned in icewater, and their numbers would have been far fewer in any given time or region when compared to their fellow predators.

Of course all creatures including humans die eventually, but burial, although practiced by some Neanderthal people, appears to be a generally recent custom. Bodies exposed in the open during the Pleistocene vanished almost immediately, bones and all, devoured by scavengers like the dire wolves and huge teratorn vultures. Any remnants of bone would soon have been gnawed away by rodents. Providing there were survivors, people who died in caves and rockshelters would have been carried outside promptly by their cavemates before the stench of rotting flesh became overpowering.

Without fossil remains, the presence or absence of *Homo erectus* in the New World can neither be proved nor disproved empirically, but other evidence strongly suggests his presence. The temporal scale of human evolution into *Homo sapiens* is still somewhat vague and uncertain, and almost certainly varied considerably in different parts of the world and under different environmental circumstances. The Neanderthal people of Europe and the Middle East are broadly accepted as representing an archaic form of *Homo sapiens*, humans with prognathous jaws and bony supraorbital ridges but with somewhat higher cranial capacity and higher domed skulls than H. erectus. They apparently appeared at some time later than 150,000 BP.

In China the early *Homo sapiens* specimens from Mapa, Dali and Xujiayao lack most of the Neanderthaloid features and are all thought to be younger than 100,000 years. They are said to already show some Mongoloid features, and the transition to *Homo sapiens sapiens*, the modern form to which we belong, occurred sometime in the Late Pleistocene but is not well dated. In southern Australia fossil remains of the so-called Kow Swamp people have been described as resembling *Homo erectus* but are dated at about 10,000 BP.

At the Calico site in Southern California every indication insists on an age for man of some 200,000 years, a minimum age for humans in the Western Hemisphere. Unless physical evolution proceeded far more rapidly in the New World than the Old, the toolmakers of Calico must have belonged to the species *Homo erectus*, as did those of the Late Stage, Locality 1 of Zhoukoudian, where both tools and estimated ages are similar to Calico's.

But is Calico really that old? This is obviously a critical point of disagreement. By at least four different means of measure; five if the newest Potassium/Argon-dated find at the foot of the fan is included, it is up to 200,000 years old: by the two radiometric dates, by soils analysis, by geomorphology and by dating of desert varnish. Furthermore, the estimates of many competent geologists at the 1970 Calico Conference placed the age of the sediments containing the lithic specimens at far more than 200,000 years; some even suggesting between a half million and a million years. Admittedly, some of the more extreme estimates may have been influenced by a wish to discredit the site as evidence of very early man in America.

Because of their importance in establishing and supporting the antiquity of the Calico site, and in a sense the whole concept of very early peopling of the New World, the above dating methods and bases for estimates need to be reviewed. The most definitive was the uranium series dating of calcium carbonate scraped off of lithic specimens near the base of the excavations and reported by James Bischoff and colleagues. Although radiometric dating must be regarded with caution, it is difficult to see how the results of the Calico age determinations could have been seriously distorted.

The dating relies on the fact that isotopes of uranium, present in ground water, will if isolated gradually change at a known rate into isotopes of thorium or protactinium. In the case of the Calico samples, rinds of calcium carbonate crystallized and later absorbed trace amounts of uranium, isolating them and beginning the transformation process. By measuring the relative amounts of uranium and the so-called daughter elements present in the sample and knowing the rate of uranium decay, the time since isolation can be determined. In the case of Calico, that time was found to be 200,000 +/- 20,000 years.

As pointed out earlier, the uranium series results did not represent the period of time since humans occupied the alluvial fan and left the stone tools on the surface, but rather the time since the tools became buried deeply enough to not only receive deposits of calcium carbonate, but time enough to allow subsequent absorption of uranium from the groundwater. An unknown amount of time elapsed from original deposition until uranium began to accumulate. Since humans would have been unlikely to occupy the region in an arid interglacial stage when aggradation of the fan was active and burial of the tools at depth occurred, they were more likely to have been there in the preceding pluvial climate stage.

The soils analyses, conducted by Roy J. Shlemon, included sediments at depth and surface soil development. These are based on such aspects as depth of soil formation, penetration of calcium carbonate and depth of calcic horizons, degree of clay formation, color and particle size. Observations are compared with soils of known age in the general region dated by radiometric methods. Shlemon concluded that soil horizons on the relict surfaces of the alluvial fan were between 80,000 and 125,000 years old. He also estimated that the lower or Yermo sediments had been laid down between 150,000 and 200,000 years ago as mud and debris flows under humid environments, a view with which I strongly disagree for reasons that will be offered shortly.

Two other bases for the antiquity of the fan structure at Calico have been cited by Theodore Oberlander. The most obvious is the extraordinarily heavy erosion of the surface there. What had once been a relatively smooth apron of sediments is now a maze of deep gullies and canyons, an effect that in his opinion must have taken over 100,000 years to produce. This estimate agrees with Shlemon's findings, and it also agrees with Oberlander's deduced age of desert varnish coating rocks on the stable surfaces above the excavations: about 100,000 years, obtained by the Coso cation leaching curve described in Chapter V.

As to the problem of what kind of climates produce heavy aggradation on alluvial fans, I hold what appears to be a minority view. During extended humid climate periods the growth of vegetation and heavy ground cover is promoted. Pollens recovered from the lower sediments at Calico indicate the presence of piñon and juniper; the fossil bones of herbivores are being found in some profusion at the base of the fan in marsh sediments of the now-vanished Pleistocene Lake Manix. Such evidence precludes the presence of barren slopes on the surrounding hills, and heavy rain on vegetated slopes produces runoff of water, not mud and boulders, and would promote streams on the alluvial fans and erosion rather than aggradation of them.

On the other hand, in arid periods with the disappearance of ground cover, a heavy thunderstorm on the slopes can move enormous amounts of mud and rock down the canyons and washes, and even in modest rains on the upper elevations the drainage runs thick with silts to be deposited as more level ground is reached and velocity is reduced. Over the centuries and millennia even widely spaced episodes of aggradation eventually produce alluvial deposits of generous dimensions.

We are of course today in an interglacial stage with arid conditions prevailing in the deserts. Twice in my own lifetime I have had the effects of heavy rains in the desert impressed upon me; once it almost cost me my life. On that occasion I was driving with a friend eastward across the low desert on the approaches to the Imperial Valley in the early hours before dawn. The date was the first day of September, the opening day of dove season in Southern California, and we were eager to reach a favorite spot before daylight. As we drove down a long incline with a barren desert range just to the north, we noticed the almost continuous flickering of lightning on the summits, although the sky was clear over us and the stars were out.

As we topped a rise travelling at high speed we were horrified to see a brown torrent of mud and rocks pouring across the highway down what had previously been a minor wash. Stopping was impossible; we plunged in and were immediately almost swept off of the road. With the engine roaring we barely managed to churn our way crabwise across the mudflow and out the other side. Such mudflows are an awesome sight, and the amount of soils removed from the mountain and deposited on the desert floor from that one episode would be incalculable.

The other object lesson came with the flood at Yuha Pinto Wash described earlier. The wash had been fairly thickly grown with desert shrubbery on its flat floor before the arrival of the storm "Kathleen." The Mexican Government had been engaged in a major project to bring water from the Colorado River to the coastal cities, and huge pipes more than six feet in diameter had been stored loosely on the floor of the wash, preparatory to their installation. After the flood had passed and we visited the scene, the concrete pipes were scattered like matchsticks downstream, and we saw many of them nearly or completely buried in the mud and silt. The upper slopes from which that mud was removed is typical desert terrain: bare of more than scattered small shrubs, and quickly eroded.

Since no one now alive has ever seen the present desert areas during a pluvial climate cycle like those of the Pleistocene, reconstruction of former landscapes and climate environments is based on logical inference from the few hints we have; paleopollens and fossil bones provide clues but leave much to the imagination. But in the case of the occurrence of mudflows, one can certainly examine regions that appear to be similar today to what must have existed in the modern desert regions during the glacio-pluvial stages of the Pleistocene.

If humid climates cause mudflows they obviously should be common in northern California, western Oregon and Washington in areas not modified by urban development of slopes or volcanic action as at Mount St. Helen. But if heavy mudflows occur in those regions they have not been reported, nor are they troublesome in somewhat less humid but non-arid regions like the piñon and juniper country of southern Utah near Beaver, surrounded by mountains and with ample rain. Put even more simply, if you pour water on your lawn water will run off, but if you pour water on bare earth, mud will run off.

There is no question that some of the alluvium revealed in the Calico excavations was deposited by massive mudflows, but these are not seen at the anthropic or culture-bearing levels, where concentrations of delicate flake tools, flakes and flaking waste were uncovered. These must clearly have been covered by far more gentle means: the normal and gradual accretion of soils in a humid environment.

The broad disagreement over whether early purported artifacts are really manmade or just naturally chipped and fractured has been belabored in previous pages and will not be addressed extensively here. The argument may never be settled to everyone's satisfaction, since recognition of very early human stonework requires careful, personal examination of the specimens in question, with a clear understanding of what Nature can and cannot do. Also needed is some familiarity with the lithic industries of Lower Paleolithic humans as well as the patterns expectable on artifacts attributable to human percussive flaking and bipolar work.

Judgments based on faulty knowledge, hearsay or casual and uninformed inspection without the required insights will continue to be made and proclaimed, but these will serve no useful purpose but rather continuation of the so-called controversy. According to Alan Bryan, ". . . if any skeptic has ever expressed any doubt about the interpretation of the evidence from a site, whether or not they have ever visited the locality, the evidence is rendered 'equivocal'." (1986:5)

Michael Moratto, in his definitive book on California archaeology (1984) makes the following observations: "The case for Buchanan Canyon being a cultural site is without merit. . . Archaeologists familiar with the San Diego materials agree that they are naturally fractured stones, and not artifacts. . . Texas Street, Buchanan Canyon and other sites of their genre in the San Diego vicinity almost certainly are not archaeological." Although Moratto has never seen the Buchanan Canyon assemblage, mostly in my custody, hundreds of readers will presumably accept his uninformed and second-hand judgment as gospel. This is most unfortunate.

All of the very early assemblages described above are indeed humanly altered lithic specimens, even those produced by random throwing. At Calico, in the San Diego coastal region, at Yuha Pinto Wash and on the varnished and sun-baked pavements covering hundreds of square miles of level desert terraces, untouched by streams or mudflows and overlooking the basins of ancient Pleistocene lakes and marshes; on the elevated flood plain of Black's Fork; all have artifacts discarded scores of millennia ago by the descendants of those Asian foragers who ventured across the lowlands of Beringia.

There are admittedly gaps in the proposed paradigm for peopling of the Americas. An obvious one is the absence still of empirical evidence for the movements of very early humans along the northern Pacific rim and up the valleys of the Yukon, the Porcupine and the Mackenzie. Such material may never be discovered and in fact may no longer exist. But in a sense all of those obviously ancient stone artifacts of which we are aware make plain that such evidence once existed before it was destroyed and obliterated by surf, foaming rivers in spring freshet and the grinding of glacial ice. No other rational explanation can account for their presence in the geographical locations where we see them today.

The original goal of the present study, begun 18 years ago in Buchanan Canyon, was to understand and explain the presence of those massive artifacts in the center of a bustling and modern city, to investigate the origins and nature of their makers, and to reconstruct if possible the landscapes and environments in which they dwelt. In gathering pertinent facts and circumstances we have ranged far afield, and enough information has been accumulated to make possible now a reasonable and even probable prehistory of the region and its earliest human inhabitants.

About 300,000 years ago, during Isotope Stage 10, the San Diego region was very different from that seen today. The climate was considerably cooler and more humid. Rainfall along the coast was more than double present amounts and snow was heavier in the mountains of the Southern California Peninsular Range, where small montane glaciers formed at the higher elevations. Winter snowstorms sometimes extended down to the coast, but in general the moderating effect of the ocean prevented severe extremes of weather. Sizeable rivers ran down to the sea in all seasons, excavating their valleys substantially in the lower reaches because of the lowered sea level, and forming deltas on the continental shelf some four miles to westward of the present beaches.

The physical features of the land behind the beaches were quite different from those of today, for the coast in the vicinity of San Diego has been undergoing slow but steady tectonic uplift throughout the period, probably amounting to more than 120 feet of elevation, so that topographical profiles from the beaches to the foothills were far lower and valley walls more modest in height. Deep canyons like Buchanan Canyon would have been far shallower in respect to their walls, and many would have had permanent streams in their bottoms. The seismically-uplifted minor plateaus like Point Loma and the La Jolla highlands would have been far less imposing, while the Coronado Islands would have been low buttes on the mainland.

The present sea bottom, relatively flat and featureless except for some nearshore deep submarine canyons, would have developed over the exposed millennia of the glacio-pluvial stage a diverse profile of stream-cut minor valleys, cliffs and escarpments, and possibly even caves in the limestones of Tertiary sea floors. As it has in all ages, sand would have been carried down the rivers to the sea; this would have arranged itself with the help of sea currents and winds into the sand beaches, dunes and barrier lagoons typical of our present coasts.

Terrestrial faunal and paleopollen records for this early period in the San Diego region are sparse if not nonexistent, but reasonable assumptions can be made, based on data from similar localities elsewhere having more information available. Areas now having approximately the same coastal orientation and climate as San Diego is believed to have experienced during the Pleistocene glacial stages can serve as models for those earlier floral environments. The coast of California from Santa Barbara to Moro Bay is suggested as meeting those requirement under the present conditions.

Here would be included conifers like Monterey pine and cypress in groves interspersed with open grasslands. Deciduous oaks, cottonwoods and sycamores would have grown in the valleys and draws, while lakes and ponds would surely have dotted the countryside in the relatively humid climate, the ponds fringed with thickets of willow and alder. A variety of berries would have included currents, gooseberries, service berries, strawberries and red raspberries.

The fauna of the region would have been little different from the Wisconsin species known from the tar pits of Rancho LaBrea, with a few notable exceptions. *Bison latifrons*, an enormous bovid almost ten feet at the shoulder and with huge, spreading horns, would have been present but would be replaced by *Bison antiquus*, only slightly smaller, during the Wisconsin. Other grazers would have included camel, horse, musk ox and mammoth, while wooded areas would shelter browsers like mastodon and deer, and ground grubbers including peccary and giant ground sloth. The ponds and marshes would have been inhabited by tapirs.

Carnivores included the sabertooth cat, a large Pleistocene lion or jaguar, the dire wolf which occupied a niche similar to that of the Old World hyena, the carnivorous short-faced bear, and probably many of the lesser predators that have survived down to the present: cougar, bobcat and grizzly. Among the birds present would have been the huge teratorn vulture, a turkey similar to the modern ocellated turkey of Yucatan, a Pleistocene stork and a goose somewhat larger than any modern species. Admittedly, listing the above without fossil remains is somewhat speculative.

The presence of people at this early glacio-pluvial stage is possible but unsupported by physical evidence, for humans would surely have lived close to the beaches as their ancestors had done over the millennia, during the slow drift around the Pacific rim. The earliest suggestions of human presence have been found at locations more likely to have been occupied during the following pre-Illinoian or Isotope Stage 9 interglacial.

Early in this period deglaciation on the continents caused sea levels to rise rather rapidly, and humans would have been forced, over several generations, to gradually retreat behind the encroaching surf lines and the estuaries creeping up the excavated and scoured-out coastal valleys. The extremely primitive tool industry excavated by Reeves at Mission Ridge probably belongs to this period and may represent a specific cultural horizon and time, while the redeposited and surface lithic materials scattered throughout the coastal region must have accumulated over scores of millennia.

Carter's Texas Street site may also date to this Stage 9 or pre-Illinoian Yarmouth Interglacial. The tools there are similar to Mission Ridge specimens in that they are principally amorphous pieces of quartzite that have either been naturally fractured or obtained by throwing, and roughly trimmed by hand-held percussion. Traditional tool types simply do not occur at either site, and both are on elevated stream terraces that would then have been down closer to the level of the estuary early in the interglacial stage, before the latter was eliminated by valley filling.

The San Diego region in the interglacial stages must have had climates and plant environments somewhat similar to present Holocene conditions, although faunal populations were quite different. The intrusion of chaparral over what had formerly been forbs and grasses would have greatly diminished the numbers of herbivores like horse and bison, as well as browsers like mastodon and deer in the coastal zone. Conifers disappeared on and near the coast except for a few Torrey pines and cypress. Cactus and succulents appeared and provided forage for camels, peccaries and ground sloths, while the juicy red fruit of nopales, called prickly pears or cactus apples, was gathered by humans in season.

In these semiarid conditions the coastal rivers sank below the sands of their beds except after sparse winter rains, leaving pools and ponds along their lengths upstream from the saltwater marshes and estuaries. These attracted animals of many kinds, from mammoth herds to small mammals like racoons and foxes. People, too, utilized these water resources in the driest seasons.

During the pluvial periods of the following glacial stages, it is not clear whether people again moved out onto the exposed landmass of the continental shelf to utilize the marine resources, gradually withdrawing to the westward, or continued to inhabit the valleys, mesas and canyons inland from the coast. Most likely both environments were exploited. At some period in the past they appear to have developed hunting skills, for in the Buchanan Canyon and other generalized assemblages, tools and implements like the skreblos or butchering tools and the spokeshaves for dressing down spear shafts strongly suggest the hunting of good-sized animals. A humid period would be a logical time for such practices to develop, for faunal populations then would be at their most generous levels.

There is also the possibility that human bands crossed the mountains and occupied the desert sites; ideal habitats for very early foragers and hunters during the pluvial conditions and rich lake environments of the Illinoian glacial stage. However, the question of how they could have known such regions and resources even existed is problematical, as is the supposition that the coast dwellers would have had any reason to leave their familiar surroundings.

During the Sangamon or last interglacial, humans, now having almost completed the slow transition to *Homo sapiens*, again were concentrated in the valleys, canyons and mesa tops, and again left their discarded and battered chopping and butchering tools in the chaparral and the dust and sand of the dry washes, to be buried and redeposited and mixed with the somewhat cruder implements of even earlier people. By now their knapping skills had improved, so that lithic specimens recovered from the lowest levels of the Charles H. Brown site in Mission Valley are so symmetrically flaked as to leave no slightest doubt as to their human origin.

Hunting skills must have also greatly improved, although stone-tipped spears still had not come into use. With increased cranial capacity probably came advances in social organization, so that expanded family bands could cooperate with other groups in the general vicinity for game drives, the building of fish weirs in the creeks and channels, and other beneficial group efforts. These advances, however, were hardly beneficial for their fellow creatures, so that the seeds of Pleistocene extinctions may have been planted far earlier than is generally supposed.

For early Wisconsin time we have the stratigraphy and artifacts of the Charles H. Brown site to consult, so far less guesswork is involved. It seems to support the belief that the people during the pluvial periods of falling sea levels followed the beaches westward to continue to enjoy the benefits of the shellfish resource, but reoccupied the Brown site thousands of years later during an interstadial period of higher sea level.

Since the winter of 1970 with its revealing glimpse on the floor of Buchanan Canyon of an unsuspected human presence apparently far back in time, great progress has been made in our slowly accumulating knowledge of ancient man in Amerasia. We now have new and far older sites in both hemispheres, and new laboratory dating methods like Oberlander and Dorn's work with desert varnish. These have added immeasurably to our understanding of human prehistory and slow expansion over vast areas of the earth's surface, and new appreciation of the ability of very early people to adapt to rigorous environments.

In the Mission Ridge and Texas Street sites, with their crude hearths and trimmed quartzite fragments, perhaps the earliest traces of humans in the California coastal zone have been revealed. Across the mountains of the Peninsular Range, the Yuha Pinto Wash site and the Miller Mammoth site have disclosed evidence of very early human presence, far earlier than had been previously suspected, while heavily varnished and alternately-flaked stone tools can be observed in profusion on desert pavements overlooking Pleistocene Lake Le Conte. The rich tool assemblages and sediments at the Calico site have been convincingly dated at more than 200,000 years before the present.

At opposite ends of the Americas are the coarse choppers at Toca da Esperanca in Brazil, dated at between 205,000 BP and 295,000 BP, and the work in the Old Crow Basin of northern Canada by Morlan, Irving and others, revealing the bone artifact industry of early people well back in the Pleistocene. Although not reported here, the investigations of other archaeologists like A. L. Bryan and N. Guidon in Brazil have already pushed back the time of first human arrival in the Western Hemisphere far beyond the 12,000 year-old Clovis stage still insisted upon by ultra-conservative academicians as representing the first Americans.

Work in east and northeast Asia has been equally significant in understanding the antiquity and movements of very early people in Amerasia. The excavation of a Soviet perma-frost site on a high terrace above the Lena River near the village of Dering-Yuryak, believed by its investigators to be a million years old or more, has exploded the myth of human inability to adapt to cold arctic environments and expand into North America at high latitudes. In today's interglacial climate, this is still one of the coldest regions on earth.

The discovery of strong similarities between Chinese assemblages dated between 600,000 and 200,000 BP and tools from Southern California sites and localities has suggested, if not a temporal correspondence, at least parallel stages of cultural evolution between those widely separated areas. The finding of massive quartzite tools, apparently identical to the cobble industry of the San Diego coastal zone, on a terrace of the Hantan River in Korea and estimated to be about 300,000 years old, and the excavation of an even older site at Nakamine on the Pacific coast of Honshu, Japan, has made even more convincing the probability of very early human expansion around the Pacific rim.

These and other developments in the relatively recent past have made evident the pressing need for reappraisal of the whole question of the first peopling of the Americas. It is clear, at least to me, that the shadowy figure that seemed to stand before me in Buchanan Canyon so many years ago, the maker and user of those massive choppers uncovered by the flood, represented only one link in a human chain that stretches far back into the distant past. The backtrail runs far around the Pacific rim, along the once exposed and uplifted continental shelves, across the fogbound lowlands of Beringia, past the rocky cliffs of Kamchatka to Japan, Korea, and finally to the caves of Zhoukoudian, the gully at Kehe Village and the incredibly ancient site at Xihoudu.

The backtrail ends there.

CAMEO

Mission Valley, the Storm and Departure

*I*t is 100,000 years before the present. Humans have been living intermittently in the San Diego coastal zone for 150,000 years. Despite favorable climate conditions in an interglacial cycle, high infant mortality and disease, particularly infections from wounds and scratches, have kept the population sparse and stable. The people are of an archaic form of the species Homo sapiens, slowly developing toward a fully modern form.

The late fall day was brilliant. The people relaxed in the clean, white sand of the beach beyond the point. At noon the sun looked down out of a clear blue sky and sparkled and shone on the towering swells that were running up from the south. The children splashed and laughed in the shallows, and the older ones poked around in the tidepools looking for sea cucumbers and small octopi. Some of the hunters had hoped to dive but the surge was strong and they stayed on the rocks and harvested mussels.

An elder hunter sat on a rocky shelf of the cliffs behind the beach. In his thirties now he was active and strong but nearing the end of his life. His barrel chest and powerful arms still gave no signs of diminishing power, and his mind was keen and lively. Only his grizzled hair and the white wisps on his chin, and perhaps his wisdom, spoke of advancing age.

As he gazed out over the beach he could see his mate and his children, and he felt a swelling pride as he gazed at the oldest son. The youth was well-formed and handsome, and soon would be seeking a mate and begetting a family himself. The elder thought with great satisfaction how pleasant was life in his world. He thought of the long line of humans before him that had dwelt in this pleasant land, and of the generations yet unborn to enjoy it.

On the beach below him, the young males were hurling their spears at a bundle of kelp for a target. They drew a line in the sand a hundred paces away and began to cast. The elder was pleased to notice how well his son did in the competition. But it saddened him when he thought of his own youth and the plentiful game of those vanished years. When he was a young man the herds of camel and horse still wandered over the mesas and valleys in far greater numbers, and deer and antelope browsed on the fringes of the broad meadows. And back in his youth, it seemed to him, the men had truly been hunters, not giants perhaps like the ancient ancestors who had killed mammoths and left their huge tusks in the canyons, but hunters who spent most of their time in the chase.

Now the men passed their days building fish weirs, and crouching hidden at waterholes hoping to spear a mule deer or peccary and follow it through the dry chaparral until it went down. They handed down stories from father to son of the ancient races who lived in the canyon, and of strange, vanished creatures that lived when the land was greener, and before the time of seemingly endless droughts. But the tales were vague and distorted like poorly remembered dreams, and only the great, ivory tusks in the canyon and fragments of old antler and bone gave them any credence at all.

But the men were still hunters first and foremost, as trembling and eager when they crouched in the ambush as had ever been any that went before them. Although they ate roots, cactus fruit and seafood, as well as lizards and snakes and crickets and anything else that was edible, they still preferred toasting the sizzling slices of meat at the hearth. They still shouted and pranced at the fires whenever big game had been killed, and bragged of their courage and skill on the game trail. They still met death in the chase, but usually now from tripping themselves in the rocks and brush and breaking their necks or limbs, and not from fatal attacks by horn and fang.

Big game hunting now was an occasional venture, a sport to engage in and a test of one's manhood but not a pursuit depended upon for the livelihood, and sometimes weeks went by when no large creature at all was killed. Although the elder thought this sad and longed for the days of his youth, his memory was playing him tricks, and the men of Buchanan Canyon even in that earlier day were gazing longingly backward in time and in the same fashion, as old men have probably always done.

The sun was warm on his back, the rippled blue sea stretched out to the bulk of an offshore island, and the people below him laughed and frolicked and dozed in the clean, white sand of the beach. But something about the swell racing up from the south puzzled the watching man on the cliff.

The tide was rising steadily, and breakers began to come rolling in where breakers had never been known before. The crescent-shaped cove below the point faced almost south, so its rocky horns shielded it from the westerly swell. It was always a favorite place for mussels and abalones, for the rocky reefs and fingers were normally washed by no more than a gentle surge. The deep green pools and channels were framed by great, billowing masses of olive brown rockweed and garnished with streamers of golden kelp, and a man could dive down in the crystal water and slip a stone blade quickly under the shell of an abalone before it could clamp down and fasten itself to the rock.

Lobsters, too, could often be found by groping into the holes and cracks in the rocks; a man in the water could open his eyes and see the dark crevices in the green dimness and wavering light. If he reached in his hand to feel around in the mossy recess, he might touch the hard, spiny carapace of the lobster, feel the creature brush him desperately with its long, waving feelers. Then a bold grasp and the mottled brown prize could be drawn out, violently jerking and flapping its powerful tail and gnashing its mandible angrily.

But that was not possible today. The strange swells kept building, running into the cove to thunder and roar in mountains of churning white spume, crashing down on the once-quiet pools and the rocks. The people gathered well up on the beach to stare at the rare spectacle. They had often seen heavy seas break on the rocks of the windward side, but these of today were different and somehow strangely disturbing, as though the familiar ocean were in the throes of some violent seizure. The swells reared and curled far out offshore over the reefs, and as they sped landward they turned into combers that rolled along with frightening power and turbulence, to run far up the beach beyond the normal highwater mark. Where cobbled shingles had been stripped of their mantles of sand, the stones went clacking and rocketing under the thrust of the violent surf.

Another strange portent was noted. The older people were finely attuned to the ways and habits of their fellow creatures, and they had never seen so many seagulls fly inland. Wave after wave of the big white birds went steadily beating their way across the shoreline all up and down the coast as far as the eye could see. Far inland the flickering wings were seen rising and falling in the still air as the flocks disappeared over the distant hills.

The shorebirds, too, seemed more nervous than usual. Thick flocks of willets and sanderlings, flying in tight, compact formations, constantly whipped over the heads of the people and went spinning over the surf and the beaches like smears of smoke streaming off in a wind, but there was no wind. The birds settled down to the sand briefly, and almost instantly whirled away, upset perhaps by the violent thrust of the sea or a quality in the air that humans could not discern.

The air felt sticky and hot, a breathless quality rare in November. As the elder hunter came down from the cliff and helped to bundle the harvest of mussels in the hides to carry back to the living place, his brown skin shown shiny and wet in the sun. He drank from the hide water pouch they had carried along, but the water was tepid and stale. The sun had been glaring down and the white sand reflected the heat in wavering shimmers, but then a faint shadow brushed the beach with a touch of coolness, and the people glanced up in surprise. A fragile mare's tail of white cloud was touching the sun briefly and dimming its brilliance, and others appeared high in the sky above the now-purple offshore island.

The mussels were bundled and shouldered, the hunters picked up their spears, women rounded up their small children and settled tiny brown infants on their broad hips. They trailed along up the shore still watching the booming surf where no surf had ever been seen, chattering and laughing in spite of the uneasy feelings that many had at the back of their minds.

As they left the sea beach and went scuffing over the dunes, they sensed the same mood of peculiar strangeness cast over the waiting land. Distant details stood out in sharp relief although the sun was now muted. Thin veils of cloud in silvery curtains drifted almost unnoticed across the sky. High aloft the feathery spindrift raced along, but down on the seared, brown surface of the land every cobweb and leaf hung motionless in the windless air.

No rain had fallen in nearly a year, and even the springs were failing. The hollow earth basin that the people had dug in Buchanan Canyon took hours to fill, and sometimes late in the day the seepage stopped altogether. Now in November it seemed that at last the rainclouds might gather again, and everyone kept a constant and hopeful watch on the sky. But the strange glare cast by the shrouded blur of the sun and the atmosphere of breathless expectancy was something even the elders had never known before.

Far out over the sea horizon still, one of the small, violent storms now called a chubasco in Mexico was churning along. Spawned in tropical waters, the vicious small hurricane had recurved to an easterly course and was heading back toward the land. As it hurled itself at the coast its cloud shield gathered and grew and a gentle shower began to fall on the land.

The people felt the cool touch of rain on their backs with exquisite pleasure. As the silvery drops pattered down, little puffs and explosions of dust jumped into the sultry air. The children turned up laughing brown faces and tried to catch drops on their tongues, and everyone smiled with relief that at last the drought was broken and there would be water flowing across the parched country again.

They walked up the canyon to the shelters under the rim of the mesa. The old people had stayed there and tended the hearths, and now the bundles of mussels were opened and the big blue shells were set round the coals to steam in their savory juices. The rain pattered down, but the fires were built up to leaping vigor and easily maintained themselves with only a little hissing and splutter of protest. As the shells gaped open the people drank the rich nectar and pulled out the orange meat with horny brown fingers.

The uneasy feelings of portent caused by the strange, brooding weather vanished as darkness came down on the canyon, and only the flames and the circle of happy, fire-lit faces and busy hands could be seen. But the rain still pattered down and dripped from the overhang, and slowly increased until muddy puddles began to form. It was clear that many would have an uncomfortable night, since there was never enough room for all to lie under the shelter. Dry wood was stacked there, and the store of cured hides was kept from the damp to protect them. Once wetted they would dry stiff as boards and need to be completely reworked.

The people lay down to nap in the wet slimy mud and the puddles, but a new discomfort arose. A fresh breeze sprang up, and from an unusual direction. It came down on the draw from the east, gusty and strong, and sent showers of cinders aloft from the sputtering fires. The smoke writhed over the ground in heavy white coils from the dampened wood and whipped into the eyes and noses of the restless sleepers, causing them to strangle and cough and their eyes to water.

The wind rose steadily, and now the rain drummed down with a force and volume none of the people had ever experienced before. The fires went out in billowing clouds of steam. Great sheets of water began to cascade down the slope and fall in a solid curtain over the projecting shelter, so that now and again cobbles and red, clotted masses of clay thudded down onto the floor of the living place.

One by one the adults got to their feet and shepherded their young back under the overhanging ceiling where they huddled for safety away from the falling rocks. The wind shrieked in a higher intensity, and blew the curtain of water back into the farthest recesses. There was no way to escape it. They could only stand soaked and streaming and patiently wait for the storm to pass.

But the storm kept increasing in fury. Now the wind was a huge battering ram against which they could hardly stand. Its full force hammered at them on their watersoaked ledge and bellowed full-throated through the dead trees on the rim. Wind and water and flying debris filled all the air space with a shouting, violent confusion that left the cowering humans dazed and bewildered. Thick, solid rivers of mud were pouring down all the slopes now, and the overhangs began to give way and fall. As great, ragged chunks detached themselves and came hurtling down, the people below them barely escaped being buried alive. They struggled out from under the collapsing shelters and clawed their way up the slope to the rim in the roaring darkness. Here they clustered together under the thrashing trees, buffeted by the hammer blows of the wind and half drowned.

Toward morning the chubasco began to abate. The wind dropped down to a fresh breeze again, and hauled around to the westward. The torrents of rain slowly lessened. By daybreak the showers had ceased altogether, although a brisk, chilly wind still whipped through the trees and around the shivering people.

As they began hesitantly to investigate their sodden and storm-lashed world, a strange, distant sound was heard. A steady roar came up from the valley and marsh, and when they walked to the rim of the mesa and looked down the canyon, they could see an enormous river of mud-thickened water and debris rushing past the foot of the draw and out toward the sea. Some of the people walked to the rim of the valley and stared in amazement. The whole floor below them and bank to bank was a roaring torrent of brown. They could see huge trees, cottonwoods and sycamores, that had been torn loose and uprooted, bobbing along on the flood. Every canyon, ditch and ravine was pouring out a cascade of muddy water and stones into the moving cauldron. Here and there on its surface the floating forms of drowned animals spun in the eddies.

The storm-battered humans gathered to watch the grim spectacle and gazed spellbound at the destruction and chaos. At last they went sadly back to the canyon to start digging out their possessions from the mountain of cobbles and mud that covered the living place. All of their hides, tools and weapons, turtle shell buckets, firemaking gear and abalone shell cups and ornaments; their stores of antler and bone; all, everything they had owned and treasured was buried under ten feet of rubble and slime.

They set to work doggedly, digging with stout sticks and their hands. It was backbreaking toil. The sticky red clay of the overhang, heavy with water and laced together with cobbles, stubbornly resisted their efforts. They floundered and scrabbled at the mound all day and still had not cleared it away. Both fire and the means to produce it were snuffed out and buried. Men, women and children lay down in the dark and the puddles and slept, exhausted and hungry.

The next day the flood appeared to be subsiding somewhat, and they decided to go to the beach for mussels before digging again, as all were suffering sharp pangs of hunger. They trailed down through the soft, thick mud of the canyon floor, a sad and bedraggled little group of miserable humans. As they came out at the bottom, a shocking sight greeted them.

Their beloved salt marsh where they and their ancestors down through the centuries had gathered succulent clams, fish and waterfowl had vanished completely, wiped out in the flood and the storm. Nothing remained but a vast brown turbulent sea stretching out into storm-built breakers across a littered mudbar, flowing out between high, rippled mud banks. Here and there stranded trees and the corpses of drowned creatures swung and fretted at the tug of the current. Vultures were circling over the carrion; some had landed on the bloating carcasses and were feasting already.

The green cord grass; the winding, silvery channels, the clam beds and hummocks; the carefully tended fish weirs; the gleaming white dunes and the beaches; all were gone now as though they had never existed. The people, even the tough, rugged hunters, squatted down in the mud and wept bitterly. The tears poured down their brown cheeks as they shuddered and sobbed. The women rocked and moaned as for the dead, and indeed Death stood before them gloating in triumph.

But at last their protesting stomachs started them moving again. The men tried to reach one of the carcasses, a fine, antlered deer, but as soon as they stepped away from the bank they instantly sank to their waists in soft mud, and only returned to firm ground with difficulty. So the hungry humans could only stare longingly at the generous store of fresh meat just out of their reach.

It was obvious that the only food supplies available to them without spears and throwing sticks were the shellfish on the rocks of the open coast. They worked their way to the rocky point and down along the promontory where the mussel colonies grew. Here at least was food that could be depended upon to keep them from starving. As long as they kept the sea at their elbows they would survive.

The surf thundered in and tossed spray high in the air over the jumbled sandstone blocks. Mountainous swells were still running shoreward, stirred up by the storm. But the tide finally drew back and let them harvest mussels enough for a meal, and they squatted among the boulders and picked meat out of the shattered shells until they felt their bellies sigh with relief.

Late in the day the people were back in the rubble and mud of the shelter under the canyon rim, doggedly picking away to unearth their belongings, and before dark they managed to find the grooved board and sticks they needed to kindle a fire. But the wood was so soaked that only a thorough drying-out in the sun would let it function again, and another miserable fireless night had to be spent, with the people huddled together for warmth in the chilly mud and the steady northwesterly breeze.

At last on the following day, after digging out all the rest of their mud-soaked belongings, the men managed to kindle a fire. They gathered twigs and chopped open dead tree limbs to get the dry, punky inner portions, and slowly added fuel until the blaze had enough heat to dry out the wood stacked around it. And now with a blazing hearth again everyone's spirits began to improve.

The males of all ages went out to hunt, but with ponds and puddles scattered everywhere over the land, the game had no need to come in to the familiar springs where it could be ambushed. Slowly the full extent of the disaster dawned on the hunters: the storm had ruined far more than the clam beds and fish weirs. The game had abandoned the area.

When they returned to the living place in the evening, seven men and three boys had been able to capture only two rabbits, a badger and eight rattlesnakes to show for their efforts. The snakes were swarming along the edge of the valley, driven out of their dens and holes by the flood. Although they were prized highly for food, a hungry hunter could easily eat the flesh of a snake in one sitting. So the rations were meager again, and the people were glum and depressed as they bolted their shares by the hearth, sucking the tiny, thin bones to lick off every fiber and shred.

It was plain now to everyone. The country they knew and had known all their lives — their world, for that matter and that of their fathers — was dying and much of it gone already, buried under the mud and debris in the valley. Like the shadowy files of their ancient, unknown kin, marching away over willow-choked floodplains and tundra and glacier-locked passes, hopefully seeking a richer land, the people would leave this canyon. Bitter though the parting might be, they would bundle their little stores of belongings and drift on, uprooting their quiet, comfortable lives and those of their children. For even though they might be able to hang on and survive in Buchanan Canyon, the vanished salt marsh might not be completely restored in their lifetimes, and this rich, fecund storehouse had stood at the center of all of their lives. Somewhere off to the south, the elders believed, another one awaited them, untouched and virgin, with its winding channels glittering silver under the sun.

So on a beautiful blue day in November the people shouldered their baggage and sadly marched off down the choked stream of the canyon, past the desolate acres of mud and the reek of the carrion, down to the sea. They stared in hard, dry-eyed silence; only the rustle and squeak of their bundled gear could be heard, and the slap and suck of their feet in the muck of the trail.

When they reached the shoreline they turned and walked off to the south.

Glossary

Alluvium.   Sand, silts and gravels deposited by running water.

Altithermal.   A period of high average temperature.

Amerasia.   A landmass formed by the connection of Asia and America in the Bering region during glacial lowering of sea levels.

Amorphous.   A random shape as opposed to a controlled shape.

Australopithecine.   An early hominid form preceding the evolution of man.

Biostratigraphy.   A means of estimating the age of a stratum in the earth by identifying the fossil species enclosed.

Cortex, Cortices.   The outer skin or rind of pebbles, cobbles, etc.

Dorsal Surface.   The back or top surface of a rock specimen.

Fanglomerates.   The mixed sand, clay and gravels in an alluvial fan deposit.

Fire Plow.   A grooved wooden board and stick capable of producing fire by friction-induced sparks in dry tinder.

Geomorphology.   The nature and study of the earth's surface phenomena.

Geostratigraphy.   A means of estimating the age of a stratum by analysis of its contained soils and geological position.

Glacio-pluvial.   A period of increased precipitation during the Pleistocene Epoch causing glaciers to form in the higher latitudes and elevations.

Hinge Fracture.   A flake scar terminating in an abrupt ridge or hinge.

Holocene.   The present of recent period after the last Ice Age ended.

Hominid.   Primates both living and extinct that walked on two legs.

Illinoian, The.   The next to the last glacial period.

In Situ.   In the place of original deposition.

Interglacial, Interstade.   Periods between glacial advances.

183

Laurentide Ice.   An enormous sheet of glacial ice up to three miles thick that covered much of Canada during glacial advances of the Pleistocene Epoch.

Loess.   A fine silt produced by glacial ice action on overlain rocks.

Mandible.   The bony structure of the jaw, especially the lower jaw.

Matrix.   The material in which objects are encased or enclosed; i.e., the soil or clay in which artifacts are contained.

Marine Transgression.   The advance inland of ocean waters during a rise in sea level caused by melting of glacial ice.

Megafauna.   The very large and mostly extinct animals of the Pleistocene, such as giant bison, mammoth, mastodon and giant ground sloth.

Midden.   A rubbish dump, especially of shell.

Morphology.   The shape of an object with particular reference to aritfacts.

Muskeg.   Thin black mud or muck caused by repeated freezing and thawing of subsoils in far northern latitudes.

Neolithic.   New stone age, following the upper paleolithic stage.

Nuclei.   Stone cores as opposed to flakes.

Paleolithic.   The old stone age in which humans produced stone tools and weapons.

Paleontology.   The study of fossil remains, primarily of bone.

Paleosol.   A very old soil.

Pedology.   The study of soils.

Periglacial.   The areas adjacent to glaciers.

Permafrost.   Perpetually frozen soils below the surface in high latitudes.

Piedmont.   The foothill region adjacent to a mountain range.

Pleistocene.   A period of alternating glacial and interglacial cycles preceding the Holocene and lasting about 2,000,000 years.

Potassium Argon Dating.   A radiometric means of dating volcanic materials.

Protein Racemization Dating.   A means of dating formerly living organisms by observing changes in the orientation of protein isomers after the death of the organism.

Quaternary.   The combined periods of the Pleistocene and Recent or Holocene.

Step Flaking.   The production of overlapping flake scars on an artifact.

Steppe.   A region of flat grasslands in the north temperate zone.

Taiga.   A region of stunted spruce trees in arctic and subarctic zones.

Talus.   Accumulations of broken rocks on slopes and at the foot of cliffs.

Tectonic.   Slow changes in the elevation of the earth's crust caused by releases of energy in the upper mantle.

Terrace.   A bench-like feature caused by lowering of sea or stream level or tectonic uplift.

Tertiary.   The geologic era preceding the Quaternary.

Thermoluminescence.   A means of determining the time of previous heating of rocks or their derivatives by high reheating and observation of degree of radioactivity emitted.

Uranium Series.   A radiometric means of dating by measuring the degree of decay of uranium isotopes into thorium or protactinium.

Ventral Surface.   The underside of an artifact, as opposed the dorsal surface, or backside.

References

Aigner, Jean S.
    1978   The Paleolithic of China. *In Early Man in America from a Circum-Pacific Perspective*, edited by Alan L. Bryan, pp. 25-41. Occasional Papers No. 1 of the Department of Anthropology, University of Alberta, Edmonton, Alberta, Canada.

Armenta Camacho, J.
    1959   Hallazgo de un artefacto asociado con mamut en el Valle de Puebla. *Mexico Instituto Nacional Antropologia e Historia*, Direccion Prehistoria Pub. 7, pp. 7-25.

Berger, Rainer
    1983   The Woolley Mammoth Site, Santa Rosa Island, California. In *Peopling of the New World*, edited by J. Ericson, R. E. Taylor, and R. Berger, pp. 163-170, Ballena Press Anthropological Papers No. 23, Los Altos.

Bischoff, J. L. , R. J. Shlemon, T. L. Ku, R. D. Simpson, R. J. Rosenbauer and F. E. Budinger, Jr.
    1981   Uranium series and soil-geomorphic dating of the Calico Archaeological Site. *Geology*, Vol. 9, pp. 576-582. Geological Society of America, Boulder, Colorado.

Bonnichsen, R.
    1978   Critical arguments for Pleistocene artifacts from the Old Crow Basin, Yukon: a preliminary statement. In *Early Man in America from a Circum-Pacific Perspective*, edited by Alan L. Bryan, pp. 102-117. Occasional Papers NO. 1 of the Department of Anthropology, University of Alberta, Edmonton, Alberta, Canada.

Bonnichsen, R.
    1979   *Pleistocene Bone Technology in the Beringian Refugium*. Archaeological Survey of Canada Paper No. 89. National Museum of Man, Mercury Series, Ottawa.

Breuil, Henri and Raymond Lantier
    1965   *The Men of the Old Stone Age.* St. Martin's Press, New York

Bryan, Alan L.
　1978　An overview of paleo-American prehistory from a circum-Pacific perspective. In *Early Man in America from a Circum-Pacific Perspective*. edited by Alan L. Bryan, pp. 306-325. Occasional Papers No. 1 of the Department of Anthropology, University of Alberta, Edmonton.
　1986　Paleo-American prehistory as seen from South America. In *New Evidence for the Pleistocene Peopling of the Americas*, edited by Alan L. Bryan, pp. 1-14. Peopling of the Americas series, Center for the Study of Early Man, University of Maine at Orono

Carter, George F.
　1950　Evidence for Pleistocene man in Southern California. *Geographical Review*, Vol. 40, pp. 84-102.
　1951　Man in America, a criticism of scientific thought. *Scientific Monthly*, Vol. 73, pp. 297-307.
　1957　*Pleistocene Man at San Diego*. Johns Hopkins Press, Baltimore.
　1980　*Earlier than You Think*. Texas A & M University Press, College Station.

Childers, W. M.
　1977　Ridge-back tools of the Colorado desert. *American Antiquity*, Vol. 42, pp. 242-248.

Childers, W. M. and H. L. Minshall
　1980　Evidence of early man exposed at Yuha Pinto Wash. *American Antiquity*. Vol. 45, pp. 297-308

Davis, E. L.
　1986　Geoarchaeology at China Lake, California. *New Evidence for the Pleistocene Peopling of the Americas*, Alan L. Bryan, editor, pp. 81-87, The Center for the Study of Early Man, University of Maine, Orono.

Davis, E. L., G. Jefferson and C. McKinney
　1981　Man-made flakes with dated mammoth tooth at China Lake, California. *Anthropological Journal of Canada*, Vol. 19 (2), pp. 2-7.

De Lumley, H., M. de Lumley, Maria Beltrao, Y. Yokoyama, J. Labeyrie, J. Danon, G. Delibrias, C. Falgueres et J. L. Bischoff.
　1988　Decouverte d'outils tailles associes a des faunes du Pleistocene moyen dans la Toca da Esperance, Etat da Bahia, Brazil. C. R. Acad. Sci. Paris. t. 306, Serie II, pp. 241-247

Dolitsky, A. B.
　1985　Siberian Paleolithic archaeology, approaches and analytic methods. *Current Anthropology*, Vol. 26 (3) pp. 361-378.

Dorn, R. I. and T. M. Oberlander
    1981   Microbial origin of desert varnish. *Science*, Vol. 213, pp. 1245-1247.

Fairservis, Walter
    1971   *The Roots of Ancient India*. The MacMillan Company, New York.

Fladmark, K. B.
    1978   The feasibility of the Northwest coast as a migratory route for early man. *Early Man in America from a Circum-Pacific Perspective*. edited by Alan L. Bryan, pp. 119-128. Occasional Papers No. 1 of the Department of Anthropology, University of Alberta, Edmonton.

Gagliano, S. M.
    1967   *Occupation Sequence at Avery Island*. Louisiana State University Press, Baton Rouge.

Gromov, V. I.
    1935   New data on the fauna and geology of Eastern Europe and Siberia: the Paleolithic of the U. S. S. R. Leningrad: Izvestiya Gosudarstvennoy Akademii Istorii Material'noy Kul'tury. (In Russian)

Hansen, G. H.
    1934   Utah Lake skull. *American Anthropology, N. S.*, Vol. 36, pp. 135-147.

Haynes, C. V.
    1971   Time, environment and early man. *Arctic Anthropology*, Vol. 8 (2), pp. 3-14.
    1974   The Calico site, artifacts or geofacts? *Science*, Vol. 181, pp. 305-310.

Heuser, C. J.
    1965   A Pleistocene phytogeographical sketch of the Pacific Northwest and Alaska. In *The Quaternary of the United States*, edited by H. E. Wright and D. G. Frey, pp. 469-483. Princeton University Press.

Hopkins, D. M.
    1967   The Cenozoic history of Beringia: a synthesis. In *The Bering Land Bridge*, edited by David M. Hopkins, pp. 451-484. Stanford University Press, Stanford.

Hubbs, C. L., G. S. Bien and H. E. Suess
    1965   La Jolla natural radiocarbon measurements IV. In *Radiocarbon*, Vol. 7, pp. 66-117.

Institute of Vertebrate Paleontology and Paleoanthropology
    1980   *Atlas of Primitive Man in China*. Science Press, Beijing, China.

Irving, W. N. and C. R. Harington
    1973   Upper Pleistocene radiocarbon dated artifacts from the Northern Yukon. *Science*, Vol. 179, pp. 335-340.

Irwin-Williams, C.
    1967   Associations of early man with horse, camel and mastodon at Hueyatlaco, Valsequillo (Puebla, Mexico). In *Pleistocene Extinctions: the Search for a Cause*, edited by P. S. Martin and H. E. Wright, Jr., pp. 337-347. Yale University Press, New Haven.

Jia Lanpo
    1980   *Early Man in China*. Foreign Language Press, Beijing, China.
    1985   China's earliest Paleolithic assemblages. In *Palaeoanthropology and Palaeolithic Archaeology in the People's Republic of China*, edited by Wu Rukang and John W. Olsen, pp. 135-145. Academic Press, Orlando.

Jia Lanpo and Huang Weiwen
    1985   The late Paleolithic of China. In *Palaeoanthropology and Palaeolithic Archaeology in the People's Republic of China*, edited by Wu Rukang and John W. Olsen, pp. 211-223. Academic Press, Orlando.

Jopling, A. V., W. N. Irving, and B. F. Beebe
    1981   Stratigraphic, sedimentological and faunal evidence of the occurrence of pre-Sangamonian artefacts in Northern Yukon. *Arctic*, Vol. 34, pp. 3-33. Arctic Institute of North America, Calgary, Canada.

Kent, Rockwell
    1935   *Salamina*. Harcourt, Brace and Company, New York.

Kim W. Y. and Chung Y. W.
    1979   *Preliminary Report on the Archeulian-type Biface Industry of Chongokni*. (In Korean with resumes in French and English) Chintan Hakpo 46,47.

Krieger, A. D.
    1979   The Calico site and Old World Paleolithic industries. In *Pleistocene Man at Calico*, edited by W. C. Schuiling, pp. 69-73. San Bernardino County Museum Association, Redlands, California.

Ku, T. L. and J. P. Kern
    1974   Uranium series age of the Upper Pleistocene Nestor Terrace, San Diego, California. *Geological Society of America Bulletin*, Vol. 85 (II), pp. 1713-1716.

Lorenzo, J. L.
    1967   Sobre metodo arqueologico. *Mexico Instituto Nacional Antropologia e Historia*. Bol. 28.

Mammoth Trumpet
    1984   Center for the Study of Early Man, Orono, Maine, Vol. 1 (3)

Minshall, H. L.
    1981   The geomorphology and antiquity of the Charles H. Brown archaeological site at San Diego, California. *Pacific Coast Archaeological Society Quarterly*, Vol. 17 (4), pp. 39-57.

Moratto, Michael
    1984   *California Archaeology*, Academic Press, New York.

Moriarty, J. R. and H. L. Minshall
    1972   A new pre-desert site discovered near Texas Street. *Anthropological Journal of Canada*, Vol. 10 (3), pp. 10-13.

Morlan, R. E.
    1978   Early man in northern Yukon Territory: perspective as of 1977. In *Early Man in America from a Circum-Pacific Perspective,* edited by Alan L. Bryan, pp. 73-95. Occasional Papers No. 1 of the Department of Anthropology, University of Alberta, Edmonton.

Movius, H.
    1948   The Lower Paleolithic cultures of southern and eastern Asia. Transactions of the American Philosophical Society, Vol. 34 (4).

Oberlander, T. M.
    1983   Fan, varnish, shoreline — possible clues to Calico. *Friends of Calico Newsletter*, Vol. 5, No. 1, pp. 4-6.

Patterson, L. W.
    1983   Criteria for determining the attributes of man-made lithics. *Journal of Field Archaeology,* Vol. 10. pp. 297-307.

Powers, W. R.
    1973   Paleolithic man in northeast Asia. *Arctic Anthropology,* Vol. 10 (2), Entire Volume. University of Wisconsin Press, Madison.

Reeves, B. O. K.
  1986   The Mission Ridge site and the Texas Street question. In *New Evidence for the Pleistocene Peopling of the Americas*, edited by Alan L. Bryan, pp. 65-80. The Center for the Study of Early Man, University of Maine, Orono.

Renaud, E. B.
  1933   *Archaeological Survey of the High Western Plains, Seventh Report.* Department of Anthropology, University of Denver, Denver, Colorado.
  1938   *Archaeological Survey of the High Western Plains, Tenth Report.* Department of Anthropology, University of Denver, Denver, Colorado.
  1940   *Archaeological Survey of the High Western Plains, Twelfth Report.* Department of Anthropology, University of Denver, Denver, Colorado.

Reynolds, T. E. G.
  1986   Toward peopling the New World: a possible early Paleolithic in Tohoku District, Japan. *American Antiquity,* Vol. 51 (2) pp. 330-332.

Rogers, M. J.
  1966   *Ancient Hunters of the Far West.* Copley Books, La Jolla, California.

Shleyukov, A. I. (Cited in Dolitsky 1985)
  1983   Termolyuminestsentnoye datirovaniyi stoyanki Ulalinka — drevneyshego paleoliticheskogo pamyatnika Sibiri (Thermoluminescence dating of Ulalinka — the oldest Paleolithic site in Siberia) in *Paleolit Sibiri* (The Siberian Paleolithic). Edited by R. S. Vasil'yevsky, pp. 31-33. Novosibirsk: Nauka.

Singer, C. A.
  1979   A preliminary report on the analysis of Calico lithics. In *Pleistocene Man at Calico*, edited by Walter C. Schuiling. pp. 55-63, San Bernardino County Museum Association, Redlands, California.

Stanford, D. R., R. Bonnichsen and R. E. Morlan.
  1981   The Ginsberg experiment: modern and prehistoric evidence of a bone-flaking technology. *Science,* Vol. 212, pp. 438-440.

Steen-McIntyre, V., R. Fryxell and H. E. Malde
  1981   Geologic evidence for age of deposits at Hueyatlaco archaeological site, Valsequillo, Mexico. *Quaternary Research,* Vol. 16, pp. 1-17.

Szabo, B. J., H. E. Malde and C. Irwin-Williams
   1969   Dilemma posed by uranium-series dates on archaeologically sig-
          nificant bones from Valsequillo, Puebla, Mexico. *Earth and Plan-
          etary Science Letters*. Vol. 36, pp. 237-244.

Tseytlin, S. M. (Cited in Dolitsky 1985)
   1979   *Geologiya Paleolita Severnoy Azii* (The Geology of the Paleo-
          lithic of North Asia), Moskow, Nauka.

Walcott, R. I.
   1970   Isostatic response to loading of the crust in Canada. *Canadian
          Journal of Earth Sciences,* Vol. 7, pp. 716-727.

Woodring, W. P.
   1931   *Distribution and Age of the Tertiary Deposits of the Colorado
          Desert*. Carnegie Institution Publication 418, pp. 1-25.

Wormington, H. M.
   1957   *Ancient Man in North America*. Denver Museum of Natural
          History, Denver, Colorado.

Wu Rukang and Dong Xingren
   1985   *Homo erectus* in China. In *Palaeoanthropology and Palaeolithic
          Archaeology in the People's Republic of China*, edited by Wu
          Rukang and John W. Olsen, pp. 79-89.

Wu Rukang and John W. Olsen, editors
   1985   *Palaeoanthropology and Palaeolithic Archaeology in the
          People's Republic of China*. Academic Press, Orlando, Florida.

Yi Seonbok and G. A. Clark
   1983   Observations on the Lower Paleolithic of Northeast Asia. *Current
          Anthropology*, Vol. 24 (2), pp. 181-202

Yoshizaki, M. and I. Masami
   1986   Badaban Locality A: recent discovery of the Middle Pleistocene
          occupation of Japan. *Canadian Journal of Anthropology*, Vol. 5
          (1), pp. 3-9.

Zhang Senshui
   1985   The early Paleolithic of China. In *Palaeoanthropology and Pal-
          aeolithic Archaeology in the People's Republic of China*, edited
          by Wu Rukang and John W. Olsen. pp. 147-186. Academic Press,
          Orlando, Florida.

Index

Filimoshki site, 44
    age, 45
fire use in China, at Zhoukowdian,
        34, 37
    at Lantian, 39
    fire plow, possible use, 37
    at Xihoudu, 38
Fladmark, Knute, 57, 58
Folsum site, 84
Friends of Calico, Inc., 107

G

Gadler, Richard, 15
gangrene, 51, 67
Gehe Village site, 37
    tools at, 38
    estimated age, 38, 95
Gif-sur-Yvette, 93
Gigantopithecus, 160
"Ginsberg" experiment, 82
    findings from, 83
Gongwangling Village, 39
    human fossils at, 39
    tools at, 39, 40
Gran Chaco, bola use at, 38
Grand Canyon, 89
Granger, Walter, 33
Great Basin and Range Province, 105
Great Basin Foundation, 112
Great Divide, 85
Great Slave Lake, 84
Greenland, 63
Green River, 85
Griner, Lynn, 62
Guanyin Cave, 149
Guidon, Niede, 172
Gulf of Alaska, 62

H

Haberer, Hans, 33
Hansen, George, 120
Harington, C. R., 82
Haynes, C. Vance, 109
Holocene, 19
Homo erectus, 35, 39
    scarcity of fossil remains, 114, 165
H. erectus pekinensis described, 41
Homo habilis, 160
Homo sapiens, 92, 165

Homo sapiens sapiens, remains at
        Shandingdong, 146
Hopkins, David, 61
Huanghe, 38
Hubbs, Carl, 69
Hubei Province, 35
Hu Chengzhi, 40
Hueyatlaco, stratigraphy, 92, 93
    tools at, 92
    age, 92
    difficulty in determining, 92,93

I

Illinoian glacial stage, 59, 82, 88
Imperial 2109, 118
Imperial Valley College, 113
Imperial Valley College Barker
        Museum, 114
Institute of Vertebrate Paleontology
        and Paleoanthropology, 35
interglacials, 59, 60
    transgressions, 64
    in deserts, 104,114
interstade, 59
Irving, William N., 82
Irwin-Williams,Cynthia, 92
isostasis, on Northwest coast, 57
Isotope Foundation, 106

J

Japan Current, 56
Jefferson, George, 111
Jia Lanpo, 34, 39, 40
Johansen, Donald, 94
Johns Hopkins University, 6

K

"Kathleen," 112
Kent, Rockwell, 63
Kern, Philip, 18
Kim Wonyon, 42
Korea, 42
Krieger, Alex, 21, 129
Ku, Richard (T, L.), 18
Kumara sites, 43, 44
Kumeyaay, eating habits, 66

L

Laboratory of Vertebrate Paleontology,